THE
INVISIBLE
PALACE

JOSÉ MANUEL TESORO

THE INVISIBLE PALACE

the true story of a journalist's murder in Java

EQUINOX
PUBLISHING
JAKARTA SINGAPORE

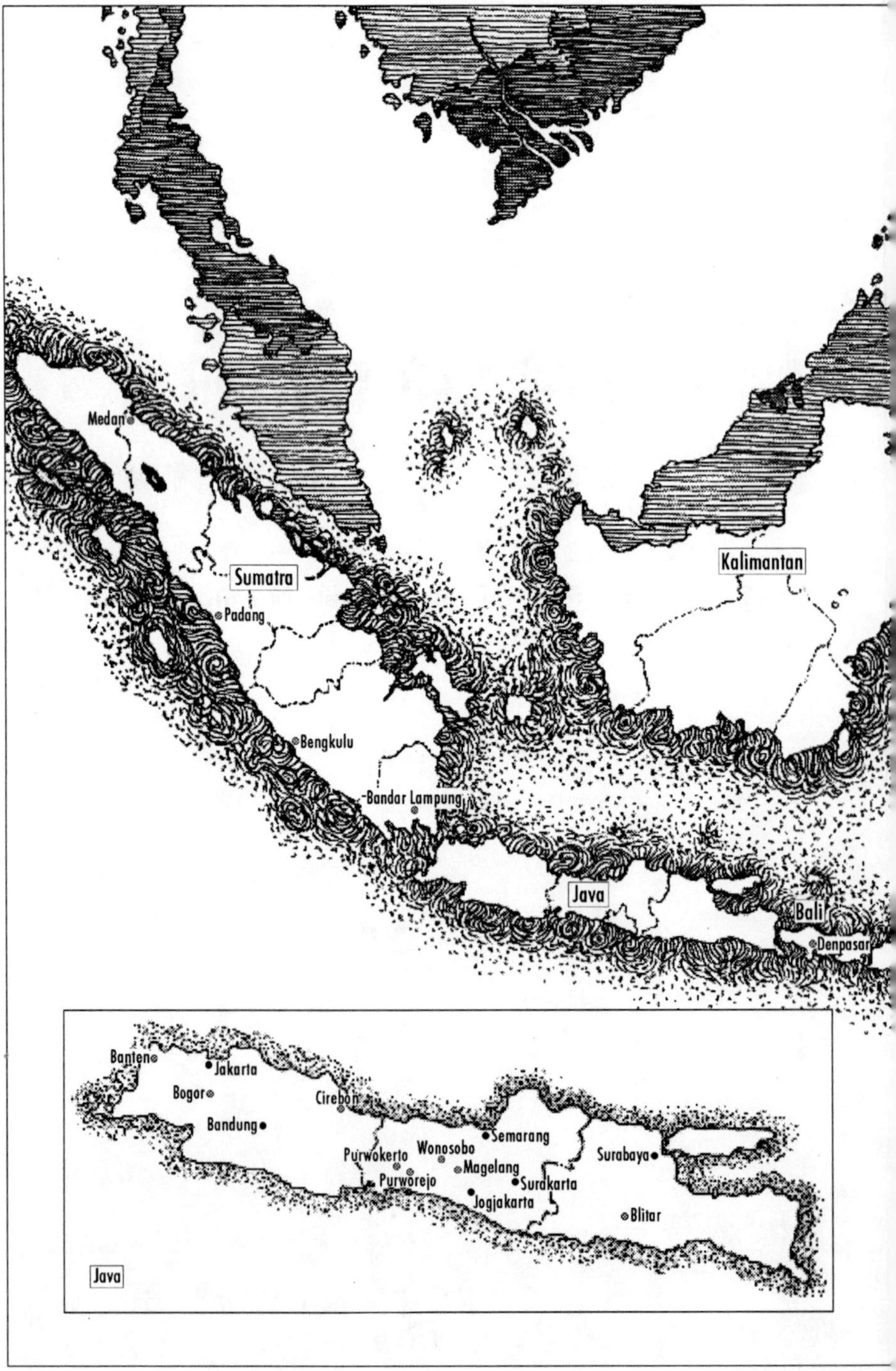

Medan
Sumatra
Padang
Bengkulu
Bandar Lampung
Kalimantan
Java
Bali
Denpasar
Banten
Jakarta
Bogor
Bandung
Cirebon
Semarang
Purwokerto
Wonosobo
Magelang
Purworejo
Surakarta
Jogjakarta
Surabaya
Blitar
Java

Map of Indonesia

EQUINOX PUBLISHING (ASIA) PTE. LTD.
PO Box 6179 JKSGN
Jakarta 12062
Indonesia

www.EquinoxPublishing.com

ISBN 979-97964-7-4

Text ©2004 José Manuel Tesoro
Illustrations ©2004 Enrico Soekarno

First Equinox Edition 2004

1 3 5 7 9 10 8 6 4 2

All rights reserved.

CONTENTS

Preface 11

Introduction: To Kick a Corpse 17

Chapter 1: Wuku Warigalit 31

Chapter 2: A Nation Always Needs an Enemy 55

Chapter 3: Carry It Out 77

Chapter 4: A Few Centimeters From Our Throats 99

Chapter 5: Puppeteers 116

Chapter 6: A Finger's Breadth of Earth 137

Chapter 7: To Teach Him a Lesson 160

Chapter 8: Political Business 182

Chapter 9: A Worm Squirms 206

Chapter 10: Sorcerors and Mystics 233

Chapter 11: Everything at the Trial 262

Chapter 12: A Country of Law 285

Epilogue: Like Dust Blown Away by the Wind 310

Sources 322

PREFACE

THIS IS A WORK OF NON-FICTION. But, like all true stories, not everything found within is fact. This book also contains fable, prophecy, rumor, fancy, recollection, conjecture, and fabrication. The mix reflects what I collected while reporting and retelling a story set in the contemporary developing world. In fact, true stories everywhere draw from a similar diversity of sources, because human beings invoke more than fact to construct or interpret their past experience, whether in the third world, the first, or in some space in-between, where most of us now live. Including such disparate ingredients in a work of non-fiction recognizes not only how people recollect and relate their personal histories, but also that in the absence of these elements, a reader never sees the full picture. Nonetheless, I have identified those assertions, anecdotes, or speculations by sources or subjects for which factual confirmation is unavailable, unreliable, or impossible to obtain. I leave it to the reader to act the judge: to weigh the testimony, consider its credibility, and then draw his or her own verdict.

I conducted all interviews with the people in this book in the language known as Indonesian, the lingua franca of the volcanic island arc that stretches across an eighth of the equator – from Sumatra, Java, Borneo, Sulawesi, and the Moluccas to half of New Guinea. All of my other primary printed or recorded sources, such as news clippings, press conference transcripts, tape recordings, legal memoranda, or court opinions, and many secondary sources I consulted were also in Indonesian. A few oral and written sources were in Javanese, which native speakers later translated for me into Indonesian. Although I missed the nuances that the individuals I interviewed, most of whom were native Javanese, could have conveyed to me through a translator fluent in their native tongue, I chose to give up some of that flavor in order to be able to converse directly with my sources.

More than two hundred million people use Indonesian daily, making it one of the world's most-spoken languages. Indonesian differs from the Malay used in nearby Brunei, Singapore, and Malaysia only in some vocabulary and expressions, much as American English varies from British English, so another twenty million people in these countries can understand it. Despite the language's immense constituency – it has almost as many speakers as French – few know it outside its home country. Since for many readers, Indonesia may already be unfamiliar territory, I have tried to make this story set there seem less alien by replacing most Indonesian words with their closest American English equivalents. I have also substituted, when necessary, sums originally denominated in rupiah, the Indonesian currency, with their equivalent in 1996 U.S. dollars.

Two key terms, however, have been difficult to translate into something intelligible to non-Indonesian readers. The words are *kabupaten*, the name given to a sub-district of an Indonesian province, and *bupati*, the chief executive or governor of that sub-district. The word *kabupaten* could be translated as "regency" and *bupati* as "regent," but neither of these words has much meaning in modern English. In some ways, a *kabupaten* resembles a county in the United States, but one with its own chief executive and legislative assembly. Rather than replace these specific administrative terms with words that might have confusing associations, I have kept *kabupaten* and *bupati* in the original Indonesian.

One final note on the language: proper pronunciation. Indonesian has long been written using the Roman alphabet. Since a national spelling reformation in 1972, English speakers can now pronounce all Indonesian vowels as short English vowels and all Indonesian consonants as English consonants, with one exception. The Indonesian "c" sounds like the "ch" in "chuckle." Readers should be aware that many Indonesians still spell their own names using the pre-1972 orthography, which draws heavily from Dutch spelling. I reproduced these individuals' names as they would write them, so readers may encounter "oe" to represent "u," "dj" for "j," "dh" for "d," and "tj" for the previously mentioned "c." When referring to the place where most of the events in this story unfolded, Indonesians follow neither the modern nor the archaic spelling rules. They write the Javanese province's name as "Yogyakarta" but pronounce it "Jogjakarta." Against local convention, I have written the name to reflect its pronunciation, except if it appears in a title. To distinguish whether the text is referring to the *province* of Jogjakarta or to its *capital city*, which shares the same name, I use "Jogjakarta" to refer to the province and "Jogja," the colloquial abbreviation of "Jogjakarta," to indicate the city.

Many people deserve my deepest thanks for helping me complete this book. I thank the Asian Scholarship Foundation and its main donor, the Ford Foundation. Two grants from the Bangkok-based foundation, formerly known as the ASIA Fellows Program, supported me through eight months in Jogjakarta and four months in the United States. I am particularly grateful to the foundation's past and present directors, Chai Podhista and Lourdes Salvador; their staff, especially Somkamol Chaiyavej; David Adams of the Institute of International Education; and Nelly Paliama of the American Indonesian Exchange Foundation for arranging the financial and institutional support that made this writing possible. The staff at the *Lembaga Ilmu Pengetahuan Indonesia*, or Indonesian Institute of Sciences; the rector of Jogja's Gadjah Mada University, Ichlasul Amal; and the Center for Peace and Security Studies' Director Syamsurizal Panggabean were my gracious official sponsors during my research in Indonesia. In the United States, Michael Dove, Harold Conklin, James C. Scott, Benedict Kiernan, Indriyo Sukmono,

Kristine Mooseker, and many others at the Yale University Council on Southeast Asia Studies hosted me in New Haven, Connecticut while I completed the manuscript at the Yale Center for International and Area Studies.

Metta Dharmasaputra and Arif Mustolih, my assistants at *Asiaweek*'s Jakarta bureau, prepared the groundwork for this project as early as 1997. Arif, in particular, continued to assist me long after he left the magazine's employment. I am also indebted to my former editors at *Asiaweek*, Ann Morrison and Zoher Abdoolcarim, who assigned me to Indonesia as a correspondent at the age of twenty-five; Alejandro Reyes, who supported my research proposal; W. Hampton Sides, who gave me advice and encouragement; and Joan Suyenaga, who oriented me to the city that would be my home for nearly a year. In Jogjakarta, the following individuals spent uncounted hours answering my questions: Mohammad Achadi, Angger Jati Wijaya, Budi Hartono, Dwi Sumaji and his wife Sunarti, Hadi Prayitno, Heru Prasetya, L.N. Idayanie, Masduki Attamani, Purwani Dyah Prabandari, Syahlan Said, Tarko Sudiarno, Djufri Taufik, Bambang Tiong, Wijiono Titet, Triyandi Mulkan, and Eko Widiyanto. Thomas Pujo Wijiyanto of the Jogja bureau of *Kompas* generously lent me his original recordings of Dwi Sumaji's 1997 trial, while Berchman Heroe shared his unpublished reportage on Bantul. At the office of the Bantul *kabupaten* government, *Bupati* Idham Samawi and his Public Relations & Information Section Director Suarman gave me their enthusiastic cooperation. The editors of *Bernas* fulfilled all my requests for assistance and tolerated my frequent impositions on their time. Finally, I am especially grateful to the Jogjakarta Police District, which granted me permission in 2001 to speak to several police officers who had been involved in the investigation of Udin's murder.

J. Joseph Errington, Ariel Heryanto, Nicole Lamy, Daniel Lev, and Angela Romano read versions of the manuscript at various stages of completion. I found their comments and corrections invaluable, especially those of Professor Lev, who advised and mentored me on this project from concept to publication. I owe five more people my thanks: John and Mark Hanusz, the book's publishers; Peter Cordingley, for editing my work at a time when it was most needed; Enrico Soekarno, whose maps and diagrams illustrate this volume; and my wife Intania, who, although my work often kept us apart, sustained me through the years it took to complete *The Invisible Palace*. Any errors in the book are mine alone.

J.M.T.
August 2004
Cambridge, Massachusetts

INTRODUCTION

To Kick a Corpse

THE ASTROLOGER WAS NOWHERE TO BE FOUND. I had risen before dawn to travel two hours by road through the parched plain of Central Java because I had been warned to arrive at the astrologer's office as early as possible. I reached Surakarta on schedule, well before the equatorial sun had burned off the coolness of the morning but also, apparently, before the astrologer had arrived at work. His office turned out to be located in a small museum in a colonial mansion, wedged between a soccer stadium and a movie theater on Surakarta's main road. A sleepy security guard directed me to a tree-shaded yard in the back. I was surprised to find that three people – an old, brown man in the stiff, black velvet Indonesian fez known as a *peci*, a chubby Chinese woman, and a man who must have been her portly bachelor son – had already formed a line before me. I took a seat in a chair beside them.

As the first hour of waiting lumbered into a second, I risked my place in line to venture into the collections. Surakarta's Radyopustoko Museum, a framed piece of paper in the front hall informed me, was Indonesia's oldest. The museum had been founded in 1890 while the Dutch still governed this Southeast Asian archipelago as its richest colony, the Netherlands East Indies. Scattered around the yard in front of the astrologer's office were moss-swaddled carvings of faceless, armless Hindu deities – an array of avatars of Vishnu, Shiva, Ganesha, and Durga. As I wandered through the mansion's gloomy interior, I passed by an orchestra of blackened bronze *gamelan* gongs. I peeked into a room where shelves of jumbled manuscripts moldered, and marveled at glass-encased arsenals of *kris* daggers with flame-shaped blades and armies of flattened leather *wayang* shadow puppets. A dust-covered model of Java's oldest mosque towered in one room. In the main hallway, a box of eighteenth-century artificial flowers sat crumbling. The fading bouquet was a gift, the label read, from Napoleon Bonaparte to a Surakarta sultan. A huge, carved ogre's head, bearded with horsehair, lurked in a darkened corner. I later learned it had once been the figurehead for a royal barge. It was said that a spirit still inhabited it, which museum employees had to appease daily with a tray of rice snacks and tropical blossoms.

These were artifacts from all the civilizations that had come to Java, the most important of Indonesia's 17,500 atolls, reefs, rocks and islands. In the eclectic, eccentric Radyopustoko Museum, prim Northern European artifacts consorted with naked Hindu carvings, pagan idols stretched out near Muslim religious paraphernalia, and the ancient bedded down with the medieval and the modern. Yet in all this religious and cultural cross-pollination, one particularly potent strain dominated. Islam had converted the majority of Java's inhabitants, and Europeans had domesticated and developed the island, but the twinned transplants of Hinduism and Buddhism, carried into the archipelago centuries ago by traders and travelers from South Asia, had thrust their roots so deep into the soil they had become inseparable from indigenous Javanese culture. The name "Java" itself comes from Sanskrit. The island's renowned art form, the *wayang*, depicts adventures drawn from the Indian epics of the Ramayana and the Mahabharata. Graven images from the Hindu pantheon still adorn hundreds of ruined brick temples scattered across the lush island. India's gods and traditions have left such an indelible mark on Java, a philosophy professor in Jogja once explained to me, that "their influence runs deep, even to this very moment."

The Hindus taught the Javanese that the moment of a person's birth determines his or her place on this earth forever. That date, hour, and second decides the relative proportion of bad luck or good fortune he or she will encounter. To become famous or fallen, sultan or servant, or even murderer or victim is not a fate an individual can truly choose. They are destinies already decided. The concept of predestination is not a hard one to accept. After all, the first step anyone takes on a journey determines where the next one falls, and that one the direction of the next, and so on until one reaches the final destination.

Yet the Hindus also whispered that inside destiny's iron law are thousands of loopholes, if one knows where to find them. There are lucky days, months, or years that can bless even the most doomed of characters. With the help of an astrologer, soothsayer, or diviner, fortune can be cajoled, bribed, and even outwitted. The astrologer I had come to meet, K.R.H.T. Darmodipuro, the Radyopustoko Museum's curator, specialized in precisely that art. He could extract, from the intricacies of the Javanese calendar, the proper choices a person should follow in matters of life, love, and destiny. Over the years, thousands have sought him out in Surakarta to ask what careers they should pursue or what kind of person they could marry. They asked for the right time to begin new businesses or embark on long journeys. They demanded advice on how to face their future properly – how to cultivate as much luck as possible inside the unseen prison providence had already erected. In other words, they wanted to have the hidden pattern of their lives revealed so they could best live them.

I, however, had come not to find out about my life, but about another's death. Not an ordinary death either, but a murder. One August night in Jogjakarta in 1996, a 33-year-old journalist's life had ended suddenly and violently. I wanted to know if there had been something in his stars or his character that had long ago fixed the manner and date of his passing. This was a society in which many took the idea of fate seriously. Since I was engaged in retelling this man's story, I hoped to find guidance from someone who knew how chance and fortune operated on the lives of the people of this island.

When Darmodipuro finally arrived, the sun was baking the carving-strewn courtyard. The astrologer, a well-fed middle-aged man with a scraggly mustache, settled himself behind his desk. His first client of the morning – the wizened brown man in the *peci* – entered and engaged the astrologer in a hushed conversation. The astrologer's first visitor seemed like a regular: familiar with the mysteries of Javanese divination, which I had only encountered in books until that point.

I knew that Javanese marked time by a calendar based on two systems, one modern and one traditional. In addition to the familiar seven-day Gregorian week, they recognized five so-called "market" days: *Legi, Paing, Pon, Wagé,* and *Kliwon*. The five market days line up with the elements of the seven-day week like the symbols inscribed in a slot machine's tumblers. So each Monday becomes a *Legi* Monday, a *Paing* Monday, a *Pon* Monday, a *Wagé* Monday, or a *Kliwon* Monday. The same system of naming applies to Tuesdays, Wednesdays, Thursdays, Fridays, and Saturdays. So in Java, a week does not repeat itself, as it does elsewhere in the globe, in the same numbing progression of Sundays to Saturdays. A week could contain, for example, a *Legi* Monday, a *Pon* Tuesday, a *Wagé* Wednesday, a *Paing* Thursday and a *Kliwon* Friday. So every seven-day week in Java can be one of a multitude of different combinations.

Each of these weeks is called a *wuku*. "The *wuku* is the same in the West as the zodiac…everyone's personality is governed by his or her *wuku*," Darmodipuro explained. Each *wuku* may be associated with a Hindu deity, a bird, a tree, or some other object of symbolic significance. A child in the *wuku* known as *Landep*, for example, has Shiva as a patron, and thus supposedly inherits that god's penetrating intelligence. Like the *wuku*, each Javanese market-day weekday has its own separate characteristics. *Kliwon* Tuesdays and *Kliwon* Fridays are thought to be especially enchanted occasions, when, all over this 1,200-kilometer-long volcanic island, mystics trek to dead temples, ancient banyans, deep caves, or overgrown graves to meditate and draw power for themselves from the day's concentrated mojo. For ordinary Javanese, these two days, which arrive approximately twelve times a year, are when fate is disposed most favorably toward them.

The combination of characteristics of both the Javanese weekday and the *wuku* help local astrologers predict the progress of a person born on a particular day, in a particular *wuku*, with mathematical accuracy. A local astrologer would laugh at the stylishly scanty advice dispensed over the Internet, such as "Scorpio: Cryptic remarks leave you wondering what you've missed. There's still time to catch up on the back-story." To a Javanese soothsayer, such fortunes are so enigmatic they are entirely useless. Consumers deserve specific instructions. Someone building a house, for example, must be told the best time to lay the foundation, through which door he or she must first enter, what incantations to murmur to protect the dwelling from thieves and what colors to paint to deliver wealth to its inhabitants.

When my turn came, I explained to the astrologer that I wanted to know a fortune. I gave Darmodipuro a dead man's birthday.

"18 February 1963…" the astrologer murmured to himself as he leafed through a massive red-bound folio. The sinuous glyphs of Javanese, derived from Indian scripts, wriggled inside boxes and lines of what looked like charts and tables on each yellowed page. Every now and then, a few recognizably Arabic numerals squirmed on a sheet, and then vanished as another heavy page fell on top of them.

Darmodipuro stopped. "18 February 1963…Oh, that fits perfectly," he said. "His day was a *Kliwon* Monday. A *sampar wangké*. If you look at the day he was born, it fits perfectly that somebody killed him."

He looked at me. "A *sampar wangké* means a very bad day." On 2 July 1990, a *sampar wangké*, more than fourteen hundred pilgrims in Saudi Arabia died in a stampede in a pedestrian tunnel near Mecca. It was the Muslim pilgrimage's worst tragedy. Ninety per cent of Indonesia's 210 million people believe in Islam. The nation's Muslims are so many that they outnumber their co-faithful in all of Egypt, Syria, Iran, Iraq, and Saudi Arabia put together. Many of those crushed and suffocated in the Mina tunnel were Indonesian. Since three out of five Indonesians are Javanese, chances were good that the mourning and wailing that followed these deaths had echoed off the red tile roofs and whitewashed cement walls of the towns and villages of Java. Darmodipuro handed me a photocopied sheet listing some two dozen dates in 2001 and 2002. Next to each were the labels "*sampar wangké*" or "*tali wangké*," an expression that he explained was similar.

"*Wangké* means 'corpse,'" he said. "*Sampar* means 'to lean on, to kick, to step on.' In the Mina disaster, people were kicked, stepped on. Hundreds of thousands." The astrologer continued. "I warned the mayor of Solo," he said, calling Surakarta by its colloquial nickname, much as Los Angeles is dubbed L.A. and as Jogjakarta is called Jogja. "Don't allow his inauguration to happen on a *sampar wangké*. They went ahead! What happened? The big market burned down. The stadium was destroyed. You can believe. You can disbelieve. But that is the reality." On *tali wangké* and *sampar wangké*, he said, one must be careful, for accidents are almost always fatal. And for those unfortunate to have been born on that cursed occasion, misfortune follows them throughout their lives like a terrible shadow.

My dead man had come into the world on such a day. Before I left, the astrologer handed me another piece of paper. Printed on it, in Javanese, was the horoscope for the murder victim's *wuku*, the *wuku* of *Warigalit*.

⁂

Three years before my visit to Darmodipuro, I was sitting in a posh Chinese restaurant in Indonesia's teeming capital, Jakarta. A retired diplomat sat with my party, and he was telling us, with obvious enjoyment, a story about Suharto, Indonesia's longest-ruling leader.

In the early 1990s, a great earthquake shook Jakarta. Inside many of the city's new skyscrapers, cracks opened up in the foundations and throughout the structures. Although few of Jakarta's twelve million residents died, the incident left President Suharto severely shaken. Raised in Central Java and marinated in its mysticism, the former general worried that the earth's convulsions might be a sign that his long rule was ending, just as earthquakes and eclipses had augured the end of so many antique kingdoms. So the president asked for help from Sujono

Humardhani, a member of his inner circle and an old friend from his barracks days. Sujono, who styled himself an expert in Javanese mysticism, knew much about such matters as omens and portents. Most importantly, his discretion could be trusted.

Sujono decided to consult an experienced diviner. The astrologer told him that the nail fixing Java to the earth had come unglued, so the island, which is about the size of Great Britain, was bobbing in the Java Sea like a ship with a loose anchor. The solution was to nail Java back into the earth's surface. Neither a five-centimeter nor a five-kilometer spike would suffice. The soothsayer told Sujono he had to cut a tree from a particular sacred forest near Surakarta. Suharto's friend was to pound the shorn trunk into the ground. That, the diviner said, would reattach Java to its foundation.

Immediately, Sujono traveled to the forest to fell a suitable trunk. Then the president's confidant brought the tree, bereft of its branches, to Jakarta, where engineers supposedly drove it into the capital's swampy substrate. When Sujono proudly told the diviner what he had accomplished, the soothsayer shook his head with disappointment. "The spiritual center of Java is not Jakarta," the astrologer informed him. Frustrated, Sujono left to retrieve a second tree for another nailing. But before he could accomplish his mission, he died. Sujono had been so obsessed with secrecy and discretion that he had failed to tell anyone – including the president – where the trunk was to go. And thus Suharto was left with the nail, and no idea where to place it in order to stabilize his unsettled nation.

I had heard many similar stories from locals, diplomats, and longtime residents. I listened to them eagerly, hoping to extract some revelation about the country's famously remote and reticent leader. I could never print these tales in the magazine where I was employed. Most of these stories interlaced fact and fiction so expertly that to separate one from the other would collapse the whole confection. But I could not afford to ignore them, for these stories helped describe and capture, better than mere statistics ever could, the country's true troubled condition.

For thirty years since the mid-1960s, a military-supported, authoritarian Cold War dictatorship had governed Indonesia. For three decades, a compliant parliament had elected President Suharto to six successive terms. No other leader, it seemed, could ever be considered. Suharto's rule had been so effective in silencing dissent and satiating his people that little news of interest or import seemed to emanate from the archipelago, the world's fourth most-populous nation. So for much of those three decades, Indonesia practically vanished off many people's mental maps. One anthropologist wrote that, for such a large, resource-rich and important state, Indonesia's "essential invisibility was something of an achievement." The country had become so ignored that one of its tiniest island provinces, the tourist paradise of Bali, came to be more famous than the country in which it was located. Another region, the eastern half of Timor island, became notorious for other reasons. Indonesia, with the tacit approval of the United States, had crudely annexed the former Portuguese colony in 1975, leading to the deaths of an estimated quarter of a million people, approximately a third of the population. Jakarta's rule was widely considered a fiasco, a shame that would end with East Timor's independence in 1999.

But when I arrived in late 1997, Indonesia, for several reasons, had started to reenter the world's stage. By the mid-1990s, Suharto was well into his seventies. He had far exceeded the life expectancy of the average Indonesian male. His people could no longer ignore the dictator's mortality, and his potential passing worried many Indonesians, for they were unprepared for a future without Suharto in charge. In particular, his generals, officials, and cronies, who had prospered under his rule, grew nervous that the privileges they had enjoyed would wane as his life force diminished. Those concerns were the reason that, from the mid- to late-1990s, the president's ministers, bureaucrats and soldiers arrested, tried, and jailed scores of Indonesians, some for just discussing what had delicately been called the post-Suharto "succession." Even mystics were not spared. In 1995, one famous paranormal went to jail for mentioning that Suharto's end was nearing. Yet the arrests of dissidents and their show trials proved less the government's strength than its insecurity. It was obvious – after three decades of apparent stability, Indonesia had to face an inevitable transformation.

As I traveled and wrote about the confused country, I kept running into other tales, some much older than the one the diplomat had told me. People I interviewed often mentioned one particular legend, which I was told had originated in the ninth century. Its author was the ruler of a kingdom in what is now East Java. The king, whose name was Jayabaya, had once described the end of the world. He had dubbed the end of days the *zaman edan*, the "age of madness." Popular during late colonial times and in the early days of independence, the various versions of the "Jayabaya prophecy," like the predictions of Nostradamus, have a disputed provenance. Few have seen the original version, which lies locked away, as it turns out, somewhere in the Radyopustoko Museum. The tale may be as recent as the eighteenth century, a proto-nationalist creation circulated by native opponents of the Dutch colonial regime. None of these facts diminished the legend's vast and continuing popularity.

Every version I have read of the Jayabaya prophecy contains a common theme: that the *zaman edan* would be identified by the rise of rampant, senseless injustice. *One day there will be disaster,* one version I had found on the Internet read:

In the east, in the west, in the south, and in the north.
Good people will suffer.
Criminals will rejoice.
When this happens, a crow will be called an egret.
The liar will be called honest.
Traitors will live in the lap of comfort.
The deceitful will perfect themselves.
The evil ones will rise to the top.
The humble will be trapped.

These tales of loose nails and ages of madness suggested that these years seemed, to many Indonesians, a time that could only be described as apocalyptic. My job as a foreign correspondent was to chronicle every step in a traumatic transition. Until early 2000, I covered riots, elections, secession, and religious and ethnic violence. But in the hundreds of stories I had encountered, I did not find any that really captured when, how, and why the tricks the Suharto government had long used stopped being effective. I was looking for a true story: one that was neither a fabrication nor a fantasy, but a story about real people who had to operate in a society in the midst of a breakdown.

I found that story in an incident that had occurred before I even arrived in the country. In 1996, I had read about a infamous murder in the city of Jogja, several hundred kilometers southeast of Jakarta, deep inside Central Java. In August of that year, unknown assailants had beaten to death Fuad Muhammad Syafruddin, a local reporter for a second-string daily. Udin, as his friends knew him, had just completed a series of stories criticizing the local government. On one level, his tale was depressingly familiar. According to statistics from press freedom organizations, between 1982 and 1999, nearly nine hundred journalists were shot, stabbed, beaten, or killed, mostly in Africa, Asia, or Latin America. From my own country, the Philippines, a few journalists seem each year to have become victims. In 1998, for example, one Filipino radio commentator died in his own recording booth. He was shot during a broadcast.

Less than one per cent of journalists killed on the job since 1992 were United States citizens. But they died largely because they practice what is essentially a foreign profession, inspired by newsroom ideals shaped in New York, Washington, and London. "We reporters, we are all Americans," an Indonesian journalist once described his position to an Australian academic. Indeed, the governments and leading elites of developing countries seem allergic to the press. Suspected and distrusted by those who should protect and value them, stymied by the rarity of accurate information, and burdened with the anxiety that they are hastening "Westernization," a journalist in the developing world can face unbearable obstacles. Murder, sadly, is one of them.

But on another level, Udin's story was distinct from the familiar parable of the martyred reporter. Where many journalists' deaths in the developing world go unsolved or uninvestigated, this one produced a murder suspect and not one but *two* trials. A few months after Udin's death, the local police arrested a high-school dropout. Although the accused had never met the journalist previously, his case went to court and became a national sensation. This journalist's murder in Java thus became an opportunity to examine more than just one untold story. In most tales of true crime in the developed world, the author shows the reader how law and order there work more or less effectively if not efficiently: a criminal commits a despicable act, which then sets the wheels of justice in motion which usually crush him. This story allowed me to use the same conventions to take a close look at the opposite phenomenon – how *injustice* functions: What happens when, in the wake of a crime, the authorities seek not to punish the perpetrator but to hide him, and not to discover the truth but to bury it.

That injustice is a feature of life in the developing world. Between 1965 and 1985, the per capita gross national product in Indonesia rose by an average of 4.8 per cent a year, faster than any of its neighbors in Southeast Asia, save Singapore. In 1970, early in Suharto's rule, two out of three Indonesians lived below the poverty line. Twenty years later, that fraction had dropped to somewhere closer to one in ten. This record, for a while, stood as proof – at least supposedly – that Indonesia had bootstrapped itself out of the last century. Yet even as the World Bank or the International Monetary Fund congratulated Suharto on his success, the country's political and legal institutions were hopelessly stunted. Indonesia's parliament was a joke, its courts were corrupt, and its police at best bumbling and at worst actively malevolent. This was development?

That the delivery of justice seemed a low priority for the developing world cannot be blamed solely on the international aid organizations or the multinational corporations that appreciated free trade and open markets more than due process or a free press. Nor should the governments that rewarded the former and paid lip service to the latter be altogether faulted. The problem cannot be ascribed either to the human-rights organizations that, over the past few decades, have raised and spent billions campaigning for "respect" of human rights and yet devoted virtually nothing to assist in the delivery of basic legal services. All of these parties were in their own way complicit. But the responsibility lies largely on the shoulders of the elites that took over after the colonial powers departed.

In 1955, Sukarno, Indonesia's first president, famously invited leaders of Asian and African countries to a historic conference in the mountain city of Bandung in West Java. Comfortably ensconced in the art deco resort hotels the Dutch had constructed, Gamel Abdel-Nasser of Egypt chatted with Norodom Sihanouk of Cambodia, while Chou En-Lai of China had tea with Jawaharlal Nehru of India. The Bandung conference had been intended to show the Great Powers that the developing world intended to take a commanding role in the global future. These leaders promised their long-suffering, newly independent people that they would achieve the wealth, stature and power of their former Western overlords in a single generation without losing their own identities in the process. It was a laudable goal, but what happened along the way was that these elites simply replaced the extractive, colonial class that departed. Their control of the new countries brought authentic wealth and power largely to themselves, while their populations received cheap imitations. The result today of these broken promises is distressing: the widespread disillusionment in the developing world with the modern institutions bequeathed by the West, from a market economy to courts of civil justice to a cosmopolitan civil society. That exhaustion with modernity has helped create, among other effects, the present-day twinned phenomena of violent terrorism and narrow religious, cultural, or racial chauvinism. Half a century after Bandung, the Third World has become not a new force in its own right but a wasteland of damaged societies and injured cultures.

Yet Udin's murder drew me in because it described something larger than either of these stories – the ossification of Suharto's Indonesia and the exhaustion of the world after "decolonization." The case revealed something fundamental about human beings. I left Surakarta skeptical about the astrologer's explanation for Udin's death. I did not believe the reporter had died, as Darmodipuro had suggested, because he had been born at the worst time imaginable. Neither was I convinced that his death was somehow a heroic sacrifice, which had become the prevailing view among the Indonesian media. What led to Udin's death was not fate, but something that resembles it: the collective consequence of individual choices.

An authoritarian government appears to be run by one man, or a ruling clique, such as that man's family, soldiers, and courtiers. But a dictatorship, in truth, survives because millions have accepted and internalized its rules and become complicit in its existence. In Indonesia, Suharto's rule lasted three decades not because he alone willed it, but because hundreds of thousands of people willingly did his bidding. That kind of collective choice resembles fate, because its visible consequences – a nation's history, or its politics, or its character – seem so fixed and immutable. But in one important way, collective choice is different from predestination. If enough people – even those who believe themselves powerless – decide to act differently, they can change what surrounds them.

Udin died for doing his job. Perhaps he did have the luck or ill fortune to live in a *zaman edan*, when a dictator's mortality had forced all individuals to make critical choices: whether they would defend the system – one they had known for decades – or try to change it. Udin's only fault, if it could be called one, was to fall afoul of people who supported a system, which, however unjust or corrupt, had given them privilege and security for three decades. The consequence was very likely his murder.

What truly intrigued me was how Udin's death gave others the opportunity to choose differently from the status quo, at a time when making that choice clearly brought personal perils, as it had to Udin himself. In fact, as do most murder victims in crime stories, the martyred reporter drops out early in this saga. I found that the true subject of this tale of a journalist's murder is not the journalist himself, but the people his death affected: his accused murderer, of course, but also the colleagues who tried to expose the truth behind his killing, the lawyers that defended his alleged killer in a system that was stacked against them, and the people of Jogjakarta who supported their struggle from beginning to end.

From the point of view of 1997, Udin's death and its aftermath did appear to represent a victory by those who supported reaction. But the fact that the following year one of the most powerful authoritarians of the post-war age had to relinquish power meant that a collective choice for change could matter. His death unmasked what Suharto and his elite had created: an enveloping system where lies had supplanted truth, amorality had replaced justice, black was called white, the guilty deemed innocent, and where criminals rejoiced and good people suffered. But instead of silencing future dissidents, the journalist's death sent the message that no matter how intimidating and encompassing the system, the only way to stop it from taking more victims was if enough people fought to change it.

In late 2000, I resigned my position at the magazine and moved to Central Java so I could investigate and examine what one man's death had set in motion – in a country in the grip of momentous change, at a time when the old rules were soon to be irrevocably altered.

CHAPTER 1

Wuku Warigalit

His deity is Brahma, whose face is handsome. The person will be the subject of much discussion. His wood is Sulastri, *without blossoms. Its character enchants those who see it. His bird is the oriole; its personality is always suspicious and jealous...*

Wuku Warigalit *is not materialistic. Its misfortune is to face obstacles.*

THE MOTORCYCLE'S HIGH BEAM sliced through the darkness that masked the road. Patches of freckled asphalt passed underneath its circumference. As the cycle rounded the road's curves, its headlight briefly swerved away from the road's surface to expose firefly-haunted ditches and gloomy thickets of sugar cane. But mostly it remained fixed relentlessly on a point a few meters in front. In the black void that surrounded the road on either side, the light it shone quickly dissipated. By day, the flooded paddies might focus and reflect the sun's brightness, making the very air above them shimmer. But at night, the rice fields turn into something that swallows light with an unquenchable thirst, like a parched ocean.

Indonesia is too vast and too poor to line its rural roads with streetlights. At night, villagers across Java leave the bulbs outside their homes switched on, supposedly to provide enough illumination to expose marauders. But the shadows that crawl from the darkened fields just wait, patiently, outside the reach of the weak porch bulbs. The dark still provides enough cover for villains either corporeal or ethereal. The wan glow thus imparts only a semblance of security. Beside the rural road, blank, naked light shone down on the barred front doors, shuttered kiosks, and lonely yards, which lay empty in anticipation like bulb-lit prison cells or barren stages. Further away from the road, across the unlit patches of countryside, Javanese village homes look like groups of fishing boats huddling together in a vast, dim sea. At night, the island no longer seems the most densely populated on the planet, but a place forlorn, abandoned, and haunted.

The man slicing his single headlight through the night was taller and much heavier than most of his countrymen. Thick-waisted, with a spreading belly, he fit snugly into the motorcycle's seat. A full helmet protected his head and face, which, if visible, would not strike many people as being particularly handsome, although its owner had been born in the *wuku* of *Warigalit*. The man's paunchy cheeks puffed out as if his mouth contained a small explosion. His head above his almond-shaped eyes had only a light dusting of hair, although his face made up the deficit with a scraggly beard and sideburns. The man's rotund build, balding crown and pear-shaped jowls made him look like a large, bearded baby.

As the man neared the city, the rural darkness gave way to the fluorescent sheen of urban commerce. The rider passed illuminated billboards, brightly lit dry-goods stores, and glowing windows, piled high with plates of sweetmeat curries of all-night Sumatran restaurants. Closer to the city, with its clusters of electrified buildings and shops and fewer darkened cane fields and paddies, the night seemed less menacing and lonely. The motorcycle rider could now glimpse, through doorways and windows, comforting scenes of relaxed domesticity: perhaps a family at home watching television, or men in *peci* and checkered sarongs sitting on mats in a small mosque, gossiping long after nighttime prayers. On the now-crowded road, families purred past him on motorcycles. Women kept one hand on their heads to stop their headscarves from flying off. Groups of youths cheered as they throttled around in convoys fueled by exhaust and hormones. Tarpaulin-draped food stalls on the populated sidewalks offered peanut sauce-drenched spears of satay, fried rice, spiced catfish, or coffee. By the time he reached Solo Road, the city's principal east-west avenue, the motorcycle rider was thick in the reassuring embrace of humanity.

The leaky, ramshackle office of the newspaper *Bernas* stood slightly back from Solo Road's row of hotels, jewelry stores and textile emporiums. Upon the rider's entrance, a passing editor joked how the heavy leather jacket and gloves the man wore made him resemble an aging British pop star. The man grinned but did not linger to banter. At the office, the man spoke to his colleagues little anyway. And tonight, he had a 9:00 p.m. deadline. A story he did not submit by that time meant missed earnings.

Udin did not receive a salary from *Bernas*, although he had worked for the Jogjakarta newspaper for over a decade, longer than many full-time staffers. One of two reporters covering the *kabupaten* of Bantul, south of Jogja, Udin was what other papers call a freelance correspondent. He was paid by the piece. In a good month, he might be able to report, write and submit about eighty stories, which could earn him the equivalent of $150, a comfortable income in his area. In the past few months, he had been hitting that target. Udin had chosen productive and profitable beats: local crime and local politics. He spent his days, Pentax camera in hand, casing the local government offices in the *kabupaten*'s capital, also called Bantul. At night, he would travel the dozen or so kilometers up from his home to the *Bernas* office in Jogja to hand in his pieces.

The *kabupaten* of Bantul was the smallest and second-poorest among the four *kabupaten* and one municipality that constitute the province of Jogjakarta. In the 1990s, the national government considered two out of three villages in Bantul among Indonesia's neediest. Bantul suffered from a problem that afflicted the rest of the island: too little land and too many people. Around 130 million, or sixty per cent of Indonesia's population, live on Java, which constitutes just seven per cent of Indonesia's total land area. If that proportion were mapped on the United States, to approximate Java's population density, the 114 million people who live east of the Mississippi would have to pack themselves into the state of New York. Since most of Java's residents live cramped in towns and villages in order to conserve land for agriculture, most visitors to the island barely notice the overcrowding. But to many Javanese, that density defines their reality.

Bantul alone supports 750,000 people. About fifteen hundred residents, on average, occupy each square kilometer. The Jakarta government's program of aggressively encouraging family planning and of resettling many hundreds of thousands of Javanese, including thousands from Bantul, on islands elsewhere in the archipelago had only relieved some of the population pressure. In the mid-1990s, by one estimate, one in four poor people in Jogjakarta province lived in Bantul. Unable to provide a livelihood to all its children, the *kabupaten* supplied the city of Jogja its surplus labor, which became Jogja's coolies, street vendors, or petty criminals.

Udin did not own land. His father, sixty-one-year-old Wagiman Dzuchoti, now an imam at Bantul's main mosque, had supported his six children as a construction worker before turning full-time to religion in his retirement. As a young man, Udin had wanted to join the military but his family did not have the right connections to secure his admission. He enrolled instead in the education department of a local university. Two years later, he abandoned his studies because his family could not afford to keep him in college. He tried various jobs, including working as a stonemason. He helped build Bantul's main mosque, where he would later attend prayers led by his father. So when he landed a job as a *Bernas* contributor, which his peers regarded as a professional position, Udin had been ecstatic. Sure, the newspaper could not offer him a regular salary, and he initially had to borrow a battered bicycle to go all over Bantul to report his stories, but he had the assurance that if he put in the effort, he could bring home enough money to start a family. In 1986, his first year on the job, he placed copies of the newspaper in front of his girlfriend at the time, Marsiyem. "See, I can write!" he had told her proudly, pointing to one of his first published stories.

Ten years later, his stories appeared so frequently in *Bernas* the novelty of seeing his name in newsprint had long worn off. Journalism did not seem too different from a trade like masonry, except that its materials were facts and quotations and its mortar the words that linked them. This night, 13 August 1996, the reporter took his usual spot near the low wooden divider separating the newspaper's editorial section from its modest reception area. He nodded politely to his seatmate, Herman Rio Itawan, the paper's senior crime reporter. A tall, gangly man with a wide grin, Herman had worked for the police for a decade before joining *Bernas*. Like Udin, he, too, was a non-salaried contributor. He had, however, the most enviably remunerative beat of all – city crime – which meant that Herman could often earn more than the paper's salaried staffers.

On this night, Herman was struggling to put together the day's stories. The words were not coming forth no matter how much the ex-cop tried summoning them. Herman looked helplessly at Udin, and asked for the other journalist's help. The big man nodded, but he started work first on his own story, which needed a headline:

> BANTUL – The armed forces faction is questioning the progress of the road-raising project in Kasihan…The project…while having as much as $140 left from a prepared budget of $27,195…has only completed 1.4 kilometers out a planned two kilometers…this must be questioned…

Udin had written dozens of stories like this. Stolen funds, shoddy projects, and unexplained anomalies in government budgets – these stories put food on his family's table. Graft in Indonesia had so many manifestations that the word "corruption" could barely contain the vast variety of swindles, conspiracies, kickbacks, and thievery practiced by those who had authority and power. The faceless people at the nameless desks of the Indonesian bureaucracy controlled the flow of money from the government to its vast population. They were the first to know of cheap loans for agriculture, of micro-loans for the poor, of government-funded scholarships for promising young scholars, or of subsidies for cooperatives. If they could not take advantage of these opportunities themselves, civil servants would offer them to their friends and relatives, so at least to keep the benefits of their position within the family circle. They also handled taxes and other government revenues, which meant that if they pocketed some, no one would be any wiser. In trade and business, the bureaucrats determined whose shipments would be released and whose would be confiscated, whose licenses would be renewed and whose would be cancelled. In this life, they could be like minor gods to other Indonesians. They decided who would prosper and who would suffer.

In the villages, the Indonesian government bureaucracy was inescapable. Anyone who wanted a job, marry, build a house, or move to another village had to visit the headman or his deputy for the necessary permits and papers – documents with august titles such as "Letter of Good Behavior" or "Letter of Clean Environment." Much of this paperwork was perfunctory. The latter certificate, for example, confirmed that the bearer had no association with the Indonesian Communist Party, which the right-wing military that ran the current government banned and then wiped out in the mid- to late-1960s. In one village in West Java, an anthropologist once counted, officials could write more than twenty-one different kinds of these types of letters.

The main offering to propitiate these petty deities was money. Village officials, for example, levied a commission for preparing land transfers. (Some officials, for an additional fee, would helpfully draw up two deeds, so an unscrupulous owner could sell the same parcel of land to different buyers.) Udin had once written about a village whose residents picketed the village office because their headman had set the fee for land registration at an outrageous twenty-five dollars and ten cents for every square meter. In December 1995, Udin wrote a story about the ex-village head of Karangtengah, in the Imogiri region of Bantul. The man had broken into the village office to burn land certificates because he feared his constituents would find out just how much he had cooked the books to line his pockets.

So a missing half-kilometer of road? That was almost laughably ordinary. Siphoning money off the budget for a dam, canal, clinic, school, park, or even public toilet – sometimes at the cost of leaving the project half-completed – was among the most elementary of scams. An official might start there, and as he was promoted up the civil service, graduate to more sophisticated swindles. In Indonesia, government assets or foreign aid would often vanish, to end up, without explanation, in the personal bank accounts of certain individuals. Or the scam could be as sly as granting a relative a profitable contract to supply snacks for one's official meetings, or to provide the stationery to one's entire department. In Indonesia, government jobholders classified their work into "wet" and "dry" positions. The "dry" positions were those where the main income was one's salary. The "wet" jobs, such as those in the public works, labor, or finance departments, sloshed with opportunities for self-enrichment. In one annually published index of global graft at the time, Indonesia consistently ranked among the top ten most corrupt countries, in the company of nations such as Bangladesh and Nigeria.

Udin found many of his stories about corruption in Karangtengah, a village so poor that Jakarta had singled it out to participate in a nationwide poverty alleviation program. The program, known by the initials "IDT," disbursed cash every year from a $213 million fund to several hundred villages around the archipelago. Officials in each community gave the poorest households between forty to fifty dollars each. These families, in turn, pooled their funds to form small businesses, such as cooking snacks or breeding livestock – at least that was the idea. In November 1995, Udin heard from several contacts in Karangtengah that many who did not qualify as needy had appeared inexplicably on the list of recipients for that village's scheduled handouts. Many in the village suspected the names belonged to friends or relatives of members of the village government. "The rich become richer, the poor like me stay poor," one villager complained bitterly to the reporter.

The following year, Udin visited Karangtengah again. This year, his contacts told him, village officials had developed a new way to skim the IDT money. Although the program's official guidelines did not instruct officials to deduct a portion of the subsidy, Karangtengah officials, Udin was told, had withheld ten per cent from each handout to cover supposed "administrative expenses." Some poor families also claimed they had received about twenty dollars, less than half of the forty-three they had been expecting. When residents confronted their village leaders about the missing funds due them, they were told the remaining money was still safely deposited in the state rural bank. But when Udin checked with the branch manager, he learned Karangtengah's IDT account had long been emptied. Udin titled his report, which ran in late July: "In Karangtengah Village, Imogiri, Bantul, Only Half the IDT Funds Have Been Given Out." In a follow-up piece, the headline had a more searing metaphor for the subtraction. The Karangtengah poor's missing money, *Bernas* blared, was like a "circumcision."

That August, Udin stopped producing his streak of stories out of the Karangtengah IDT controversies. Five sour-faced *kabupaten* officials had showed up at the *Bernas* office. The bureaucrats complained to Subadhi, the paper's aged assistant managing editor. The *kabupaten* of Bantul, they said, found Udin's coverage of the Karangtengah IDT program both inaccurate and harmful. If the editors did not change the paper's reporting, one official threatened, *Bernas* would have to deal personally with their superior, Bantul's *bupati*, Colonel Sri Roso Sudarmo.

"'Din, don't be so daring in your stories!" Udin's wife, Marsiyem, had pleaded with him when he told her what had transpired at the office.

"What can I do?" he had answered. "It's the truth."

But behind his façade of confidence, the threat of a lawsuit worried him and broke his concentration. During their meeting with Subadhi, the officials had agreed to end their dispute if the paper printed a letter to the editor. On 9 August 1996, the paper did publish the officials' explanation. The Karangtengah villagers were actually supposed to receive only twenty dollars each, not forty-three. Still, Udin promised Marsiyem, the reporter planned to visit Imogiri on 12 August to mend ties with the officials there personally. Dealing with officials in the future would be easier if they were not hostile. But, perhaps because since the letter was published no other Bantul official had visited *Bernas*, the reporter delayed his planned encounter. He had become occupied with other stories, including this one on the missing half-kilometer.

As he was writing, Udin heard loud voices coming from the reception area.

"Is Djoko here?" a man was asking the receptionist. The visitors were looking for Djoko Mulyono, a quiet thirty-seven-year-old reporter from East Java. He was the newspaper's other freelance Bantul correspondent.

Herman looked up from his computer. "'Din, you know these guys?" he asked. "Why are they so loud?"

Udin shrugged. The noisy voices receded. But after a few minutes, the receptionist approached. Djoko could not be found, he informed Udin, so the men now wanted to see him. The burly reporter got up and left the area to meet the visitors. Herman stood up to peer over the wooden divider. He watched Udin exit the building with the two strangers. In the paper's dim parking lot, the three men held a hushed but animated conversation. They were too far away for Herman to hear any of their words or see their expressions.

After a quarter of an hour, Udin returned to his seat. The Bantul reporter's demeanor had changed. He seemed worried; his nerves appeared shot with anxiety. Udin stood up from his computer and switched to another. He asked the crime reporter for a cigarette, which Herman thought was unusual, since Udin usually offered the smokes from his own pocket. Curious about why his friend, who a few minutes earlier had seemed so focused on his work, now appeared scattered and frantic, Herman asked the Bantul reporter if he had trouble.

"Just a land thing," Udin replied.

"If it's Djoko's land, then why are you so nervous?" Herman ventured.

"It's nothing," Udin insisted. The reporter returned to his rapid typing.

He had finished only one of his stories when he rose, picked up his jacket, and announced that he was going home.

"Wait!" said Herman, "I thought we were going back together!" Herman had wanted to sip tea with Udin at one of the sidewalk food stalls after their deadline. Besides, Udin still had to help the crime reporter write his story. With the Bantul correspondent gone, the ex-cop would have to do his article himself.

"But..."

But Udin was already out the door, and, although Herman did not yet know it, he would be the last person at the newspaper to speak to Udin alive.

If Javanese astrologers posit that the moment of birth decides one's fate, there is a good argument that the place of one's birth has an influence that is just as powerful and equally inescapable. Udin had been born on 18 February 1963, a *sampar wangké*. But his destiny would probably have been different had he been born somewhere other than in the conservative, traditional province of Jogjakarta. Encompassing approximately 3,170 square kilometers, roughly the same size as the U.S. state of Rhode Island, Jogjakarta is Indonesia's second-smallest province after the national capital district. The province's borders enclose an area roughly the shape of a triangle clipped out of the lower half of Central Java. Much of it is flat agricultural land, except around its main geographical feature, which lies at the triangle's apex. An active volcano, Mount Merapi, rises about three kilometers above sea level. The northern part of the province slopes upward its near-perfect cone. The capital city, Jogja, sits due south of Merapi, sandwiched between the volcano and the Indian Ocean, which locals call the Southern Ocean.

Jogja's geographical center is a walled area one kilometer square below Solo Road. The complex contains the palace of the province's sultan and the homes of his relatives and servants. Its walls embrace two banyan-shaded squares, one each on the northern and southern sides of the palace

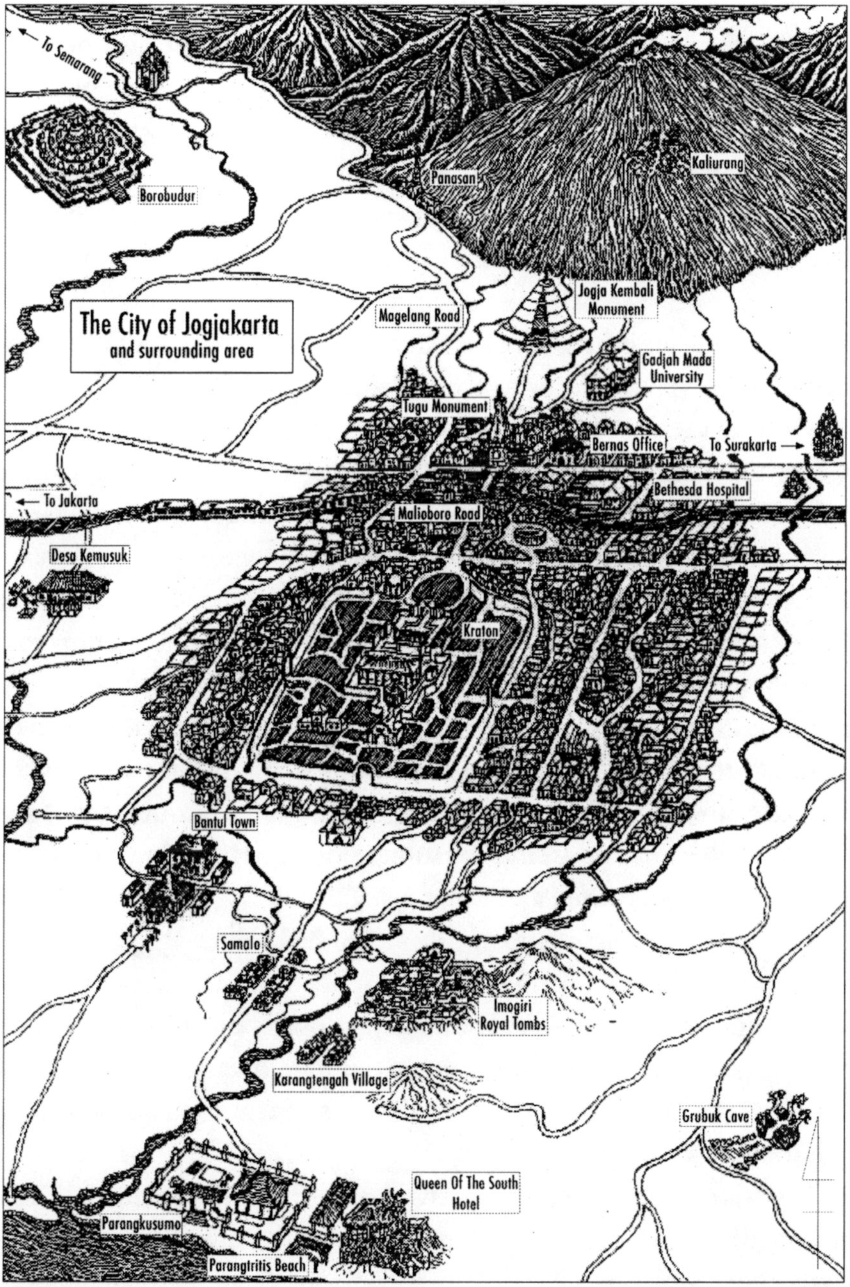
To Semarang
Borobudur
Panasan
Kaliurang
The City of Jogjakarta
and surrounding area
Magelang Road
Jogja Kembali
Monument
Gadjah Mada
University
Tugu Monument
Bernas Office
To Surakarta
To Jakarta
Bethesda Hospital
Malioboro Road
Desa Kemusuk
Kraton
Bantul Town
Samalo
Imogiri
Royal Tombs
Karangtengah Village
Grubuk Cave
Queen Of The South
Hotel
Parangkusumo
Parangtritis Beach

proper, which, many years ago, once hosted battles between captured tigers and water buffaloes for the sultan's amusement. A skein of pencil-thin alleys and narrow roads, hemmed in by cramped homes built by generations of palace servants, connect the two squares. Stout, bleached battlements encircle and defend the entire labyrinth, turning the area into a cramped, Javanese version of the Forbidden City. Inside the walled town-within-a-town, each home rises no taller than a single story, so none of the sultan's servants would sit on a higher level than their lord and master.

Just as both the province and the city share the same name, the sultan's palace and the walled city that surrounds it are both called the *kraton*. To a visitor, the whole place seems quaint and timeless. The residents of the *kraton* hang caged songbirds above their roofs or inside the eaves of their picturesque houses. Horse-drawn carriages clop through the *kraton* alleys, which, until a multilateral aid organization stepped in to build one, did not have proper drainage or sewage systems. The *kraton* boasts several nineteenth century public clocks imported from Europe, but each tells a different time. All appear to be broken.

Although bureaucrats housed elsewhere run the province, the *kraton* serves as the sultanate's spiritual center. Among the ideas the Javanese had imported from India was a belief in divine kingship: that a ruler exerted both political power and religious influence. Court astrologers had carefully chosen the city's location midway between a volcano and an ocean, symbols of fire and water. Each pavilion, gate, and courtyard of the *kraton* had been meticulously positioned so that the parts as well as the whole structure formed a mandala. The court's mystics believed that by designing the palace as a massive cosmic diagram, the sultan's home could harness the natural energy of the universe to augment his power, so he could shine aristocratic Javanese civilization and advanced culture into the barbaric countryside.

The *kraton*'s antique patina deceives many visitors into assuming Jogja is a medieval city. The town, however, only dates from the mid-eighteenth century, when the Dutch, in a classic divide-and-rule colonial tactic, distributed the lands of Mataram, the last major Javanese kingdom, between two squabbling branches of the royal family. One branch of the clan built its court in Jogja, while the other founded a new palace in Surakarta, also known as Solo, sixty-three kilometers to the east. After independence, the Indonesian government placed Surakarta's territories under the administration of a new province encompassing Central Java. But Jogja's own independence continued, largely due to its canny maneuvering of its cosmopolitan then-sultan, Hamengkubuwono IX. The sultan understood that when the Dutch left, his kingdom would not survive if his court sided with the foreigners, as sycophantic Surakarta long had. When Indonesian nationalists declared independence from the Dutch on 17 August 1945, Hamengkubuwono IX volunteered his city to serve as the embattled new republic's capital. While nationalists resisted the Dutch, who had returned after the Second World War to reconquer their resource-rich colony from the occupying Japanese, the sultan allowed a nationalist foundation to teach law and literature in the *kraton*. Hamengkubuwono IX thus helped found Gadjah Mada University, the infant country's first Indonesian-run institution of higher learning. In 1949, after years of battling exhausting guerrilla warfare and international criticism, the Netherlands recognized Indonesia's independence. Before departing to the colonial capital of Batavia, which would be renamed Jakarta, the victorious nationalists gave Jogja – and its sultan – a reward: autonomy. While Surakarta would be absorbed and completely stripped of its political identity, Jogja would become its own self-ruling province, an island of kingship in a republican ocean, a pocket of the past in a newborn nation.

Like the principalities of Monaco or Liechtenstein in Europe, Jogjakarta took pride in being among the last autonomous kingdoms in Southeast Asia. But for the people who are born or who live in Jogjakarta, that special status can sometimes seem less a blessing than a nuisance. Other places in the archipelago welcomed the opportunity independence provided to start a new history under a new national identity. But like many places that constantly look back to a storied past, Jogjakarta seems uncomfortable in the present and uninterested in the future. So Java's old traditions and institutions retained its hold on Jogjakarta.

Central Javanese society, classically conceived, follows a hierarchical model. The royalty and the aristocracy formed the highest tier, the farmers and the merchants sat below them, and the peasants and paupers struggled to stay on the lowest rung. This model, encouraged by the court, taught that stability and order required strict adherence to social rules, because conflict would never exist if each accepted his proper place in society. The deep-seated caste distinctions emerged even in the Javanese language. The tongue has several styles of speech to express gradations of status, from flowery High Javanese to the crude Low Javanese of the streets and markets. When one Javanese wants to show respect to another, he or she speaks in nasal, multi-syllabic High Javanese. Familiarity, on the other hand, permits the earthier Low Javanese version. The sultanate famously conserves its dances, literature, and other artistic traditions against innovation. For example, compared to the brilliant, busy batik motifs of the north coast trading ports of Java, such as Cirebon or Pekalongan, which had long absorbed Chinese and Western colors, designs and techniques into their cloths, Jogja's style of batik has long stayed limited to monochromatic, court-approved repeating patterns.

Although by the mid-1990s, Jogja had become home to about 1.4 million people, the city still kept time according to its courtly, small-town, schedule. Surrounded by a grid of rice paddies which look, from the air, like a verdigrised, cracked mirror, the city rises and goes to bed according to its own agricultural clock. Its inhabitants complete most of the day's important work by noontime, when the bristling heat forces everyone to flee under the shade of mango trees or inside the cool stone walls of their houses. In the equatorial climate, days and nights vary little with the seasons, so each day seems identical to the one before it. The sun beats down regardless of whether it is July or January. Night arrives brusquely around 6:00 p.m., in April or in September.

The booming population did force Jogja to develop, but it did so in the awkward, graceless way of an adolescent. Fast-food and department store franchises opened branches on Malioboro Road, the main avenue connecting Solo Road to the *kraton*. Weedy housing complexes and strip malls sprung up along the avenues leading out from the palace complex. But since many farmers could not bear to give up their valuable land, three-story buildings were erected beside cultivated rice paddies, and water buffaloes to this day plow lazily through the mud just one block from Jogja's municipal hall. Much of the city now looks like a Frankensteinesque patchwork of urban blocks and rural hamlets. Often, a peek behind a built-up, urban façade of shop houses and mechanic's garages reveals a sea of emerald green rice stalks, rippling like water as a breeze passes across them.

Public transportation never quite caught up with the city's expanding borders. The *becak*, a version of a rickshaw which is mounted on a tricycle, remains Jogja's main form of public conveyance, the best alternative to the city's thieving, expensive taxis and creaky, smoke-belching buses. Propelled by the powerful legs of its operator, often a sun-browned man with bad teeth, a *becak* takes twenty minutes to half an hour to travel a kilometer. So those who could afford the down payment bought private transportation, which in the 1990s was something also two-wheeled but fuel-powered. Japanese-brand motorcycles replaced the bicycles once favored by Jogja's citizens. In 1996, Jogjakarta had over 330,000 motorcycles, a number that almost equaled its entire population of cars, trucks, and other four-wheeled vehicles. Most thoroughfares in the city have at least one Yamaha, Suzuki, or Honda dealer. Their stock rolled across Jogja's streets, clogging each city intersection like flies on a papaya. Surrounded by hundreds of the vehicles, Jogja's children grew up understanding motorcycles instinctively. Some can even pinpoint a motorcycle's year, make, and model from the pitch of an engine's purr or the sound of its firing pistons.

Jogja's main industry, aside from tourism, is education. Perhaps because the sultan had been so supportive of native learning, Jogja became

Indonesia's foremost college town. In the mid-1990s, the city hosted over seventy institutes of higher education, the students of which accounted for as much of seven per cent of the city's population. Around the campus neighborhoods packed with cheap student restaurants, computer cafes, photocopy stores, and stalls selling pirated software, the city did seem younger, more forward-looking and less mired in its traditions. But outside these academic ghettos, Jogja was still the overgrown rural Javanese town of farmers, small traders, and an aging aristocracy. Trapped in the past, Jogja became for many a stultifying prison. But it is exactly such places that often produce dreamers and rebels.

Udin lived in Bantul, about halfway down a two-lane provincial highway known as Parangtritis Road that snaked south from Jogja through the middle of the *kabupaten*, just as a sliver of water buffalo horn forms the pliable spine of a *wayang* puppet. Udin and Marsiyem paid about fifty dollars a year to rent a small house beside a furniture store in Samalo, a hamlet about thirteen kilometers south of the *kraton*. Officially, Samalo was part of Patalan village. But in Indonesia, a "village" is a loose term that could encompass any number of spread-out, isolated communities. Samalo, more precisely, was a group of houses sprinkled among the irrigation canals, sugarcane fields, and rice paddies on the outskirts of Bantul town, the *kabupaten*'s capital. Farmers and minor civil servants, who worked either at offices in Jogja or in the nearby fields, made up Samalo's resident population. The couple's neighbors included two women who ran a restaurant across the road from the couple's home that served steaming bowls of noodles. Right next door to Udin lived the journalist's cousin, Sumaryati, and her husband Sujarah, who made his living driving a truck for a snack company. Sumaryati operated a small store from the front of their home, from which she peddled Giv soap, cartons of tea, and boxes of matches.

Udin had his own business, too. He, a neighbor he had brought in as a business partner, and the twenty-nine-year-old Marsiyem developed

THE INVISIBLE PALACE 45

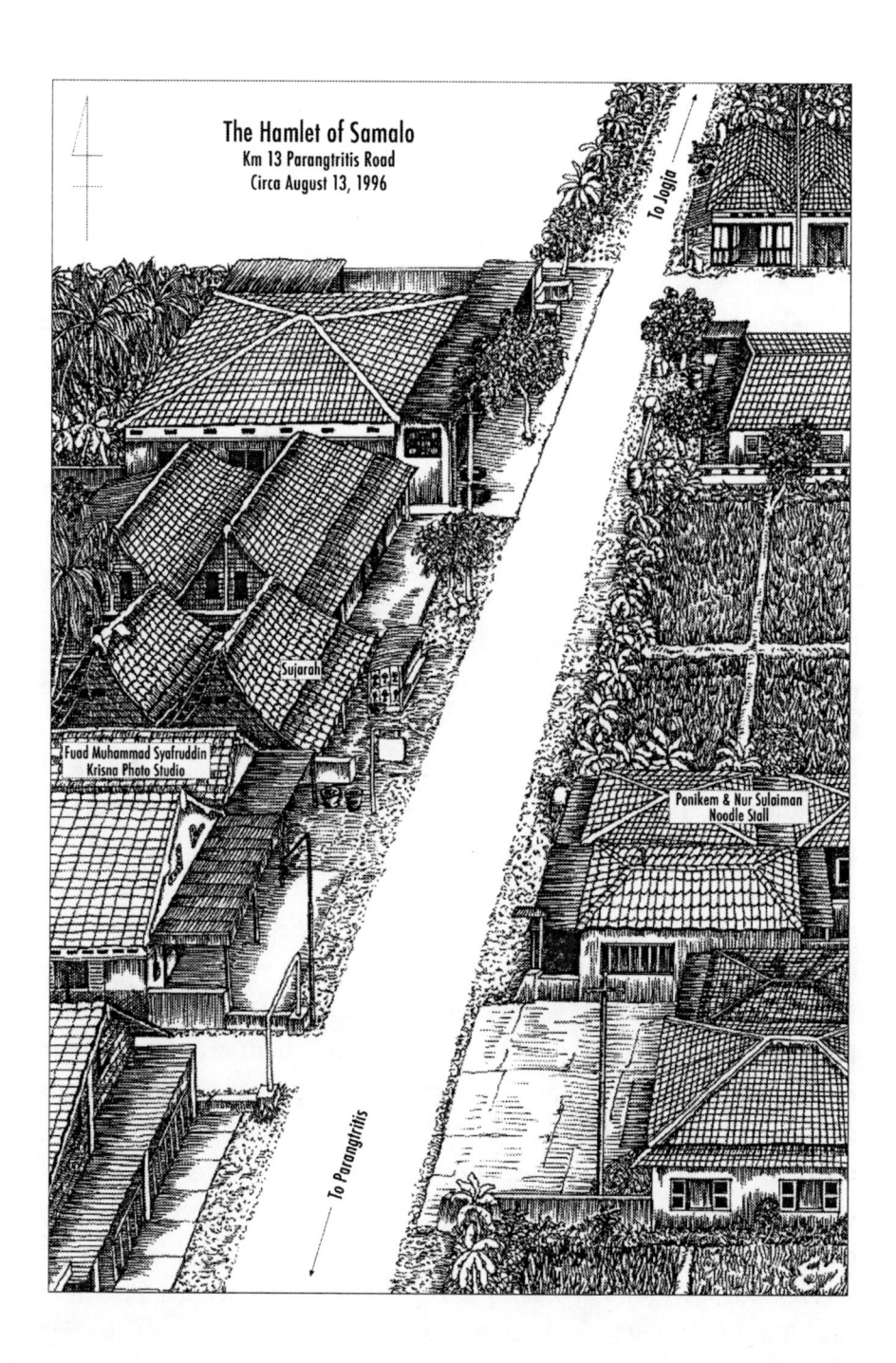

film and printed photographs for customers from their home. In a room in front of Parangtritis Road, the couple also sold picture frames and albums from dusty glass cabinets. As the business prospered, their stock expanded to include stationery, plastic flowers, and other cheap household trinkets. Behind the shop, Udin set up a portrait studio. He had an artist decorate the walls with painted backdrops for his customers, who might want to pose for their portraits in front of a serene rose sky over distant mountains, or under a pair of doves fluttering over a faux window decorated with blooming flowers.

Samalo turned out to be an excellent location. Although Parangtritis Road ends where the island does, at the edge of the Indian Ocean, a fair amount of people traveled down the highway. The road's destination, Parangtritis, was famed throughout Java: six kilometers of concrete-colored sand surrounded by rock crags and bordered by a brackish stream. By no means can the grey-sand beach be called beautiful. Unlike lusher, cleaner coasts further east, such as those on Bali or the eastern islands, no reefs or lagoons shelter Parangtritis from the open sea, so tall waves crash upon the shore, making the beach regularly too rough for swimming. When the water recedes, it exposes areas as broad as two hundred meters, and then covers them up in a vast rush of surf, creating an undertow that makes the beach sometimes even too dangerous for wading.

Yet Javanese visit Parangtritis not for what they can see, but what they supposedly can never see: the realm of an ancient goddess named Nyai Roro Kidul, who predates Islam and perhaps even Hinduism on Java. Locals venerate her all along the island's southern coast. Often called the Queen of the Southern Ocean, she supposedly rules over the spirits of the island's trees, mountains, and rivers. These spirits had to move to the ocean depths because humans had crowded them off the island. Her palace, legend has it, lies somewhere deep underwater just off the beach at Parangtritis.

Nyai Roro Kidul, her legend also says, makes Parangtritis perilous to swimmers. In 1994, seven people drowned at her beach. The following year, the ocean claimed thirteen more lives. Then in 1996, in the most shocking display of her power, twelve children drowned in a single day. Although a sign outside the beach's often-unmanned safety post warns visitors against swimming in the choppy waters, on any given day, couples recklessly invite their children into the surf to paddle, even as the receding tide tugs insistently at their ankles, and the water pulls at their clothes and blouses. It is said that the reason that so many drown at Parangtritis is so Nyai Roro Kidul can have a constant supply of servants and soldiers to populate and defend her palace. If the Queen spots a person on the beach who she desires, she will open before that individual a vision of a tree-lined avenue leading down into the ocean. That person, irresistibly drawn down the path, will believe he or she is entering a magnificent city when in reality his or her lungs are filling with water.

Despite Parangtritis' dangers, both physical and metaphysical, enough people visit that a sizable tourist industry has sprouted to fulfill the visitors' needs and desires. Cement-brick boarding houses, built on the sand, provide passable lodging, thatched-roof restaurants offer a decent repast, while bars, brothels, and gambling dens market other, less wholesome entertainments. The prostitutes of Parangtritis offer erotic encounters for about six dollars, sometimes with the room included. Their grimy buildings encroach on the sand, obscuring whatever natural attraction the beach possessed with the miasma of commerce. Plastic straws, cigarette butts, and abandoned rubber slippers litter the goddess' dunes, while hawkers or horse cart-drivers tramp up and down the frontage of her Southern Ocean.

Notwithstanding the degeneration of the beach, Parangtritis still draws both serious worshippers and curious tourists eager to encounter Nyai Roro Kidul. On *Kliwon* Tuesdays or Fridays, aspiring mystics may meditate naked on the sands in the surrounding caves. Their requests to the Queen vary from a simple wish to be granted to the endowment of a supernatural power. On those days, heavier-than-usual traffic passes down Parangtritis Road. In 1996, the thirteenth of August fell on a

Kliwon Tuesday. But since Javanese consider a market-day weekday to end not at midnight but at sunset, by the time Udin reached his house after fleeing his disturbing encounter at the office, *Kliwon* Tuesday had long gone. Parangtritis Road was quiet and deserted.

The *Bernas* reporter called his business the Krisna Photo Studio. Krisna was his eldest: a daughter born eight years earlier formally named Zulaikha Dita Krisna, but nicknamed "Yuli." The couple had one other child: a two-year-old, Wikan, which was short for Zulkarnaen Wikanjaya. When Udin returned home, both children had already gone to bed. Marsiyem was ironing the family laundry. The four of them lived in the one remaining room in the house not devoted to the portrait studio. Barely twelve meters square, their living space fit two dressers, a desk for Udin's computer, and a small table for his citizens band radio.

Using a dresser to create a divider, Marsiyem had carved out space in the back for a basic kitchen. That day, she had been so busy with the chores she had not prepared any food for her husband's dinner. She offered to buy a bowl of noodles for Udin from the ladies who ran the restaurant across Parangtritis Road. But the reporter said he was sick of eating their food, which he and Sujarah consumed far too often. Udin said he only wanted to go to bed. He had had a long day, and rest would be welcome.

"Only five more pieces to iron," Marsiyem promised her husband.

Udin changed into a shirt and a sarong. He switched on the computer to play some computer chess. To pass the time, Udin also turned on his citizens band radio. The apparatus often came in handy for stories. Once, while chatting with other radio amateurs, he had found a disgruntled member of the *kabupaten* assembly. From him, Udin obtained some useful leads on local political rivalries. At home, the worry had fallen from Udin's shoulders. His wife was near. Their children slept safe in their shared room. The pressed laundry gave off a pleasant, clean scent. He was secure. No one could touch him.

A thin, pretty woman with high cheekbones and light, clear skin, Marsiyem had dated Udin for about two years before their marriage.

The couple had first met during a village volleyball practice. At the time, she had been a high-school student, and Udin a novice journalist and *Bernas* distribution agent. She found the big-bodied man considerate, understanding, and charmingly shy. He was so shy, in fact, that whenever they quarreled, he would insist on writing her a long letter instead of discussing their differences in person. When they were dating, he wrote at least six of these bashful missives to apologize for minor spats and quarrels.

On their early dates, the couple strolled along Parangtritis. They paid a few coins to the *kabupaten* at the entrance for access to the beach. As long as they avoided the food stalls and hawkers, they paid virtually nothing for an afternoon of sea breezes and conversation. On their nights out, Udin invited her to watch action movies at the Widya Bioscope in the *kraton*. The loud explosions and the actors' pointless exertions bored her, but she went along because she liked him. First of all, he came from a pious Muslim family, as she did. Secondly, he was full of promise: he was a diligent worker and he had a decent, respected job. When the couple married, they dressed up in Javanese finery. Udin wore a high black hat and had gold tips attached to the top of his ears, a Javanese symbol of wisdom. Marsiyem wore her hair pulled back and studded with gilded hairpins. She had her forehead painted with stylized bangs, so she looked like a life-size version of a shadow puppet.

When Marsiyem heard three loud raps – rapid and insistent – at the door, she still had three of the children's shirts to finish ironing. She set her iron on its bottom, crossed through the dark portrait studio and unlatched the front door. She glanced at the clock hanging on the wall of the storefront. The two hands told her that the time was 10:40 p.m.

"Who is it?" she called out.

She cracked open the door and saw a fit, good-looking youth about 1.68 meters tall. He was dressed all in red. The bandanna around his head had been cut from cloth dyed a deep blood color. His shirt, buttoned all the way up to the collar, was of a shade of crimson that was slightly lighter. His round face had unblemished skin and a pencil-thin mustache.

He spoke in the nasal tones of High Javanese: "It's me, ma'am."

"What do you need?" she responded in the same polite language.

"Is Udin in?"

"What do you want?"

"I want to leave my motorcycle with him," he said. "I can't put this into the muffler." For a moment, a rod of metal about the thickness of her thumb flashed in the darkness. The material of its manufacture resembled stainless steel, but she could not make out from what part of the vehicle it came.

"Where is your motorcycle?"

"Oh, over there." He nodded towards a point somewhere up the dark, empty road.

Marsiyem closed the door. Perhaps if Udin had gone to bed, she would have ignored the interruption or asked the visitor to leave a message. She hated to disturb her husband when he needed his rest. But Udin was still awake, waiting for her to finish. So Marsiyem told him he had a visitor. "I don't know who or where he's from," she said. "He just wants to leave his motorcycle with you."

Before leaving the room, Udin changed from his sarong into a pair of brown khakis, and buttoned a green shirt over his white singlet. Marsiyem turned back to her laundry. The iron was still hot; she could finish her ironing shortly. After a few moments, she realized that her husband had not invited the polite man inside. In fact, she could not hear Udin at all.

She set aside her iron and moved toward the front door.

At the same moment, Udin's neighbor Sujarah sat moaning next door. He was miserable. The thirty-two-year-old had been sick to the stomach since morning. At work, he had felt weak and dizzy. All he could bear to put in his mouth was a cigarette or some water. No solid food could stay down his esophagus. He had not felt any better when he got home that afternoon. Usually, to make some extra income, he sold motorcycle fuel to travelers along Parangtritis Road from a kiosk in front of his house until 10:00 p.m. This night, he felt so sick he had closed down the kiosk two hours earlier than normal.

Sumaryati insisted he eat something. She bought noodles from across the road, but the food failed to banish the ache in his belly. The snack-company driver wanted his day just to end. Then Sumaryati poked her head through a doorway to say that while she was in the toilet, she had heard a loud thud outside, as if a thick rice sack had fallen on the pavement.

A second later, they both heard somebody screaming. Sumaryati ran outside. On the other side of the low wall that separated their front yard from the Krisna Photo Studio, she saw Marsiyem cradling Udin's limp body. The reporter lay on the ground unconscious. Blackish blood leaked from his head. The liquid pooled on the concrete and spattered the clean clothes he had put on to meet the visitor.

Sumaryati fled back inside to tell Sujarah. Her husband quickly reached for the long farmer's blade he kept around to protect himself from the thugs who often robbed homes in this part of Bantul. Sujarah had warned Udin several times that he should always have a weapon ready to fend off these hoodlums. Well, his neighbor had ignored his advice. Still, Sujarah thought, whoever had felled Udin could not have traveled far. If he was quicker, the snack-company driver might be able to catch him.

When Sujarah reached his front yard, he could not see anyone running along the road's shadowed shoulder. Across the street, the women who ran the noodle restaurant were standing just outside their shop, transfixed by the blood-spattered scene before them. Marsiyem was shrieking for someone to find a car to bring Udin to a hospital. Sujarah knew that two houses away lived Udin's half-brother, who owned a car. Sujarah sprinted up Parangtritis Road to find him.

At that precise moment, two vehicles appeared on Parangtritis Road from the direction of Jogja. One was a Jeep, the other a motorcycle. As the vehicles passed the scene in front of the Krisna Photo Studio, the driver and the rider both spun around. The driver of the Jeep halted his car in front of Udin's house. Four young men exited. The rider let a sixth young man, his passenger, off the motorcycle before speeding back north towards Jogja.

Marsiyem begged the six men to help. They grabbed her husband's legs, while Salim Ma'aruf, a neighbor who had appeared beside her, supported Udin's back and arms as the group carried him into the vehicle. The reporter's blood was getting on everything – on the young men's clothes, on the car seats, and on Marsiyem. She cradled Udin's head, from which much of the blood seemed to be spurting. Liquid dripped from the *Bernas* reporter's ears, while blood in his throat gurgled horribly. As they stretched him out in the back of the Jeep, she asked Salim to get into the car. She did not recognize any of the men, so she wanted someone familiar to accompany her.

"Hurry! Hurry!" Marsiyem shouted at the driver.

Udin's large body barely fit inside the vehicle. His legs dangled out the rear window. In the car, Udin had difficulty breathing. The passengers in the Jeep felt like they, too, were suffocating. The air inside was spiced with the salty, coppery scent of blood.

As soon as the car pulled into the small hospital of Bantul, orderlies wheeled Udin into the emergency room. Marsiyem waited anxiously outside. She realized that she recognized one of the young men who had helped her. He was Sri Kuncoro, who went by the nickname "Kuncung." He was the man on the motorcycle that had sped away. Apparently, she learned, he had tried to pursue the assailant, but returned when he lost the trail. Kuncung also happened to be the nephew of Bantul *Bupati* Sri Roso.

The Jeep's driver tried to clean Udin's blood off his car's floor mat, while his friends washed their hands and arms in a hospital sink. Marsiyem turned to Kuncung and asked him to return to Samalo to pick up Udin's half-brother, who lived a few houses down from the Krisna Photo Studio. Another young man offered to locate Udin's father, Wagiman. The imam lived in a neighborhood just north of Samalo named Trirenggo.

"No, that's not needed. This will be nothing, you see," Marsiyem answered nervously. Udin suffered from diabetes as a result of years of sweet tea and snacks of sticky rice. His diet had left him dependent on medicines to moderate his high sugar level and blood pressure. Asthma had forced him to avoid the fragrant clove cigarettes favored by his neighbors, but the tobacco he smoked was not any better as an alternative. She had thought that perhaps if tragedy came to Udin, it would come naturally, as an attack of wheezing or coughing, or a spell of severe dizziness and fainting. She never dreamed that trouble would come dressed in a crimson shirt, wearing a blood-red bandanna, and that she would open the door to it.

Finally, a doctor appeared. He told Marsiyem the hospital could not handle someone in as serious a condition as what Udin had suffered. The reporter needed to be brought to a larger and better-equipped facility in Jogja. The doctor's diagnosis worried Marsiyem. She suspected the Bantul doctors had already written off her husband's life, if they were so hastily handing him off to another hospital. The clinic had readied an ambulance to take the victim to Bethesda Hospital, a Protestant-run institution that was a block away from the *Bernas* office on Solo Road. Although the ambulance had room for one person other than Marsiyem, none of the youths wanted to accompany her. One said blood scared him. Aside from Kuncung, Marsiyem recognized only Salim, who ran a satay stand a few dozen meters south of Ponikem and Nur Sulaiman's noodle restaurant. Roused from his bed by the commotion, Salim had come running up the road dressed only in his sleeping sarong. He did not have time to slip a shirt over his naked chest. When Marsiyem turned to ask him to accompany her to Jogja, Salim protested that he was not wearing a shirt and could not go to the city. To end the discussion, one of the young men handed him a jacket to clothe his bare torso. Salim got into the ambulance with her.

Less than an hour had passed from the moment her husband had been attacked to their departure from the Bantul hospital. But to Marsiyem, in those moments, her future had been irrevocably altered. A haze coated her senses. Even if someone had spoken directly to her, she would have heard or noticed little. But she remembered one phrase that sliced through her shock like a scalpel. In the crush of people at the hospital, someone had commented:

"*Mas Udin nek nggawé berita kendel banget.*"

She understood that sentence clearly. That person had said, in coarse Low Javanese: "The stories Udin wrote were just too daring."

CHAPTER 2

A Nation Always Needs an Enemy

SEVERAL CENTURIES AGO, a small, nondescript hill some forty-three kilometers northwest of Jogja lay bare and open to the sky. In contrast to the flat land on which much of Jogjakarta is nestled, this area of Central Java is hilly and densely forested. Perhaps among the scores of misty hillsides here, this particular mound alone had that perfect shape: gently convex, like a drop of water. Or maybe it stood out just a little, rising out of a patch of plain that isolated it from its fellows. Whatever the reason, within a few decades, the hill had disappeared. Laborers had encircled and piled on top of it tons of black volcanic rock, enough to cover 55,000 square meters. The monument they built to Buddhism in Java rose six stories high. The entombed hill now supported three terraces of stone, most of them carved to depict scenes from the past lives of Siddhartha Gautama. At Borobodur's pinnacle, seventy-two hollow stupas sheltered seventy-two serene images of Buddha.

The Buddhist kings of the thirteenth-century Sailendra dynasty had ordered this edifice built here as proof of their piety and their political domination of Central Java. But within a century, their grand project had a rival. A competing line of Hindu kings, the Sanjaya dynasty, had erected their own temple-mountain further east, on the plain between what are now Jogja and Surakarta. Near a river whose waters had been diverted to pass beside the temple complex, the Sanjaya lords had ordered three tall peaks of stone erected at a place that would later be called Prambanan. Each spire would be a shrine to one of the Hindu trinity of Brahma, Shiva, and Vishnu. Artisans encrusted the towers with carvings no less detailed than those at Borobodur, but these ones depicted scenes from the Hindu epics. Dozens of smaller, miniature shrines ringed the base of the three central towers, much like the other monument's stupas. Also intended to be a mandala – a palace of the religious imagination – Prambanan, the Hindu Sanjayas' creation, mimicked and perhaps even mocked the Buddhist Sailendras' Borobodur. After the collapse of both dynasties, their temples fell into ruin. After their reconstruction this century, Borobodur and Prambanan now rank among the main attractions for tourists to Jogja. But most visitors are probably unaware of both places' histories. The temples, which seem so serenely spiritual, were grand attempts at political one-upmanship.

When sovereigns change – from Buddhist to Hindu, or Dutch to Indonesian, from one president to his successor – they inevitably insist on distinguishing their rule from that of their predecessors. The measures they adopt might be as minor as changing a personal style, from lofty to folksy, or from devout to secular. Or, like the Sanjayas and Sailendras, they might build grand monuments to their great vision for society. Rarely do these moves alter the essential dynamic between the rulers and the ruled. The person paying the foreman might change, but for the workers, the stones have not become any lighter or the lifting any less taxing. And money still goes missing from the monument's budget.

When Indonesia's first president, Sukarno, declared independence, his people thought they could now be part of something truly new, a civilization finally free of the ancient feudalism of their sultan-strewn past or the economic extraction of their recently-ousted colonial oppressors. What the Dutch had left the people of the former East Indies was indeed unprecedented: a country that was nearly the size of a continent, although fractured by several seas, straits, mountains and jungles. Over several patient centuries, the Dutch had assembled a collection of islands spanning a distance that, if superimposed on Europe, would cover more than a dozen countries between Tehran and London. The vastness of its territory was the new nation's greatest strength and its most fundamental weakness. Home to three hundred ethnic groups who spoke more than two hundred languages, the new country threw together Muslim Bugis with animist Papuans, Hindu Balinese with Christian Bataks, and in the polarized political mess of the mid-twentieth century, radical Communists with devout Islamists and secular nationalists. After independence, Indonesia had become a "country." Its future as a nation looked much cloudier.

Acclaimed president at the age of forty-four, Sukarno devised one solution to Indonesia's problem of self-definition. The cultural, ethnic, and religious differences were too vast and complex to manage. The best he could do was to override them. Partly, he fell back on the ruling philosophies of the old Javanese sultans and Balinese kings, which was to use mandalas, monuments and magical symbols as a kind of political theater to dazzle their subjects. So Sukarno littered Jakarta with heroically posed, larger-than-life statues. His muscled giants breaking manacles of colonial oppression, or thrusting a bowl of frozen flames in the air, or pointing confidently towards the cosmos, still mark the crowded, polluted capital. The new nation might not have the security of a single culture, religion or ideology. But it could have monuments, a flag, a lingua franca, and an Independence Day – just like every other normal country.

Thus every 17 August, Sukarno gathered Muslims, Communists, Christians, and whoever else was now "Indonesian" in the center of Jakarta. Wearing a *peci*, a pair of dark glasses and a gleaming white tropical suit, he strode out before the throng to deliver an impassioned speech filled with dramatic, demagogic flourish. He thundered explicit comparisons between his Indonesia and the Great Powers: "America and France consecrate the month of July, China and the Soviet Union – October…so we hallow August, the month of our Proclamation!" But, skilled as he was as an ideologue, orator and propagandist, Sukarno was no administrator. He preferred the glamour of developing a unifying ideology and the exhilaration of leading such a large and promising nation to the bleary drudgery of budget-balancing and legislative drafting. Civilian politicians obliged by handing him a ceremonial role as head of state, while a prime minister and parliament handled day-to-day governmental functions.

But the parliamentarians themselves were not any more effective as leaders. Preoccupied with partisan maneuvering and greedy for the post-independence prizes of influence and power, they could rarely agree among themselves over which policies the new nation should follow. Between 1945 and 1958, Sukarno presided over more than seventeen different cabinets. His administration was in perpetual disarray. The country suffered from failed harvests, frequent rebellions, and rampant corruption. Sukarno's decision in 1960 to govern as a dictator and dissolve the inconvenient, incompetent, and fractured legislature led to further disaster. Without parliament, Sukarno allowed his ego to run rampant, while continuing to ignore the hard-nosed policy design and execution required of any effective leader. In the absence of a credible economic plan, inflation doubled between 1961 and 1964, before shooting up sevenfold in 1965. As the price of food and clothing rose far beyond the reach of their salaries, office workers hauled away their desks to sell secondhand, stevedores stole from shipboard cargoes, and soldiers set up roadblocks to extort money from travelers. On Java, a local Communist Party swelled with desperate and landless peasants. By the mid-1960s, the Party had accumulated an estimated three and one-half million members. The Indonesian Communist Party became the world's third-largest socialist organization after those of the Chinese and the Russians.

Frustrated by failure at home, Sukarno turned his anger towards the West. A decade earlier, he had revealingly told a visitor: "A nation always needs an enemy." Like many leaders, he understood that nothing unites a people more than a threat, even one half-imagined. In quick succession, the president challenged the Netherlands, Britain, and the United States. In 1964, he withdrew Indonesia from the United Nations and other multilateral organizations. Sukarno vowed to establish a rival world body to replace these imperialist-dominated groupings. His anti-U.N. would be called the "Conference of New Emerging Forces" and would group the Third World nations whose leaders he had hosted in Bandung. In 1965, Sukarno supported attacks against the U.S. embassy in Jakarta, the Peace Corps, and properties owned by American oil interests.

In a way, Sukarno was right. As the post-colonial world divided into opposing Cold War camps, one led by the United States, the other by the Soviet Union, the developing world's independence had become an exhilarating, short-lived illusion. The superpowers, like trigger-happy border sentries, believed no category existed other than friend or foe. Neutrality was not acceptable. Yet, at the same time, the aging and ailing Sukarno had become his own worst enemy. Like other third world independence leaders, he had become so enamored with his own visions of his country's future that he preferred those to the problem-ridden present. The military, racked with ideological and factional conflicts, fretted over the president's growing infatuation with the Indonesian Communist Party as a potential popular base. At the beginning of 1965, reports circulated in Jakarta that Sukarno had taken ill. Rumors of an imminent military takeover followed.

On 30 September 1965, several young officers kidnapped and killed six senior generals. The mutineers drove their captives to a marshy Jakarta suburb and dumped their bodies down a dry well known as the "Crocodile Hole." In a subsequent radio address, the rebel leader claimed his group had been protecting Sukarno from an imminent coup by an anti-Communist "Council of Generals." But the rebels had left one important general off their hit list. Third down in the army's chain of command, the missing general's name was Suharto.

Suharto, who at the time of the abductions had been a middle-aged officer, had distinguished himself during the anti-colonial struggle. On 1 March 1949, he had led a counterattack against Dutch forces that had occupied Jogja. By seizing the Indonesian capital, the Dutch had hoped to secure their reconquest of their colony and assure international recognition of their de facto authority over the former Dutch East Indies. When Suharto, then a twenty-eight-year-old lieutenant colonel in charge of the city's security, helped recapture Jogja for six hours, the infant republic demonstrated to the world that the Indonesian revolt would not be so easily extinguished. Later that year, diplomatic pressure led by the United States forced the Netherlands to recognize Indonesia's independence. Since that key battle, Suharto had maintained a low, apolitical profile, an attitude that might well have helped him survive and steadily rise through the heavily-politicized military. His humble, unassuming style might also have influenced the plotters to make the fatal mistake of overlooking him. But, in the light of how events turned out, decades later many Indonesians would wonder whether Suharto had led the plotters to believe that he would not challenge their plans, part of a meticulously diabolical plan to assure his rise to power.

The day after the putsch, Suharto, as the remaining most senior military leader, marshaled the army and crushed the rebellion. The military naturally acclaimed him its hero. At the time, so little was known about Suharto that the Central Intelligence Agency could only tell Washington that the general was "considered to be an anti-Communist." Suharto quickly proved that assessment correct. Whatever the true reasons behind the failed coup – whether the plotters were part of an internal power struggle within the military or ignorant pawns in a clever power grab engineered by Suharto – he and his fellow right-wing generals seized the opportunity to blame the Indonesian Communist Party for encouraging the officers to turn against their superiors. Army-controlled papers spread tales that Communists had flocked to the Crocodile Hole to torture and castrate the captured generals. (These tales were later disproved by the military's own autopsies.) Indonesians were told that every dead general – there were six of them – had to be paid with the lives of 100,000 Communists.

The military banned the party and rounded up over a thousand leftist leaders. A week after the failed coup, mobs attacked and incinerated the Indonesian Communist Party's Jakarta headquarters. In Bali, parts of Sumatra, and much of East and Central Java, mobs started to slaughter the party's members – including many who were not Communists at all. The bloodletting allowed many to act on personal grudges as well as local rivalries. People turned against their own relatives, friends or neighbors. In Central and East Java, youths, out-of-uniform soldiers, and members of Sukarno's own Indonesian Nationalist Party hunted down thousands of people accusing of being party supporters. In the massacres, people used farm implements as weapons: machetes, scythes, knives, bamboo staves, or hammers. Plowshares became swords; fields were turned into boneyards. High school students joined in. Teenage boys licked their victims' blood from their knives as a precaution so that the spirits would not later attempt vengeance on them. The killers hid the dead in dry wells, caves and creek ravines in the green Javanese landscape. So many decaying corpses floated down East Java's Brantas River that the residents of the port city of Surabaya, on the eastern edge of Java, had to push bodies from the sides of the city's canals each morning.

Within months, between 100,000 to half a million people died in one of the largest yet least-known or understood bloodbaths in modern history. That the Communists put up so little resistance to their mass execution seemed, at the time, proof of their complicity in the failed coup. Yet most people had joined the Indonesian Communist Party because it had promised them a share of land – something that would effect real change in their lives, instead of the promises Sukarno and other politicians were offering. And none of the victims had told the young officers to kidnap and kill their superiors. But the deed had been done: the world's third-largest Communist Party had passed into history.

The coup had also irreparably damaged Sukarno. The independence leader had been caught flat-footed by the crisis. Foolishly, during the putsch, he had consorted with the rebels at their south Jakarta headquarters, and then snubbed the reactionary military by skipping the murdered generals' funerals. Although after the coup, the president tried to pretend as if nothing had happened and that his power and authority remained unchallenged, once the vast Indonesian Communist Party had been eliminated, no other force was more powerful in the country than the military.

In fact, an extralegal "Council of Generals," known officially as the Committee for the Restoration of Peace and Order, did come into power. Established to mop up the Communist threat, the Committee could conduct searches without warrants, ban newspapers, arrest citizens and detain suspects for indefinite periods without trial. Even after the Indonesian Communist Party had been eradicated and its leaders convicted in a series of show trials, the Committee remained. Paradoxically, although the Committee had been established ostensibly to "restore peace and order," it justified its own existence and the necessity of military rule by continually identifying other threats from which the country had to be "protected." Sukarno had given good advice, indeed: "Every nation needs an enemy."

The military persuaded Indonesians, for example, into believing that the Communists had not been eradicated but merely driven underground. Given the ruthlessness with which the military had dealt with its nemesis, that possibility was unlikely. But the propaganda was so effective that in 1985, twenty years after the massacres, one of out of three Indonesians continued to maintain that Communism remained the greatest threat to the country. Another survey of educated Indonesians taken in the mid-1990s showed that many Indonesians still believed that the Communist threat remained real. By that time, though, the government had long moved on to other threats, such as Islamists, pro-democracy activists, or leftist journalists.

In the 1960s, however, the generals clearly could not govern indefinitely by committee. They needed a president. So on 11 March 1966, the military forced Sukarno to relinquish his authority to the forty-four-year-old Suharto. The independence leader died four years later. Suharto did not attend the funeral.

As Sukarno had before him, Suharto promised Indonesians change. He established himself as Sukarno's polar opposite, both in his private character and in his plans for the country. Diligent and a no-nonsense manager, Suharto, the son of an irrigation official in Jogjakarta, had made a success of himself through military service. So he preferred concrete, disciplined action to grand strategy. Suharto did continue, however, the tradition of one-man rule that the independence leader had brought back after a brief fling with parliamentary democracy. For like Sukarno, Suharto – and the right-wing generals – chose authoritarianism as the best way to impose unity on their frustratingly chaotic, centrifugal country.

The strategy they adopted could charitably be called a soft fascism. By 1973, the president had forced the cacophonous, post-independence menagerie of unions, lobby groups, and organizations to shut down or merge into a more manageable handful, so that only one group spoke for each respective segment of society. Civil servants could form only a single bureaucrats' union, while all their wives had to enter one official women's organization. Workers and journalists were each allowed one officially recognized union. There was one farmer's group, one chamber of commerce, even one toothpaste manufacturers' association. The Indonesian Communist Party remained banned; ex-members and their descendants or relatives barred by regulation from joining the civil service, the military, and practically any remunerative private employment. Suharto permitted only three political parties. The Unity and Development Party replaced the gaggle of Sukarno-era Muslim parties. Sukarno's emaciated power base, the Indonesian Nationalist Party, and several small Catholic and Protestant parties were forced to merge into the Indonesian Democratic Party, known in Indonesian by its initials: PDI.

The third political grouping, Golkar, was an entirely new creation. Controlled by the military – six out of seven early top leaders were from the armed forces – and supported by the bureaucracy, Golkar had the benefit of bottomless funds and nearly limitless government favor, including a rule that civil servants were prohibited from voting for another party. It would become the ruling cabal's political vehicle in parliament. Although it functioned practically like one, Golkar was not officially called a political party. The distinction permitted Golkar to organize branches at the village level, an activity that was off-limits to the other "political parties." Thus for much of the population, Golkar became a dominating influence. Through a combination of largesse and intimidation, the ruling party ensured that Indonesian voters chose no other party. And just to make sure, during elections for the reconstituted parliament, which happened once every five years, local officials counted invalid and blank ballots as votes for Golkar. Naturally, from 1971 onwards, Golkar won landslide majorities in every local assembly or legislature, from *kabupaten* to the national level. Golkar's dominance was one reason why for thirty years, the Indonesian parliament never passed legislation independent from that suggested by the executive. These two branches of the government became indistinguishable from each other.

With so much stacked in its favor, the ruling party's regular victories turned elections into empty rituals. In Java's feudal past, tyrants had insisted on submission. But modern elections, which both the post-colonial world and their former rulers believed were an indispensable requirement to be a modern nation, made – in the absence of a fair multiparty system – an additional, perverse demand on the citizenry: "consent" to their own repression. The politically aware withheld their vote in mute protest. But every five years, the rest dutifully voted and had delivered to them the inevitable government victory – a victory that their leaders then presented to the population and the outside world as confirmation that their authoritarian policies had popular legitimacy.

If this system bothered the United States or other foreign powers, those countries did little substantively to show their disapproval. Suharto's impatience with left-leaning third world politics and, especially, his eradication of the Indonesian Communist Party had endeared him to the developed world. "Indonesia: The Land the Communists Lost," chirped *TIME* magazine in the 1960s, "The West's best news for years in Asia." The taps of loans and aid money, shut off in the last years of Sukarno, were reopened. In 1969, developed countries, prodded by the United States, lent Indonesia over half a billion dollars, the first of annual aid disbursements that by 1986 had reached $2.5 billion yearly, making Indonesia the fifth-largest third world borrower. Japan became a particularly important benefactor. Tokyo provided a third of Indonesia's aid budget and made the country into the second-most important destination for Japanese investment after the United States. With the critical help of these foreign loans and handouts, Suharto plugged Sukarno's massive deficits, which had been eating up two-thirds of the state budget. Between 1965 and 1968, a team of U.S.-trained Indonesian economists wrestled Indonesia's annual inflation down from six hundred per cent to a more manageable ten per cent annually. In the first dozen years of Suharto's rule, Indonesia's economy expanded by seven per cent each year. As the decades passed, the fact that Suharto had come to power in the midst of a mass slaughter seemed increasingly insignificant to both his own people and the foreign governments that supported him. That he had instituted an airless, undemocratic regime also seemed irrelevant. Indonesians had stability, and for the West, a strategic oil-producing country had been kept out of the hands of Communists and firmly in their pockets.

To a population exhausted by the political and economic dislocations of the Sukarno era, the order and development that Suharto offered seemed like a godsend. Millions enthusiastically embraced the new dispensation. Under the government's guidance, villages from one end of the archipelago to the other began remaking themselves in one state-suggested image, so as to contribute to the impression of a more orderly Indonesia. Each community learned to line their roads with low concrete walls and build public buildings in an unlovely, brutal, yet functional style. Yearly competitions awarded municipalities that achieved a certain, nationally-determined level of "cleanliness." The country's diversity of culture, politics, and religion was tamed, ordered, and literally made uniform. Each of the three political parties even had an assigned color. Supporters of the Unity and Development Party always wore green, the color of Islam; leaders of the nationalist-democratic PDI required their members to sport red clothing. Golkar officials and cadres, meanwhile, paraded and rallied in sunflower yellow. The civil service also had its own color, which was, fittingly, gray. Even people usually unconcerned by politics and governments – such as *becak* drivers – had uniforms made so they could feel like they were a valued part of what Suharto had started calling "The New Order."

At his death, the lusty Sukarno had left four wives and several mistresses. Suharto had always been loyal to a single plump, moon-faced woman from a noble Surakarta bloodline who supported her husband and spoiled her children. Her name was Siti Hartinah, nicknamed Tien. As the old dynasties and Sukarno had done, the Suhartos continued building monuments. Most of their structures were devoted to the heroic exploits of the Indonesian military, such as Suharto's "General Attack" and the crushing of the 1965 coup attempt. There was one monument, which was conceived and planned by the schoolmarmish, matronly Tien, that best encapsulated the Indonesia her husband and his army were busy fashioning.

The "Beautiful Indonesia-in-Miniature Park," inaugurated in 1975, occupies over a hundred hectares not far from the Crocodile Hole. Its centerpiece is a complex of twenty-six pavilions, each representing one of Indonesia's provinces before the annexation of East Timor. Every pavilion represents each region's traditional architecture. Thus, ornate temple portals frame Bali's pavilion, while high, gabled roofs crown West Sumatra's mansion. Inspired by Disneyland, the park was a place where Indonesia's wild cultures and fractious politics were made to appear domesticated by a single governing intelligence. Suharto's rule was an impressive monument, and as every year passed, his one-man, one-party rule, supported by Western aid and investment, seemed even more rock-solid. It would take many years before people realized the structure's insides were hollow.

The day after the assault, *Bernas* did not run a story about Udin. The reporter had always tried his best to make deadlines, but this story – the one in which he was the subject – had happened too late to make the presses. The paper's front page on 14 August 1996 printed no news about what happened the night before at the Krisna Photo Studio. So most *Bernas* employees did not learn about the tragedy until they arrived at work that morning.

What they heard upset them. The beating Udin received had cracked his skull. A shard of bone had punctured his brain, causing massive bleeding and sending Udin into a coma. A doctor who examined the reporter after his arrival had jotted down that his condition was "serious, unconscious, and restless." At 8:30 a.m. that morning, Bethesda doctors had operated on his head to relieve a massive hemorrhage. They drained a couple of cups' worth of his blood. By the time his friends and family were allowed to visit Udin in the intensive care unit, doctors had swaddled the reporter's body, head, and hands in bandages so he looked embalmed, like an Egyptian mummy. A trickle of blood still dripped down his earlobe.

Many *Bernas* reporters headed first to visit Udin's colleague, Djoko. The other Bantul correspondent came from East Java, a region whose inhabitants are known throughout the country as coarse, talkative, and quick to anger. Djoko, however, was withdrawn, shy, and soft-spoken. He seemed more suited to be an accountant than a reporter. The assault on Udin had left him even more timid and quiet. Although Djoko knew a lot about Bantul, to each of his fellow reporters' questions, he gave the same answer: He knew nothing about what had happened to Udin, nor would he guess who might be behind it.

All Djoko could tell his colleagues was that several days earlier, Udin had mentioned he had received a disturbing piece of news. The Jogjakarta provincial military command wanted to question Udin about his Karangtengah IDT coverage. Such a request was not unusual. Like many leaders – and not only those of developing nations – Suharto distrusted his own people. Since civilians had bungled the country for the first two decades of independence, Suharto's military decided that it should now "assist" civilians in running the nation. Rather than concentrate its forces in headquarters and train them on bases, Indonesia's armed forces stationed soldiers in every town and province to form a sort of government-within-a-government. Military garrisons thus shadowed the civilian administration of provinces and municipalities. One step down on the administrative hierarchy, military sub-districts kept watch over *kabupaten* like Bantul.

It became impossible to distinguish where military authority ended and where civilian power began. Even in the nominally-civilian administration, active generals and colonels dominated. Although they were supposedly on active duty, these officers also served as ministers, governors, or senior managers in state-owned companies. In 1969, more than half of Indonesia's mayors and *bupati* came from the ranks of the military. Two years later, Suharto gave the armed forces even more power. In 1971, he permitted unelected, appointed military representatives to occupy a fifth of the seats in the five-hundred-member parliament. By the early 1980s, one in three cabinet members and one in four provincial governors was an active officer. "Under colonialism, we had a governor-general," wags joked. "Now that we're independent, we have general-governors."

To Suharto, who had been in the army since he was a teenager, effective leadership was about inculcating rules, respect, and discipline in an unruly population. The method he and his generals chose was inspired by their military training: propaganda and, if that was insufficiently persuasive, censorship. In 1965, the year he seized power, Suharto shuttered forty-six pro-Communist papers, which meant closing one in three newspapers in the country. Over the next decades, he and his advisers built a lasting and subtle system to control the media. His Information Ministry guided how Indonesian journalists covered their country. Its bureaucrats instructed the media to contribute to the country's development by advancing positive, uplifting news about Indonesia's accomplishments and refrain from exposing its seamy underbelly of corruption and political repression. Under this so-called "development journalism," reporters avoided critical coverage of government officials and institutions, which was thought to erode faith in the authority of government leaders. The Information Ministry would even dismiss graft with a glib, culturally relativist explanation. "A gift…in certain societies, if accepted, can be considered as corruption," one ministry pamphlet reasoned, "but in other societies, rejection can be considered an insult." Thus, that Udin's allegations of the misuse of IDT funds had attracted the attention of the local New Order military bureaucracy was understandable, even expected. The question was whether that attention was connected to the assault Udin had suffered.

The reporter's friends and colleagues wanted to learn more about the loud strangers who had visited Udin not more than an hour before the assault. They retrieved the names of the guests from the receptionists' records: "Suwandi" and "Sukrisno." At Djoko's home, *Bernas* staffers pressed the Bantul reporter to tell them more about these people. Udin's colleagues wanted to know if Djoko had been working on any sensitive stories. Perhaps Djoko had offended these men. So they had come that night to punish him but had tragically mistaken Udin for Djoko.

Mistaken identity turned out to be a dead-end hypothesis. Suwandi was a member of Bantul's *kabupaten* council. He was also a land broker, as was Sukrisno. To earn money on top of his fees as a *Bernas* contributor, Djoko moonlighted as a real estate agent. So he knew both these men. Since the two also knew him, when the two men wanted to see Udin, they clearly knew which Bantul reporter they wanted.

The injured reporter had mentioned to Herman he had a "land problem." Udin and Marsiyem were indeed looking for land along the road to Parangtritis. At *Bernas*, it was no secret that Udin's Krisna Photo Studio had become a profitable enterprise. People always needed photos: for school identification cards, job applications, weddings, and government paperwork. By 1995, five years after he and a neighbor had opened it together, the shop was earning about eight dollars a day.

In some months, Udin and his partner could take in the equivalent of two hundred dollars in profit.

Sujarah, his neighbor, often joked that Udin's expanding waistline tracked his growing wealth. He noticed that Udin could trade in his motorcycle nearly every other year for snazzier models. In 1996, the reporter had enough cash to buy a computer in addition to a bright red Honda Tiger motorcycle, the best and most expensive model then available. Udin could also afford to make repairs to his rented family home. He put plastic sheeting under the disintegrating clay roof to keep the rain out of the bedroom, and erected a tin awning in front of the store to protect his customers from the heat. But he and Marsiyem thought that it would be better to invest money soon in a place of their own rather than continue improving their rented property.

Although they knew Udin was looking to buy land, *Bernas* staffers could not shake their suspicions about his meeting with Sukrisno and Suwandi. The following assault of the reporter had tinted any event that occurred before it with strange and ominous colors. His friends' minds contained countless questions. Why had the assailant not tried to rob Udin's home? Why had nothing had been stolen from the wounded reporter? The crime had happened so swiftly and so violently. It seemed less born of passion than of premeditation.

At first, the management of the newspaper seemed uncertain how to approach the assault on a *Bernas* employee. The paper's publisher, a cautious fifty-five-year-old businessman named Kusfandhi, employed 130 or so people. Some sixty percent of his employees were editors and writers. Many of them spent their days outside the office. To him, the assault seemed regrettable; but it could have been an ordinary crime. He assigned it the same significance he would have if a photographer's pockets had been picked or a secretary's bag snatched at the market.

Kusfandhi's newspaper in fact covered crime extensively. The dozen or so pages *Bernas* published daily of local political, business, and social coverage also came heavily seasoned with stories of crime and the supernatural, both particularly popular topics among readers in Java. Occasionally, a story would mix magic and criminal mischief:

> **Corpse's Shroud and Thumb Stolen**
> **Residents Nervous: Signs Point to a Sacrifice**
>
> BOYOLALI – The residents of Keposong village, Musuk, Boyolali, are nervous following the theft of a burial shroud and the left-hand thumb of a dead baby...According to local belief...stealing a burial shroud and a left thumb was a condition for a sacrifice. Especially if taken from a corpse that had died on a *Kliwon* Tuesday...

The paper devoted several column inches on its front page to crime. The story of the day could be one of Jogja's frequent hit-and-run accidents, motorcycle thefts or school-test scams. But once in a while, the lead crime story would be about a murder. In March of that year, someone had stabbed a Bantul man as he was fixing the electric box outside his house during a power outage. The police arrested the victim's wife and her lover. In April, children in Jogja had stumbled on the body of a blind masseuse in an alley near their schoolhouse. Police arrested the victim's unemployed husband, who had stabbed and strangled his spouse after she had complained too often about his consistent lack of employment. The man had told *Bernas* that, after murdering his wife, he had thought of throwing himself down a well. But, he explained, "I cancelled this plan because I probably wouldn't die – just drink a lot of water."

Kusfandhi's paper perhaps covered so much crime not just because it sold issues but because lovers stabbing cuckolds or henpecked husbands strangling their wives were events that were generally apolitical. The Information Ministry had armies of bureaucrats whose single occupation was to monitor local media and report to their superiors any violations of government expectations. Should a print, television, or radio outlet publish or broadcast a story the government found subversive, a bureaucrat would immediately place a phone call to a representative of the offending publication or station. The conversations were invariably polite, but the message conveyed was not: retract, desist, or face sanctions.

The Information Ministry wielded two important powers with which it could punish the media. The first was a monopoly on newsprint, which allowed the government to deny paper to publications it deemed irresponsible. The second was an exclusive authority to grant publishing or broadcast licenses, without which no media company could legally operate. Just two years before, in 1994, the Ministry shut down three magazines, including the influential, twenty-three-year-old newsweekly *TEMPO*, which had a stature in Indonesia analogous to *TIME* in the United States. The closure threw over four hundred journalists and staff out of work. The magazines' fault had been to publicize a feud between a cabinet minister and the military over arms purchases. Kusfandhi may have thought if the assault on Udin was an ordinary crime, then a brief mention would be more than sufficient. If the assault was somehow more than what it appeared – something political – then any mention at all could be dangerous to the paper's survival.

Kusfandhi's initial reservations about expending too much ink on the beating sat uncomfortably with many people in the newsroom, among them Udin's editor, thirty-one-year-old Heru Prasetya. Thin, slight and with a shock of thick black hair, in a style that had gone out of fashion a decade earlier, Heru had since 1993 edited the "Around Jogjakarta" page. In other words, he ran the section of the paper that most often printed Udin's stories from Bantul. In those years, Heru and Udin had become close friends. The first time Heru had met the Bantul correspondent, he had felt intimated by Udin's size and glowering silence. The editor soon learned, however, that Udin's reticence masked a self-effacing shyness that resembled Heru's own. They even shared the same sense of humor – a preference for wry one-liners that would send their friends into peals of laughter.

Like many of his colleagues, Heru insisted that Kusfandhi and *Bernas* devote many more column inches to the assault on Udin. So the following day, on 15 August, a photograph of the bandaged and comatose Udin appeared on the front page of *Bernas*, along with several stories that detailed for readers what the paper's reporters could discover at the time about the incident.

The correspondents learned that Udin's assailant may have visited Samalo one day earlier. On the night of 12 August, Sujarah had met a man who had been looking for Udin on Parangtritis Road. The stranger resembled the one Marsiyem had described at her door. The driver had been eating in the noodle restaurant across from the Krisna Photo Studio near midnight. He looked across the street and saw a fit, attractive youth walking back and forth in front of Udin's home. The man wore white sneakers, blue jeans, and a black T-shirt stretched tight over a set of taut muscles. In one hand, he carried a white motorcycle helmet.

As Sujarah watched, the stranger knocked on Udin's door. Receiving no response, he bent over to peer through the keyhole. Sujarah knew that people visited the reporter at all hours. But something in the stranger's actions stirred his suspicions. Sujarah decided to cross Parangtritis Road and confront the young visitor.

"Is anything the matter?" he asked the young man.

"Is Udin in?" was the answer.

"Yes, should I call him?"

"No need, I'll just come back later. My motorcycle has broken down over there," the youth replied, gesturing to a motorcycle parked down the road towards Parangtritis. Before Sujarah could add another word, the man hurried away.

But well past midnight, after Sujarah had gone, the stranger had apparently returned. This time, he encountered the noodle restaurant's elderly cook, Ponikem, and its owner, Nur Sulaiman, who were closing up their eatery. Neither got a good look at the young man's face, since now he was wearing the white motorcycle helmet he had been carrying under his arm an hour earlier.

The stranger asked the two women if they knew Udin, and inquired if they knew where the journalist was this evening. Ponikem asked why the man was looking for the reporter. The young man repeated his story about the broken motorcycle, and added that he wanted to borrow a wrench from the reporter. He showed her a length of pipe that gleamed before he slipped it back into his jacket. What Ponikem found odd, she later told the police, is that when she told the man that a short way up Parangtritis Road there was a garage that could repair his motorcycle, the man just walked away. Ponikem recalled that the youth spoke in scrupulously polite Javanese, just like the man Marsiyem found at her door the following evening.

Although the neighbors could provide information about their encounters on 12 August, the reporters who assembled *Bernas*' first report on the crime could not get as many details about the night of the assault itself. On 13 August, Udin's neighbors said, none of them had gotten a good look at the reporter's assailant. Sujarah and Sujarwati had been inside the house, while Ponikem and Nur Sulaiman – whose kitchen sat directly opposite the Krisna Photo Studio – claimed their attention had been directed elsewhere at the critical moment. The cook said she had been washing dishes, while Nur did see Udin speaking to someone in front of his house but she turned away to call her daughter, who had been helping in the restaurant that evening. She spun back to look at the Krisna Photo Studio only when she heard Marsiyem's wailing.

Nur Sulaiman's daughter, Ayik Fatonah, also said that she saw little. Like her mother, she had been looking at the Krisna Photo Studio at the very moment Udin emerged to speak to his assailant. Yet at that instant, she told reporters and police that, she, too, had turned away. She added, however, that immediately after the assault, she had heard the sound of a Yamaha motorcycle in the distance.

So the only person who had seen Udin's assailant's face directly was Marsiyem. To the police, the reporter's wife described the youth as being of a particular height, with a trim, athletic build. His skin, she said, was a light brown – the color of a ripe *sawo* fruit – and his features were distinguished by his thin mustache and clear complexion. Nur Sulaiman's daughter Ayik was also able to describe the man she had seen standing outside the photo studio. She thought, however, he was about two centimeters shorter than Marsiyem's description. Although the man Marsiyem had seen on 13 August wore red clothes and a red bandanna, and the one Sujarah and the two noodle-stall women encountered on 12 August had on a dark shirt and a white helmet, their builds were close enough – and their stories about a broken motorcycle nearly identical – that reporters concluded they had to be the same person.

In Indonesian police slang, if a suspect cases a scene before committing a crime the act is called "batik," perhaps because planning a caper was a lot like drawing patterns on cloth first in wax before dying it. Perhaps the youth's plan had been to assault Udin that very night, 12 August. That was, after all, *Kliwon* Tuesday, a day that brought good fortune to the law-abiding and to criminals alike. A crime committed on a *Kliwon* Tuesday often gave the perpetrator the best chance for a successful heist and a clean getaway. But since Udin had failed to come to the door, the assailant might have delayed his assault until the following evening.

What reporters found interesting was that all four – Sujarah, Ponikem, Nur Sulaiman and Ayik – were certain that Udin's visitor had not been alone, either on 12 August or 13 August. He had an accomplice. Ponikem told police that after the young man left her on 12 August, "he went to his friend who was waiting with a motorcycle." Nur's daughter Ayik also insisted that she had seen a second figure lurking in the roadside darkness, several meters south of the Krisna Photo Studio. Sujarah also told investigators that on 13 August he was convinced that "this person was not alone. He must have had a friend waiting for him in the distance."

The presence of an accomplice, the existence of the "broken motorcycle" cover story, and the appearance of the mysterious youth a night before the assault convinced *Bernas* reporters that what had happened to Udin could not be a case of mistaken identity or even an aggravated robbery. It seemed something far more evil: an intentional assault on a defenseless individual.

CHAPTER 3

Carry It Out

IN THE MID-1990s, the kind of generational change familiar to journalists and editors worldwide had reached the *Bernas* newsroom. In the not-too-distant past, newspaper reporting had been a middle-class occupation whose members had made up for their lack of a formal education with street smarts and gumption. Now even at Jogja's second-best daily, journalism was increasingly populated by men and women with fancy educations who treated reporting as if it were some kind of profession or, even, a craft or perhaps a "calling."

For *Bernas*, the transition to a different breed of journalist began at the start of the decade, when the largest circulating national newspaper, *Kompas*, bought thirty-five per cent of Kusfandhi's newspaper. *Kompas*, profiting off its domination of the capital, had wanted to acquire footholds in provincial markets. It had already purchased shares in regional papers in Sumatra and Java, and had begun revamping each paper's management. The new investors injected a professional spirit and style into the once-stodgy *Bernas*, a fixture of the Jogja media since the 1950s. The paper's name, originally an acronym for *Berita Nasional*, or the "National News", had become *Bernas*, which conveniently happened to be an Indonesian word that means "firm" or "straightforward." *Kompas* provided a new headquarters building for the paper on Solo Road as well as several editorial advisers from Jakarta. To bring fresh energy into the newsroom, the new managers offered staff members over the age of forty-five early retirement so it could hire younger – and incidentally cheaper – journalists.

The new recruits included Udin's editor, Heru. He and his fellow new hires differed from the paper's grizzled veterans in several ways. Many had finished college and had chosen journalism as a career, unlike the previous batch of reporters who, like Udin, came from working-class backgrounds and had stumbled into the profession. Heru's background was solidly middle-class; his father had been a schoolteacher. As a student, Heru had devoted much of his spare time to writing short pieces for various pamphlets and papers. He would later admit he had no idea what a journalist's life required. But he knew he wanted to write, which was a sufficient enough reason to submit an application to the newspaper.

Heru took his job as editor seriously. He and other journalists had learned to measure their performance as reporters against the textbook standards of journalism, including its code of ethics that supposedly transcended national boundaries. Heru, for example, always pressed Udin to get both sides of a story before he would allow one of the contributor's pieces into the paper. Although *Bernas* paid staff members a pittance – when he started in 1990, Heru made the equivalent of ninety dollars a month plus benefits – Heru would never trade the high ideals of his profession, no matter how attractive the incentive. "One of the best editors at *Bernas*," one young *Bernas* reporter would call Heru. "His idealism was strong. He was often promised 'rewards' to fix stories. He never accepted. He never wanted that kind of money."

But many of the paper's older editors and reporters – and some of the new generation – saw their job as far more prosaic: to get a newspaper out and sell it. To do that successfully, certain unavoidable rules had to be followed. The Suharto government's system of censorship and propaganda did not just rely on the Information Ministry's power. Another important element in the government's press-control scheme was the Indonesian Journalists' Union, or PWI, the only organization permitted to represent journalists. If the Information Ministry's duty was to watch media owners, the PWI's responsibility was to keep tabs on reporters. Since 1969, the government has required every employee of the media industry to join the PWI. Conversely, any journalist expelled from the union could expect to be fired from his or her position. For editors and writers who embraced the regime, membership in the PWI brought great rewards, including overseas training junkets or assistance to relatives in finding jobs or schooling. But to the emerging young generation of reporters, the PWI represented a betrayal of the public trust. To them, the union was made up of people who had traded the objectivity and fairness required by their positions for the steady work assured by subservience and collaboration.

The best example of what one could achieve by being a loyal PWI member was Harmoko, the PWI's ex-president. Harmoko, a former caricaturist, ran the most successful newspaper in the country: *Pos Kota*, or "City Post." The tabloid served its readers the usual broadsheet fodder: a raunchy menu of celebrity scandals, miracle babies, headless corpses, gang rapes, and drug rings. Its editorials were staunchly anti-Communist and pro-Suharto. As head of the PWI, Harmoko aligned the union even more closely with the interests of Golkar, the military and the president. Harmoko's reward for his loyalty was appointment as Information Minister, one of the few non-soldiers to hold such a sensitive post. He also received elevation to parliament as a Golkar representative. Harmoko apparently used his influence profitably. Supposedly, during his tenure at the Information Ministry, he and his relatives acquired shares in thirty-one newspapers, TV stations, and magazines. The deals were on a quid pro quo basis: a ministry license in exchange for share of the profits.

Under Harmoko and his successors, the PWI ensured that the Information Ministry's policies and guidelines were followed. The union expected its members to practice "development journalism," which meant extolling the government's virtues and ignoring its flaws. According to this philosophy, criticism in the media damages the people's fragile faith in their government, thus it was best to abstain from examining policies too closely or to engage in attacks on public officials, even those known to be corrupt or abusive. Discouraged from writing informed dissent or from exposing official malfeasance, most Indonesian journalists produced insipid stories that read like press releases. Bound by the PWI and the Information Ministry, even private publications read like the state-run media.

Since one out of four print media organizations in Indonesia did not pay their staff a decent living wage, many reporters also engaged in a practice common in most developing countries – they accepted money in exchange for favorable stories. To ensure favorable coverage, government agencies, private companies, or wealthy individuals regularly handed out envelopes of cash during press conferences. Sometimes the bribes came in less public forms, such as a basket of gifts sent to an editor's office or a direct transfer into a reporter's bank account. For journalists with families to support, or who had grown used to the additional income, the envelopes became a feature of their day-to-day reporting. To the new breed of Indonesian journalists, nothing else symbolized how deeply their colleagues and their profession had been co-opted than these packages. The bundles of cash were nothing less than an outright purchase of a reporter's integrity.

The new, more professional *Bernas* paid higher salaries to its staff members so that they could refuse the envelopes. The management also instituted a system in which reporters could turn over what money they received, so an administrative assistant would return the cash to its source or donate it to charity. Not every journalist, especially those who had come to expect the handouts as a perk of their profession, followed the new policy. So some of the paper's more aggressive young staffers started posting the amounts they received on the paper's bulletin board to shame the senior reporters who were reluctant to give up what had been part of their earnings.

This subset of the younger generation of reporters had crossed the line between objective reporting and outright activism. The paper also hired reporters who were working their way through college. While someone like Heru might be content with preserving and promoting the best of journalistic ideals within the established system, these youths would not be satisfied with anything less than the system's destruction. Among them was Mohammad Achadi, a raffish twenty-four-year-old farmer's son and ladies' man with long hair and fashionably tattered clothing, who had joined the paper in 1994. Achadi had spent his entire education at Islamic boarding schools and was a student at a Muslim teachers' training college in Jogja. Despite his religious background, Achadi described himself as more a leftist than an Islamist. On campus, he and his friends had once distributed T-shirts emblazoned with the words of a radical Latin American Catholic bishop: "I feed the poor and they call me a saint. I ask why they are poor and they call me a Communist." For his campus magazine, Achadi had recklessly written a story detailing the Suharto family's corruption, a topic most mainstream media knew to treat gingerly. The local military command noticed. His college rector banned the publication and Achadi endured a police interrogation.

Achadi and his peers preferred sacrifice to selling out. Achadi had so little money he ate and slept at his campus mosque or in the *Bernas* office, where he kept his belongings stored in cardboard boxes among stacks of back issues. Although he and his friends earned two dollars a story at most, they regularly turned in every envelope they received. In a kind of slacker protest, they also neglected to send their membership applications to the PWI, although they continued working as full-time journalists. They quarreled constantly with Kusfandhi, whom they accused of being too concerned with his profits than with the advancement of his newspaper or its workers. *Bernas* circulated about 64,500 copies, about 30,000 issues fewer than *Kedaulatan Rakyat*, or "People's Sovereignty," which, although founded later then *Bernas*, had become Jogjakarta's paper of record. More radical than Kusfandhi's generation or Udin's or Heru's, the twenty-something student reporters treated the newspaper like they did their universities: as a coliseum for the clash between their rebellious, untainted idealism and the co-opted establishment of their elders.

Since the PWI was the government's recognized representative for journalists' interests, the union launched the media's official inquiry into Udin's beating. On 14 August 1996, the day after the crime, the union's Jogjakarta chapter formed a five-member "Fact-Finding team" to prepare a report for the PWI's Jakarta headquarters. Masduki Attamani, a well-liked and respected senior journalist from the national wire agency and a former *Bernas* employee, led the team. Other members included a *Bernas* editor, Putut Wiryawan, a fifteen-year veteran of the paper, and Asril Sutan Marajo, Jogja correspondent for the Semarang daily *Suara Merdeka*, or "Free Voice." Asril, in particular, had extensive contacts within the provincial police from his position as the PWI's police liaison.

Putut and Asril asked the *Bernas* archivist to gather Udin's articles from the previous twelve months. By perusing the murdered reporter's pieces, which bore his sole or joint byline, the PWI team thought they might locate a list of personalities who might have held a grudge against the reporter. But many of Udin's stories since the previous August could be considered controversial. One of his pieces, for example, had exposed a Karangtengah village official's affair with one of his constituents. The reporter had also embarrassed a bureaucrat who had overcharged for land certificates. And Udin had skewered a local bigwig who had swindled farmers out of their cattle and exposed a Bantul detective who had been accused of destroying evidence.

But the only people who had ever threatened Udin directly were bureaucrats from the Bantul *kabupaten*. The paper's publication of the *kabupaten*'s letter to the editor had apparently not ended the local government's displeasure. The PWI team discovered that the *kabupaten* had nonetheless gone ahead with its plan to go after Udin and his newspaper. A reporter for the *People's Sovereignty* had chanced on an official request by the *kabupaten* to the Bantul police to attend a 13 August meeting to discuss what to do with *Bernas* and its meddlesome Bantul correspondent.

In the past year, Udin had focused his readers' attention primarily on the activities of Bantul *kabupaten*'s governor, Sri Roso Sudarmo. A fifty-year-old artillery colonel, Sri Roso had been born in Bantul, in a part of Patalan village not far from Samalo. Once he joined the military, however, Sri Roso spent much of his professional life throughout Java. He returned to Jogjakarta when he was assigned as the province's garrison commander, a position from which many soldiers had launched successful careers in the civilian administration. It seemed almost predestined when, in 1991, Bantul's assembly appointed him *bupati* of his native *kabupaten*.

With military efficiency, the stone-faced colonel transformed the sleepy town of Bantul. For years, the place seemed less a town than a collection of large government buildings planted into the rice paddies. Under his administration, Bantul became a fastidiously clean local capital, proud of its shady main avenue lined with orderly whitewashed buildings. His office, a complex of palatial edifices surrounded by a one-square-kilometer wall, was the town's most notable feature, much as the *kraton* defined Jogja.

In 1995, Sri Roso had unveiled an ambitious development effort. The previous year, his administration had started planning a modest project in Parangtritis. The government wanted to build a children's swimming pool to protect visitors' offspring from the treacherous ocean and the appetite of its voracious queen. The pool was to cost an estimated $35,000. Several months later, however, that modest effort had expanded to a massive megaproject. A rich Jakarta conglomerate had suggested to the *kabupaten* that it could profitably build and manage a vast tourist development in exchange for the right to use over two hundred hectares of state-owned property along the Parangtritis coastline. The project, which would supposedly rake in billions of rupiah in tax and excise revenue for the local government, was to include a hotel, several vacation villas, an amusement park, and a seventy-six-hectare golf course. Worth an estimated forty-three million dollars, Sri Roso's office promoted the development as a way for the *kabupaten* to earn an estimated annual income of over a quarter of a million dollars, in addition to the tourist dollars the resort would attract to the local economy.

But the administration had to eject several dozen families who lived on the property before construction could commence. A few days before the groundbreaking ceremony for the project, Udin had arrived at the area to find about sixty residents demolishing their own homes, nail by nail and plank by plank, after Sri Roso's government had given them a week's notice of their eviction. Scattered on the gray Parangtritis sand, as if deposited from a shipwreck, were bits of building materials mixed with personal belongings. In such a short time, many had not been able to find new lodging. Now homeless, the evicted residents pitched tents or makeshift shelters from the remains of their old houses. "We don't own an inch of land anywhere," one woman told Udin.

Udin's story helped fuel public opposition to the project, which had been rumbling almost as soon as the development was announced. Some Bantul citizens complained that the proposed site plan encroached on a section of the Parangtritis beach known as Parangkusumo, an area considered especially sacred to Nyai Roro Kidul. They complained that the complex threatened not to make the beach a holier and more spiritual place but to increase clientele for the area's gambling dens and brothels. Local environmentalists protested that the golf course would be built on top of the habitat of a species of rare turtles, and that the planned development footprint would almost certainly eradicate Parangtritis' geologically unique sand dune formations. In fact, they pointed out, several times before, the *kabupaten* had cleared out the Parangtritis area for ambitious but ultimately-aborted developments. In 1992, for example, the local government razed forty-six stalls to build a "ritual tourist park" which never materialized. Two years later, more people were evicted for a planned but never finished amusement center. "For whose benefit is this development?" one member of the *kabupaten*'s local council asked Udin rhetorically. "A huge investment means nothing if the public suffers."

The Bantul council was a body of forty-five people tasked to oversee and approve the work of the *kabupaten* government. It was set up much like the national parliament, with representatives from the Unity and

Development Party, the PDI, Golkar and the military. Although Golkar and the military held twenty-seven seats in this assembly, the council still often clashed with Sri Roso. Some of the friction came out of the personal rivalry between the *bupati* and the council's chairman, Kamil Sugema, a crusty old colonel from West Java. Kamil appeared to be Sri Roso's chief rival for the *bupati* position when Sri Roso's term expired in May 1996.

But the straight-backed, humorless Sri Roso also had an imperious personality more suited to barking orders at the garrison headquarters than backslapping politicians in the halls of the local assembly. Shortly after he became *bupati*, Sri Roso brushed off a reporter requesting time to do a profile of him for Bantul's residents. "I am a native Bantul son. I know all of Bantul's nooks and crannies," Sri Roso said curtly. "So why do I have to introduce myself?" The colonel treated the Bantul assembly with similar high-handedness. Although in public, the executive and the legislative branches of the *kabupaten* government showed camaraderie and unity, council members complained in private that Sri Roso rarely invited them to local government functions. And when the council did make an appearance, they felt snubbed as the *bupati* hogged the spotlight and the credit for the *kabupaten*'s development.

Sri Roso and the council squabbled most bitterly over the money the *bupati* had spent to upgrade his office complex. To complete the project, which had begun in 1992, Sri Roso borrowed twice the amount the council had authorized. All told, the renovation of the complex may have cost as much as $4.9 million, a shocking amount for the second-poorest *kabupaten* in Jogjakarta. When they attended the office's unveiling, council members gasped at the *bupati*'s extravagance. Thick, hand-carved pillars of solid teak held up the foyer of the main building. At the center of the complex, Sri Roso had built a massive marble-tiled Javanese ceremonial pavilion, several times larger than even those found inside the sultan's own *kraton*. Its three-tiered roof could comfortably shelter several hundred people. The *kabupaten* also spent $25,000 on a *gamelan* gong orchestra, which provided official occasions with a traditional soundtrack. The assembly members made polite, admiring noises about the refurbished complex. But in March 1996, when Sri Roso returned to Kamil and his council with a request for funds to improve his own official residence – including $17,000 to replace his floor with ceramic tiling – they rejected the proposal.

No one could quite explain to the council why the renovation cost so much. Many observers naturally guessed that the figures had been inflated to cover kickbacks and payouts. Jogja reporters had heard from their sources among the local business community that in Bantul, every winning bidder on a state-funded construction project had to pay a series of commissions. Two per cent of the project's value would go to the *kabupaten*'s secretary, three per cent to the public works department and four per cent to the *bupati* himself. Contractors had a nickname for the scheme: "2-3-4," after a popular brand of clove cigarettes. If that information were true, then close to $200,000 of the $4.9 million renovation could have gone into Sri Roso's pockets. But this was just rumor. No source ever produced evidence that Sri Roso had been involved in corruption on that scale. Yet in 1998, a disgruntled Bantul public works employee publicly accused his department chief of pocketing three per cent of every major project's value. She promptly sued him for slander.

The close link between development and corruption formed the unspoken subtext that informed the questions surrounding the Parangtritis megaproject. Sri Roso's stubborn refusal to answer the critics only strengthened suspicions that the *bupati* had much more at stake in the resort development than the good of the *kabupaten*. His spokesman arrogantly told journalists at one press conference: "Go ahead if you want to give some of your input. But what is clear is that we will forge onward. If everyone puts in their opinions, do we have to accept them?" One *Bernas* reporter would later meet a public works official who claimed that the Jakarta conglomerate behind the project had already distributed over one million dollars to Jogjakarta officials from village bureaucrats in Bantul to the inner reaches of provincial governor's office to ensure that the project would move forward.

Sri Roso did not bother masking his annoyance with the local media, which had liberally aired the public's suspicions and questions. In November 1995, the *bupati* complained to a *Bernas* reporter: "I don't want to see any more news in the papers about the megaproject." At one meeting, Jogja journalists learned, Sri Roso had swiveled his head around to see if there were any reporters present. "If there aren't any, that's fine," he supposedly said. "I hate journalists."

Yet if criticism of the Parangtritis megaproject had appeared in several different newspapers, then why had Bantul authorities chosen *Bernas* and Udin as specific targets for legal action? The PWI team dug deeper through Udin's pile of articles. Throughout much of 1996, Udin had devoted several dozen pieces to that year's elections, both those for village chiefs and for Bantul's next *bupati*. In addition, he had covered the campaigning that had started for the following year's national parliamentary elections. In none of the three situations Udin had covered did Sri Roso or the Bantul government appear in a flattering light.

In Indonesia, the job of elected village headman, which lasts for eight years, is an attractive one for aspiring villagers. Although unpaid, the headman's job offers ample opportunities for self-advancement, through corruption and control of several hectares of village land, traditionally set aside to produce income for village leaders in lieu of paying them a salary. The locals cultivate the land and distribute the income from the crops to the village bureaucrats. But in many Javanese villages, unscrupulous headmen sell the land entrusted to them, robbing the villages of their communal possession. Others have found ways to keep control of the land within their family indefinitely, such as backing relatives to assume their offices when their terms expire. This control of Java's most precious resource – arable land – in addition to the state funds, projects, and permits that were already in their position's portfolio often made village chiefs the richest individuals in any rural community.

Winning these prized positions requires a significant investment. A bid for village chief might cost a candidate tens of thousands of dollars. Much of that money does not go to recruiting campaigners, printing posters, or rewarding voters. Candidates must often use the cash to hurdle one preliminary obstacle: the local candidate screening committee. That body, composed of bureaucrats from the local government, evaluates whether a candidate's educational or political background permits him or her to enter an election. Even before a single ballot is cast, a select group of senior officials decides who would make an acceptable chief. Such vetting ensures that whoever wins the election would be loyal to the government.

Their essentially predetermined nature, coupled with the personalized politics of small communities, made village polls particularly susceptible to controversy. Election scandals supplied constant fodder for Jogja papers and for rural reporters such as Udin. One perennial source of scandal was the activities of election "brokers." Since candidates could not be seen lobbying screening committee members directly – and since many had no personal connections to the bureaucracy in the first place – middlemen emerged to channel bribes from candidates to committee members. For a price, these brokers could persuade committee members to overlook a candidate's criminal record or unfinished high school education. They could also persuade committees to disqualify a candidate's strongest rival by rejecting his application outright or "discovering" he had relatives in the banned Communist Party.

One such broker, reporters had heard, was the tall, thickly built local land broker Sukrisno, one of the two men who had spoken with Udin in the *Bernas* parking lot shortly before the reporter was assaulted. Sukrisno, a menacingly large man famously easy to offend and difficult to placate, was known to be a close and loyal supporter of Sri Roso. An aspirant in a village race in Bantul would later claim to one Jogja reporter that he had paid Sukrisno $1,500 to bribe two screening committee members. His application had failed, and a relative who never graduated from high school went on to win the election. The loser believed his rival had paid ten times more than he had to Sukrisno. But the land broker, if asked, denies possessing any authority to fix elections.

The election of a *bupati* follows much the same model. At the kabupaten level, an "election" still means that the government chooses a local official first before presenting him for acclamation. The main difference is that the process now involves the central government directly. Before the election, a *kabupaten*'s council draws up a slate of three candidates. Given the dominance of the military and Golkar in the national and local legislatures, the personalities on that list will often come from the armed forces bloc or the local bureaucracy. In Bantul, for example, the candidate suggested to the *kabupaten* assembly by the provincial military command almost always wins nomination. Once the local assembly gathers its slate of candidates from its various factions, it submits the names to the Interior Ministry, which approves the list and sends them back to the council. The assembly then chooses the winner. Since the Interior Ministry must confirm the *bupati*-elect before he can assume office, the identity of the victor is often determined well in advance of his elevation. So for ambitious civil servants or soldiers, what matters most to one's political career is not the support of one's constituents, as it would in a true multi-party democracy, but the favor of influential decision-makers in Jakarta located in such institutions as the Presidential Palace, the armed forces headquarters, the Interior Ministry, or Golkar's central office, all of whom have a say on who can be a *bupati*. Just as village chief candidates had to bribe the screening committee members even to have a chance to contest an election, candidates for *bupati* also had to plot to win or buy the favor of superiors to make it past the shadowy, informal process of being anointed a candidate and then the Interior Ministry's equally murky vetting process.

In December 1995, some six months before the end of Sri Roso's term, Udin had predicted in an article that whoever succeeded the *bupati* would be from the military. In early January 1996, Udin had concluded that the two strongest candidates for nomination were the two rival colonels, Sri Roso and Kamil. The following month, the Bantul legislature indeed nominated three military officers. But, surprisingly, none of them was Sri Roso or Kamil. Instead, the front-runner was the head of a *kabupaten* assembly in Central Java province. "The commander has decided Colonel Iwan Supardji will be permitted to be nominated as *bupati*," the Bantul assembly's chief military representative told Udin. At the end of March, the assembly dutifully submitted Supardji's name with two other candidates to Jakarta and waited for the expected approval, followed by Supardji's inevitable election. No one knew why Supardji had been named to replace Sri Roso. The choice of Supardji had come from the local military, which presumably had received it from both men's superiors. The assembly representatives had satisfied themselves that they were doing what the central government required of them: to provide the imprimatur of popular legitimacy on leaders chosen undemocratically.

The expected approval never arrived. Instead, the Interior Ministry sent a note informing the Jogjakarta governor that Bantul's list of candidates was unacceptable. Although the Bantul assembly's own military representative had seemed so sure a few months earlier that approval had already been granted for Supardji, the assembly was now being told that armed forces headquarters had now denied the colonel permission to serve in a civilian position. The note from Jakarta naturally infuriated the assembly. Supardji's name had been delivered through the usual channels. Then armed forces headquarters and the Interior Ministry changed their minds, and assumed the Bantul assembly would meekly swallow the slight and start the time-consuming process all over. Although in this process, the council acted much like a rubber stamp, the sudden reversal of what was supposed to be a foregone conclusion disturbed and distressed the representatives. One councilor complained to Udin that he and his fellows were being treated "just like puppets." But another representative told the reporter that he recognized the real authority to appoint and elect Bantul's leader was located elsewhere than in the *kabupaten's* assembly, and that they had no choice but to follow. Strangely, however, whoever decided such matters seemed confused and conflicted. "What is clear," he said, "there is a conflict of interest within the 'hidden institution.'" Nonetheless, the council could not question the Interior Ministry's decision. They extended Sri Roso's term for several weeks until they could complete another election.

Yet now Udin's sources were telling him that Sri Roso's reelection chances had suddenly been reinvigorated. The Jogjakarta provincial military command had dispatched a new set of names, which now included Sri Roso. As the incumbent, he seemed virtually assured of Interior Ministry approval. Then, near the end of May, after the Bantul assembly dutifully submitted the new candidates to Jakarta, several council members, including Kamil, received a copy of a letter that shocked them more than the Interior Ministry's unexpected rejection of their previous candidate.

The hand-written note had read:

DECLARATION

I, the undersigned
Name: Sri Roso Sudarmo
Rank: Artillery Colonel
Office: *Bupati* of Bantul *Kabupaten*

Truthfully state that I am ready to donate funds to the Dharmais Foundation in the amount of 1 (one) billion rupiah should I be chosen as *bupati* of Bantul for a second term (1996-2001). The said obligation will be carried out/ undertaken by Noto Suwito. This declaration I have made willingly and without duress.

The amount mentioned in the letter amounted to about $428,000. The paper came stamped with a seal, the kind used to make binding legal documents in Indonesia. Four signatures appeared on the bottom to lend further authority to the note. One was the unmistakable, expansive flourish of the promisor, Sri Roso. Two others named Anggoro and Suwarno had signed the document as witnesses: these were names no assemblymen recognized. But the remaining signature everyone knew. It sat over typed letters that spelt the name "Noto Suwito."

His name, and that of the Dharmais Foundation, told representatives everything they needed to know about the nature and intent of the document. In 1975 Suharto had founded the Dharmais Foundation as a charity to fund orphanages. Three years after its founding, Dharmais' capital had been reported to amount to a paltry $16,000. Yet within two decades, Dharmais had accumulated an estimated $385 million, an increase of over 24,000 per cent. However, since mainly Suharto's children and closest friends sat on its board, no one outside that charmed circle knew how much Dharmais was truly worth. Although the foundation had expanded its purview to include such activities as building and funding the country's main cancer hospital in Jakarta, its increased profile could not completely explain why Dharmais had grown so wealthy. With that money, Suharto could have clothed, fed, and educated every orphan in the country, with more to spare for each child's descendants.

The truth was that Dharmais was not really a charity. Its main role was to act as a kind of unofficial Suharto bank. It received donations from favor-seekers or businesses that had prospered off the government. Dharmais then lent that cash to Suharto cronies or invested it in their companies to generate vast financial returns for Suharto's inner circle and political apparatus, such as Golkar, whose campaigns the foundation funded. At around the time of the Udin killing, Dharmais was poised to become even richer, this time from contributions taken directly from the national treasury. In the mid-1990s, Suharto had instructed the government to donate to Dharmais two per cent of all personal income taxes collected.

Noto Suwito was Suharto's younger half-brother, the only member of the president's immediate kin who had remained a permanent resident of Jogjakarta. Suharto had been born in 1921 in a rural area outside Jogja. Five weeks later, his parents divorced and then remarried other partners. The president-to-be was handed back and forth between foster families. His father's three marriages, his birth mother's two unions and a foster mother's family produced a family tree like a spreading banyan. By one recent count, Suharto had ten foster siblings and twenty-one half-brothers and sisters. When Suharto became president, his relatives moved to Jakarta to take advantage of their proximity to power. Noto Suwito, the sixth child of Suharto's mother's second marriage, chose for his own reasons to stay in his home province.

Since the 1970s, he had been village chief of Argomulyo, a pleasant settlement near the main road heading west out of Jogja, just within the northern border of Bantul *kabupaten*. His home, an estate of several buildings built or bought over the years from neighbors, sprawls across several lots. Like many in Suharto's family, Noto Suwito had acquired sizable business interests during his half-brother's regime, rumored to be in minerals, oil, and timber. He used some of his money to dispense loans to people who came from all over Java. He gave outright donations to the particularly needy. From his pen issued letters of recommendation that could secure jobs at state-owned companies, admissions to a prestigious university, or election to coveted government positions. It is unclear what Noto Suwito received in return for all his largesse. Like his half-brother, he won reelection virtually unchallenged. Although he lived simply – the unremarkable exterior of his home gave no hint of his rumored personal riches – he probably did not need favors or money. Perhaps he played the patron because he enjoyed the sense of power another man's gratitude or fear gave him.

The note signed by Sri Roso had been dated 2 April 1996, which was two weeks after the assembly had submitted its first list of candidates. The letter coincided with the reversal of approval for Supardji and the *bupati's* subsequent electoral resurrection. At the end of May, with days left before the second *bupati* election, Kamil asked Sri Roso to explain the letter. Whether or not Sri Roso's account satisfied Kamil, his assembly elected Sri Roso to a second term on 3 June 1996.

But the scandalous document did not remain a secret for long within the upper reaches of local Bantul politics. Udin had received a copy of the letter and wrote a story about it that bore his byline. On 29 May, *Bernas* printed that article with the headline: "Bantul Parliament Receives Anonymous Letter." Udin's story did not mention Sri Roso or the Dharmais Foundation by name. He simply wrote that a candidate had offered a "well-known" organization in Jakarta over $400,000 in exchange for his election. But he had told the newspaper's readers more than enough to set tongues wagging and to embarrass Sri Roso and those who supported his government. On the day of the *bupati*'s reelection, two young men had been discussing the suspicious letter in a Bantul food stall. Their conversation stopped when a plate of rice and goat satay came flying at them. The man who threw it at them was real estate broker, alleged election fixer, and Udin's late-night visitor: Sukrisno.

Bernas had been the only paper in the province to run the story about the *bupati*'s "One-Billion Rupiah Promise." But after he secured his second term, Sri Roso pretended as if nothing had marred the credibility of his reelection. He insisted he would see through the Parangtritis development during his second term. "Don't you dramatize this planned project," he admonished reporters after his inauguration. "All the development done by the *kabupaten* government is clearly for social prosperity." The *bupati* also had a new project that kept him busy: his campaign for the following year's nationwide parliamentary elections.

Although the parliamentary elections, so tilted in favor of Golkar, were by any measure just a cynical fiction, Suharto came to rely on the poll returns as a measure of how well his system was working. The more votes the ruling party secured, the stronger they believed their grip on power. Perhaps he and his officials even ended up thinking their landslides were deserved and willingly given. In 1987, Golkar had won over seventy-three per cent of the national vote. But in 1992, its share had slipped to sixty-eight per cent. Shockingly, one in three Indonesians had voted for the two minority parties. Although Golkar still held a commanding majority in the national and local legislatures, the government feared that if the slide continued, one of the minority parties might be emboldened enough to support a challenger to Suharto's presidency. Because what mattered more to the military and the bureaucracy was not who supported them – that were expected – but who did not.

So like many public officials at the time, Sri Roso participated enthusiastically in the nationwide campaign to secure a win for Golkar for the coming 1997 election that would reverse the unhappy trend indicated by its slipping figures. In late June 1996, the *bupati* organized a rally for the ruling party, which Udin attended. In a 29 June story, titled "The Colors According to the Bantul *Bupati* Sri Roso Sudarmo," Udin described how Sri Roso, who as *bupati* was supposed to treat all parties neutrally, had obliquely criticized Golkar's rivals: the Unity and Development Party and the nationalist PDI. "Imagine if these decorations were green," Sri Roso had told the crowd, pointing to the ruling party's yellow flags and banners. "Would they be as bright as the yellow you see here today?" He added: "Let's just think rationally…if you choose red, doesn't it make your eyes hurt?" Udin reported that a jeer had come from the crowd. "Yeah," a heckler had cried. "When the rice is yellow on the stalk, that means it's about to fall!" The crowd had responded with laughter.

In early July, Sri Roso summoned seventy-five village chiefs to Argomulyo, where he personally swore in Noto Suwito to another term. The citizens of Argomulyo had reelected the president's half-brother resoundingly in the village election: ninety-seven per cent of them had cast their votes for him. The meeting was supposed to be closed to media, but Udin had slipped in as one of the crowd, and later printed what he witnessed in his newspaper. At the rally, Sri Roso had asked the village chiefs to do all they could to secure victory for the ruling party. "Your main role is to win votes for Golkar as much as two hundred per cent," he told them. "So if we lose one hundred per cent, we still have one hundred per cent left!" Indonesia's decades of stability, the *bupati* explained, had been the direct result of Golkar's leadership. Later that month, Sri Roso told village officials that they would receive bonuses equivalent to $850 if they secured a landslide. "If there are red banners already up, just leave them alone. Don't be so obvious taking them down," he advised them. "If reporters spot you, they won't let you forget it."

Udin's coverage of the rally at Noto Suwito's home in Argomulyo had brought the first complaint by representatives of the Bantul *kabupaten* government to *Bernas*. Sri Roso's spokesman had complained that Udin had infiltrated a private meeting. Assistant managing editor Subadhi responded drolly: "If the meeting involves the public interest, whether it is 'closed' or not is debatable." Reporters heard soon after the incident that Sri Roso had told Bantul civil servants to cancel their *Bernas* subscriptions.

Perusing Udin's articles left the PWI team with more questions than answers. Did Sri Roso's well-known annoyance with the media coalesce into specific hatred of Udin after the Bantul correspondent's stories had cast doubt on the legitimacy of his reelection and mocked his attempts to secure victory for the ruling party? Had Udin's published coverage of the IDT irregularities in Karangtengah – a minor matter, compared to his other stories – been the last straw? Had Sukrisno, a Sri Roso loyalist, been dispatched to *Bernas* to intimidate the reporter? During that meeting in the parking lot, had Udin resisted the threats, which forced the *bupati*'s people to deliver later that night a more pointed lesson? Finally had the presence of Sri Roso's nephew, Kuncung, at the scene of the assault, been planned to ensure a clean getaway for the perpetrators?

At this point, the reporters could only speculate. Only one journalist – their original source – had seen documentation indicating the lawsuit the *kabupaten* was preparing. Several months later, however, a contact in the Bantul police leaked to journalists a revealing series of memos from the *bupati*'s office. The paper trail confirmed that a litigation preparation meeting had been planned. Although no mention is made of assault or murder, the documents also showed that Sri Roso knew exactly who had been making trouble for his *kabupaten* and how strongly he had felt that Udin had to be punished.

The first date on the documents was 19 July 1996, almost a month before Udin had been beaten. That was the day a district official complained to the *kabupaten* government about *Bernas*' negative coverage of the IDT program. Sri Roso's aide, who had received the report before the *bupati*, had attached a memo to his superior. "It is really not fair if false reports are always forgiven," he advised. "This needs to be handled."

The *bupati* responded two days later with his decision:

"Lawsuit against reporter/*News*. Prepare it."

When another district official submitted a report complaining about the erroneous *Bernas* IDT stories, Sri Roso established a firm deadline for his flunkies to carry out his instructions: 17 August, Indonesia's Independence Day. "Verify this wrong news," the *bupati* had written, his pen pressed firmly into the paper. "Prepare the charges against the editor or the news source. Make it clean. Before the seventeenth."

Sri Roso's aide then dispatched an internal auditor to Karangtengah to prepare an analysis of the IDT program. By 6 August, Sri Roso had received the auditor's report, which said that no evidence indicated that the IDT funds had been corrupted. This was the document the *kabupaten* needed to nail the reporter and his paper in any legal proceeding. But by this time, Independence Day was less than three weeks away. To underline his concern about his self-imposed deadline, the *bupati* scribbled his thoughts directly on the auditor's report. His comments were addressed to his deputy:

"I have ordered a lawsuit prepared against the editors. It has not been done."

But on 8 August, it appeared his aides still did not feel the required urgency, because on that day, Sri Roso shot off a separate memo addressed to the *kabupaten*'s legal department, with more explicit and detailed instructions:

> According to the agreed-on plan, coordinate the proper departments, including the public prosecutor's office and the judge. Prepare a letter to *Bernas'* editors on our objections. Copy it to the local security authorities. Make a serious effort to bring the lawsuit to court if it fulfills the legal criteria.

He added one final word – a verbal punch – to his memorandum. In Indonesian, it read: *Laks.*

"Carry it out."

CHAPTER 4

A Few Centimeters from Our Throats

THREE DAYS AFTER THE ASSAULT, on Friday, 16 August, Udin's editor Heru found himself in a small house on the outskirts of Jogja, near the road that leads from the *kraton* to the royal tombs at Imogiri. In the gloom of its interior, a woman sat at a table decorated with fresh flowers. Her pudgy form stiffened into a trance as Heru watched. In a high-pitched, unnatural voice, like that of a child, she breathlessly told him, "The suspect rode his motorcycle north. He was looking for a side street. He threw the weapon in the nearby paddies. Look for it."

Heru had come here on the invitation of a friend, who had told the editor that this woman could channel a spirit that dwelled in a tree in her yard. With her close connection the spirit world, Heru's friend asserted, she could obtain information about the assault on the *Bernas* reporter. Raised a pious Muslim, Heru did his best to pray five times a day and visit a mosque every Friday. He never visited any of the hundreds of mystics, mediums, sorcerers, psychics, or paranormals that infested his home island. These men and women practiced a craft that brushed uncomfortably close to what an imam would call blasphemy. *Mushrik*.

Religion demands faith, the abject surrender to a divine power that can seem remote and indifferent. These magicians, these *dukun*, also admit the existence of larger powers. But in contrast, they promise that supernatural forces can be manipulated, wielded, or turned to serve the immediate, material ends of ordinary mortals. In Java, a *dukun* could be anyone of any ethnicity, as long as the *dukun* had a natural talent for the arcane arts or a native grasp for manipulating the world of the spirits. There could be Arab, Chinese, or Indian mystics, or *dukun* who moonlighted as shopkeepers, schoolteachers or even notaries. That an ordinary Imogiri housewife could also be a *dukun* did not surprise Heru. Even allegiance to formal religion did not disqualify one from being a *dukun*. Jogja boasted several priests and imam reputed to have the power to heal the blind or track down missing persons.

Like a doctor or lawyer, a *dukun* adopts a specialty. Some focus on treating poor body image and sexual dysfunctions, such as infertility and impotence. Their practice is particularly well developed. They prescribe incantations and prayers along with breast creams and penis pumps. Other more traditional mystics, meanwhile, perform an ancient art known as *susuk*, which involves inserting a needle somewhere in the body to give its bearer special powers, such as irresistible beauty or superhuman strength. Certain *dukun* focus on *klenik*, or black magic. This is graveyard magic; the kind conjured with handfuls of dirt from the cemetery or from the thumbs of infant corpses. *Klenik* is a deal with the devil: the commission of the unspeakable motivated by greed or revenge or anger. Examples of this kind of magic might be curses laid on cheating partners or special formulations to achieve invulnerability to ordinary weapons. Although government regulation expressly forbids *klenik*, *dukun* who specialize in it openly advertise their mastery of the dark art. They present themselves slyly as counter-black magic consultants for people unfortunate enough to be targets of hexes. Magazines, tabloids, and newspapers like *Bernas* earned significant revenue from printing advertisements of *dukun* services and products, such as oils, belts, rosaries, and *kris* that offer protection from all sorts of terrors, be they enemies, bullets, fires, sharp objects, accidents, diseases, or crop failures. Judging by the ink and pulp devoted to pages and pages of commercials in local media peddling ancient sexual secrets from China, India, or Egypt; amulets, cures, and enchantments; and even "long-distance" treatment (after the receipt of a suitable bank transfer) by a *dukun* too distant for a client to see personally, magic in Indonesia is big business.

As Heru listened to the medium, his skepticism sprouted. He tried testing the *dukun*'s insight with questions to which he knew the answer. When she insisted that the Krisna Photo Studio faced west on Parangtritis Road, his doubts about her powers blossomed. From the countless times Heru had sipped tea in Samalo with Udin and Marsiyem, he knew the couple's home faced east toward the sunrise. "A shame," Heru thought. The medium had told him that Udin would recover and identify his attacker. Another *dukun*, "Engineer" Gembong, considered among the city's most skilled mystics, had also predicted the same thing that morning. Heru had more faith in God than he did in these sorcerers. Still, a part of him wanted to believe them.

Heru and Udin had been a team. The stories that had appeared on the "Around Jogjakarta" page were as much his as they were the Bantul reporter's – he had guided their reporting and edited the copy. Many of Udin's headlines had been formed on Heru's word processor. But it was Udin who was now lying in Bethesda Hospital. That morning, doctors had inserted a tube through Udin's throat to assist his breathing because the reporter's drafts of air had grown shallow. After the operation, the journalist's condition showed little improvement. Udin's big, gentle body was failing. When Heru returned to the office from his visit to the medium, he found the newsroom somber and uncertain. Udin's colleagues had learned that at one point that day, the reporter's pulse had faded to a point where doctors could barely feel it.

Heru, Achadi, and the paper's other junior journalists had scheduled their usual friendly game of Friday afternoon football against the computer science students from a school not far from the office. The reporters never won, but they always looked at the match as an opportunity to let off some end-of-the-week steam. They had been looking forward to today's game at a dusty field down in Bantul. But Udin's deteriorating condition forced them to reconsider whether the game should take place. Then news arrived at the office that Udin's condition had improved. His pulse had quickened and his breathing had returned almost to normal. His doctors felt confident enough to declare the worst over for the wounded reporter. Cheered, Heru joined the other young staffers, most of whom were closer to Achadi's generation than his own, for the half-hour drive down to Bantul.

They reached the field at 4:15 p.m. Triatmoko Sukmo Nugroho, a twenty-eight-year-old reporter everyone called "Moko," changed into his playing clothes. Moko turned over his office-supplied pager to Purwani Diyah Prabandari, nicknamed "Ndari." The bright twenty-four-year-old worked on the paper's international news desk. Draped in her headscarf and a long-sleeved shirt, Ndari had not planned to join the game, but to watch, cheer, and look after everyone's clothes and belongings from the sidelines. Forty minutes into the game, Moko's pager buzzed with a message: At 4:55 p.m., Udin's heart had stopped beating at Bethesda Hospital.

Ndari ran onto the field. Shocked into silence, Heru, Achadi, Moko, Ndari and the others returned to their vehicles. As Moko started the engine, he thought: "*What had Udin done wrong, to die like this?*" The young man prided himself on his ability to restrain his emotions. When his parents had passed away, he had not wept. But now, he could not hold back his tears. They streamed down his face as he pulled the *Bernas* white passenger van onto Parangtritis Road for the drive back to Jogja.

By the time the young staffers reached Bethesda, news of Udin's death had spread by phone and pager through the community of journalists in the city. A crowd had gathered in front of the intensive care unit inside the hospital's maze of interconnected pavilions. Outside the ward, the junior journalists saw one of the newspaper's secretaries embracing Marsiyem tightly. Tears flowed down the young widow's cheeks. When Udin had breathed his last, his wife had been beside him.

Muslim tradition required that Udin's remains be buried within a day of his death. After an autopsy of his body, an ambulance conveyed his corpse in a light wooden coffin to the *Bernas* office, where it was laid in the newspaper's reception room, not far from the very computer where he typed up his last stories. In his honor, his friends sang "Fallen Flowers," a song honoring dead heroes which dated back to the Indonesian Revolution. Then the ambulance carried the coffin to Udin's home, where, led by his grieving father Wagiman, Jogja's reporters prayed in congregation for the soul of Udin and the welfare of his family.

The next day, 17 August 1996, the fifty-first anniversary of Indonesia's independence, a grave had been prepared in Trirenggo's small village cemetery. The heat of the day beat down on the crowd gathered in the treeless square, among the narrow mold-covered Muslim twinned tombstones that covered each grave like upside-down stone benches. Villagers and family members mingled with journalists, some of whom had come to cover the burial but had attended mostly to mourn their fallen colleague. As several strong young men, sent by the Unity and Development Party to serve as pallbearers, carried Udin's coffin into the graveyard, several people had to support Marsiyem, who was too weak with bereavement to stand. Her daughter Yuli wept alone in her grandmother's lap. As Udin was lowered into a hole dug near the graveyard entrance, the mourners threw perfumed rose petals on his coffin, a funerary rite performed throughout Indonesia. The *Bernas* photographer Tarko Sudiarto dabbed at his own glistening eyes as he took the pictures of the mourners.

The reporters scanned the crowd for Sri Roso. Regardless of whatever conflict he might have had with the *kabupaten*, Udin had been so well known to the Bantul government that his family and colleagues assumed the *bupati* would attend and deliver a short eulogy. When the *bupati* failed to appear, journalists thought the absence seemed significant, as if Sri Roso had intended to slight the man who had undermined support for the colonel's megaproject, publicized his heavy-handed campaigning for the ruling party and exposed his promise to pay a billion rupiah for his reelection.

Sri Roso's absence seemed even stranger because on 16 August, the day before Udin's death, *Bernas* publisher Kusfandhi and his senior editors had visited Sri Roso to discuss their concern over what had happened, and to ask the *bupati* to ensure the safety of Djoko, the remaining correspondent. The *bupati* had said at the time that he was aware of the incident on Parangtritis Road. The day after the assault, on 14 August, two employees of his *kabupaten* had visited Djoko to confirm reports that Udin had been injured. Yet one of the editors, Subadhi, who had accompanied Kusfandhi, had the impression the *bupati* cared little about the tragedy that had occurred in his community. Sri Roso seemed much more upset with the *Bernas* editors for their paper's coverage of his politics and policies than about what happened to their reporter.

Sri Roso complained about the paper's portrayal of his government, especially its reporting on the IDT poverty alleviation fund and his reelection. The *bupati* of Bantul was "assistant to the Father of Development," Sri Roso said, using a phrase often associated with Suharto. The colonel seemed to consider himself an extension of the president and thus entitled to the same degree of respect and unquestioning deference. Subadhi never heard Sri Roso ask about the reporter's condition. The *bupati* also waved away the editors' suggestion that the attack might have been spurred by one of Udin's stories. "It is too premature," Sri Roso said, "to connect the attack with Udin's reporting or his profession."

So at the funeral, in the *bupati*'s absence, Udin's colleagues and relatives read their own reminiscences about the reporter. The activist-turned-journalist Achadi seized the opportunity to make a point about the Indonesian media. His words augured Udin's transformation from a working family man to a secular martyr. At his death, the reporter now symbolized the struggle of his entire profession. "The sword hangs just a few centimeters from our throats," Achadi declared. "But let us be clear. It is one thing to be powerless under threat. It is another to just give up." That the day Udin was buried was Independence Day, Indonesia's most hallowed secular holiday, seemed somehow significant. Udin's death had galvanized journalists in Jogjakarta. This single assault on this single reporter had now become an incident that did violence against the national media and against the very ideal of a free press. By no stretch of the imagination could Kusfandhi still consider what had happened to Udin as an ordinary crime. As the soil was shoveled on top of the reporter's flower-strewn coffin, the case now clearly involved the far more serious matter of a politically-charged murder.

∞

The police investigation had begun the night of the assault, on 13 August 1996. Three night-duty officers from a post about seven kilometers from Samalo, summoned by the hamlet's neighborhood watchman, arrived at the scene shortly before midnight. They found the Krisna Photo Studio's door unlocked, and the fifteen-watt lightbulb outside still blazing. A crowd of onlookers from Samalo and nearby hamlets had gathered around the spot where Udin had fallen. If the young man in the red bandanna or his accomplice had left any traces of their presence, those clues were now buried under cigarette butts and slipper scuffles. One neighbor had mopped up much of Udin's blood with a mixture of soil and sand, further destroying the crime scene. The officers sketched the Krisna Photo Studio and its front yard, noting the position of Udin's body as witnesses had described it to them. Their brief report ends with the conclusion: "The scene was already destroyed while the victim was no longer at the site."

On 14 August, Bantul's Chief Detective Edy Hidayat, ordered his men to retrieve from Marsiyem and Bethesda Hospital the clothes the reporter wore the night he had been assaulted. Hidayat had appointed a team of nine Bantul policemen and three police intelligence agents to handle the Udin investigation. Over the following days, the detectives questioned Sujarah and the three noodle-stall workers. The Bantul police had also ordered the autopsy on Udin before his remains had been turned over to his family. The inquest, which lasted two and one-half hours, established that hemorrhaging in and around the brain had caused Udin's death. The same blunt object that had fractured the reporter's skull had apparently bruised and wounded other areas on his head, torso, limbs, and lower body.

Unlike the intricate, overlapping network of services and agencies that keep civil order in the United States, the Indonesian police follows a simple hierarchical structure that crosses jurisdictions. Edy Hidayat's boss, Bantul Police Chief Adé Sudarban, reported to the Jogjakarta provincial police, which in turn followed orders from the Central Java Police District, based in the north coast city of Semarang. All three police forces were part of the Indonesian National Police, headed by a police general named Dibyo Widodo. Although the assault had occurred in Bantul, the case was of such importance that any one from the provincial, district, or national police could be called to assist in the investigation.

A salaried class of law enforcers – a modern police force – had appeared in the West by the eighteenth century. But in those parts of the globe that the West colonized, police arrived only with the colonial powers. When the Dutch first came to Java, they found the countryside ruled by gangs of thugs, bandits, and local strongmen, known as *jago* in Central Java and by various names elsewhere in the island and around the archipelago. Each village needed a *jago*, whose muscle protected his community the way the stereotypical Mafia don defends his neighborhood. As a reward, *jago* could thieve from other, less well-guarded villages and his village would look the other way and continue to shelter him. To carry out his twin duties as policeman and thief, a *jago* mastered martial arts and magic, especially *klenik*, for protective spells and useful divinations. As long as one community's protector could be another's invader, the balance of forces kept a fragile kind of order in the precolonial countryside. This motley group was the first kind of "police force" most Javanese knew: a cross between bounty hunter, security guard, and gangster.

The Dutch established urban constabularies to protect their white governors, settlers, and traders. But for the rest of the vast population, they had neither the desire to develop a rural police force nor the manpower to import one from Europe. So they and their local aristocratic collaborators found it easier to maintain the *jago* system. In addition, they gave the goons some new duties, including tax collection, espionage, or the manipulation of village elections. It was only in 1905, well after their hold on the islands was secure, that the Dutch authorities sidelined the *jago* and founded a trained local police force and professional intelligence-gathering agencies. They introduced a police academy, smart uniforms, and new forensic and surveillance technologies, such as the science of *vingersporen*, or fingerprinting. But along with the new clothes, new responsibilities, and new statutes, the promising local youths hired to form the new force did not completely reject the heritage of the *jago* even as they hunted the bandits to extinction. To do its job, the police married local criminal investigation customs with modern forensic science. Long after independence, professional police still looked for the traditional omens of impending crime, such as a cat baring its claws or the gluttonous call of a gecko. Up until today, Indonesian police regularly consult *dukun* during the investigation of a crime, much like Western police departments use psychics. But where the latter is a reluctant convert to paranormal services, the former is an enthusiastic consumer. *Dukun* are far cheaper, more plentiful, and less finicky than fingerprints, ballistics, or DNA experts.

True professionalism remained a distant goal. But for a brief number of years after independence, the police, though poorly trained, managed to be a serviceable force. The post-colonial politicians who ran the government, however, could not resist the temptation to use the police force to arrest opponents and harass critics, as well as to soak up the country's surplus labor. Keeping officers underpaid and the force underfunded ensured the elite that the police would be dependent on whatever government was in power. Most police officers in Indonesia have not completed a degree beyond elementary or junior high school. Despite the greater risks, longer hours and tougher demands of their profession, law enforcement officials receive the same pay scale as the bureaucrat behind a desk. When a detective opens an investigation, he or she receives a budget of only five thousand rupiah – an amount, in

1996, equivalent to less than two dollars – that is intended to cover all expenses involved in the case. Indonesian police officers are often not embarrassed to cadge contributions from crime victims – what one detective has delicately described as "acquaintances' money…money from outside" – so they can perform the duties for which the law has tasked them.

Partly as a result of lax discipline and partly because of the force's perennial poverty, many officers have found it more profitable to subvert the law than to uphold it. For a fee, for example, officers can revoke arrests, lift detentions, or cancel investigations. Conversely, they can be hired to issue arrest orders for one's enemies or extend their imprisonment. Police officers moonlight as security guards and sometimes as hit men. Although inadequate training and poor pay is likely most to blame for police excesses, some officers do relish the brutality and the power their position gives them. Even in legitimate investigations, psychological harassment, torture, and summary executions have become acceptable crime-fighting tools.

Once police services started to go to the highest bidder, there was little to protect the population at large from the perversion of police authority. In 1970, a case in Jogjakarta revealed the emerging pattern of New Order police practice. That year, a seventeen-year-old girl named Sum Kuning had been on her way home from selling eggs at the market when several youths abducted her. They dragged her inside a car. She felt a damp hand cover her nose. As she drifted into unconsciousness, hands grabbed at her sarong. Her kidnappers raped her repeatedly before robbing her of the few rupiah she had earned that day. After Sum Kuning poured out her story in the presence of a reporter, the provincial police command, instead of investigating the rape, arrested her for making a false statement in public.

In 1970, Jogja had still been predominantly a town that was ruled by bicycles. Only officials, military officers, and the wealthy could afford private motor vehicles. Her rapists were thus likely the joy-riding teenage children of generals, colonels, businessmen, or the local aristocracy. But instead of pursuing powerful and well-connected suspects, the police tried to silence and discredit the rape victim. They kept Sum Kuning under house arrest for over a month, subjected her to daily interrogations, and then declared that she had sex with a street hawker and had lied about her rape to hide her own immoral behavior. Detectives arrested her supposed lover and presented both him and Sum Kuning to the press so reporters could hear the couple's confession. The two claimed the police had tortured them to admit they had sex with each other. After a trial that riveted Jogja's attention for months, a court acquitted the teenager and the vendor. Sum Kuning's rapists were never apprehended.

In 1967, Suharto merged the police with the military, making it part of a massive bureaucracy dominated by the army. Although the police formed the single largest component of the military – by the 1990s, 175,000 of the 450,000 members of the armed forces were police officers – the best facilities and opportunities still went to the army generals and their soldiers. Though mistreated, the police became an integral part of the New Order's wide-ranging secret infrastructure of surveillance and intimidation. To silence government critics, military security or police intelligence would stone homes of dissidents or spread gossip to discredit them. They might hire transvestites or madmen to infiltrate student demonstrations and disrupt rallies. The secret police operatives could assume many guises, from student activist to Islamic scholar, from *becak* driver to street sweeper.

As a result, Suharto's New Order achieved an effective omnipresence: its agents were both everywhere and nowhere. In the absence of information or rules about what the government could or could not do, ordinary people never knew what lay behind the events that unfolded around them. If a reporter's motorcycle is forced off the road, or someone hurls a rock at the roof of the home of a critical academic, it is not always because the secret police had planned it. But just as no one could be sure if a neighbor was an informant, no one knew whether an event had been engineered or had happened spontaneously. Thus it seemed safer to be obedient than to make trouble. On Java, people had long believed they shared their surroundings with spirits and ghosts. Similarly, under Suharto, Indonesia lived with the shadow of secret agents and the rumor of conspiracy and surveillance.

The system's very disregard of any and all rules kept a perverse kind of order. Many in Jogjakarta still remember the "*Petrus*" murders of the early 1980s. "*Petrus*" stands for *penembakan misterius*, or "mysterious shootings." In 1983, as Indonesia's parliament elected Suharto to a fourth five-year term, the country had hit a rough patch. A global recession had led to an oil price collapse. Government revenues from oil declined from almost nineteen billion dollars to $6.9 billion by the middle of the decade, which put the government in serious financial difficulty. The government reduced politically sensitive subsidies on energy and food and devalued the rupiah, permitting the national currency to lose more than a quarter of its value against the U.S. dollar. Prices inevitably soared, as did crime and unrest in Indonesian cities.

Then, beginning in Jogja, the military put a brilliant idea into effect. To control crime, why not just eliminate the criminal? The authorities required suspected malfeasants and ex-convicts to register for regular inspections. Those who failed to appear promptly were judged de facto guilty. Soldiers and police disguised in dark uniforms without insignias hunted them down. They left the criminals' corpses beside bridges, on the banks of creeks, in alleys near markets, floating in ponds, or stuffed into sacks by country roads. The pilot program was a success. Crime in Jogja dropped dramatically.

From Jogjakarta, the operation spread nationwide. Sites that in the 1960s had been used to bury dead Communists were reopened to receive what the government considered human refuse. One location was Grubuk Cave, a deep limestone cavern in a remote part of Jogjakarta that opened to the surface through a gaping sinkhole above an underground river. Soldiers and police dumped dozens of bodies down that hole, to be flushed out through to the Indian Ocean – a literal sewer for the waste of society. Deliveries to that location of captured or executed individuals followed a strict, military schedule. Residents could count on the army trucks coming in on Fridays and Sundays. The government refused to confirm or deny that its soldiers and patrolmen were behind the killings, although many years later, in his memoirs, Suharto took credit for coming up with the idea for the mass extrajudicial executions.

The widespread, "mysterious" murders had the desired effect. They struck fear even into would-be criminals. Convicts scheduled for release begged prisons to allow them to stay for their own protection. Those who had been recently freed committed minor crimes so they would be returned to the relative safety of police detention. Tattooed young men, who feared their tattoos might make the executioners mistake them as ex-convicts, sliced their own skin off to erase what might mark them for elimination. In the two years between 1983 and 1985 in which the *Petrus* were the most plentiful, the death squads reportedly eliminated over five thousand people. Some estimates place the number of victims at as many as ten thousand. When hospitals and morgues complained that they could not afford autopsies and funerals for the scores of corpses, the killers considerately left banknotes tucked in their victims' pockets. But after a while, the constant murder no longer seemed extraordinary. Mutilated corpses became so common that children on their way to school ignored the disfigured or decapitated bodies.

Then the murders stopped, like a sudden, passing rain shower. The killings, however, had inscribed on Indonesian society a chilling message. The police and military clearly put a higher value on order than law. Their refusal to be bound by rules that bound others made the line between law enforcer and lawbreaker frighteningly thin. As the years of the New Order turned into decades, the distinction between police officer and perpetrator became altogether blurred. One recent case in particular demonstrated how little respect the Indonesian authorities had, by the 1990s, for the constraints of law and legal rights, perhaps even for the bounds of morality. In 1993, the corpse of Marsinah, a young worker involved in a watch factory strike in East Java, was found in ditch beside a teak plantation. An autopsy showed that some object had been thrust into her vagina with such force it had broken her uterine wall and shattered her pelvis. Marsinah had disappeared after threatening to lodge a legal complaint against the local military command for pressuring the strike's leaders to resign from their jobs even after the strike had been settled.

Although police pledged to investigate and catch the killers, they focused most of their efforts toward establishing that her death had no possible relationship to her complaint against the local military. Detectives rejected any suggestion that her activities in the local labor movement had caused her death. She was probably the victim of a quarrel over inheritance or an ill-fated love triangle, the police asserted. The local military command helpfully arrested eight people, including Marsinah's employer, the watch-factory owner. The detainees later testified that soldiers and intelligence agents had beaten them with the butt of a pistol, pummeled their legs, or electrocuted their genitals to force them to sign confessions to her murder. But the East Java courts dutifully declared each one of them guilty. Most were sentenced to jail for between seven and twelve years. The factory manager and owner each received seventeen years in prison.

Although the *jago* had long passed into history, the way Suharto's government had turned the police and the military into enforcers of order above law passed on to the authorities the most poisonous element of the *jago*'s ambiguous inheritance: that double identity of protection and of threat.

After Udin's funeral, Bantul policemen visited Wagiman's house to ask his permission to enter the now-shuttered Krisna Photo Studio, which Marsiyem had abandoned after her husband's death. Udin's elder brother accompanied them to Samalo, where several plainclothes detectives were already waiting to enter the reporter's home. After a thorough search, the detectives zeroed in on Udin's notebooks and papers. One of them asked if the police could keep Udin's documents. Udin's older brother nodded to indicate they had his permission.

The detectives had told Udin's family they had come on the orders of one Edy Wuryanto. Bantul Chief Detective Hidayat had appointed the thirty-nine-year-old sergeant major to head the homicide inquiry. Edy was considered to be the sharpest investigator in Bantul, if not in all of Jogjakarta. Since his assignment to Bantul, Edy's exploits had become legend. Supposedly, he had solved the perplexing homicide of a Bantul teenager, beaten to death with a bamboo cane. Edy figured out that the culprit was the teenager's jealous transvestite lover. After Bantul police had spent months trying to locate who had dumped the body of a local thug down a well, Edy was able to pin the killing on several disgruntled villagers who had grown tired of the hoodlum's extortion. Other murders he had solved included the killing of a taxi driver on Gadjah Mada University property, the murder of a test-preparation center director on Solo Road, and the case of a sarong-wrapped corpse found bobbing in Bantul's Cangkringan River.

A short, dark-skinned and crafty man with perpetually greasy hair, Edy preferred to conduct his investigations incognito. For his undercover sleuthing, he had prepared several alternate personalities, complete with official identification cards for each identity. Once, Edy dressed in the sun-bleached tatters of a *becak* driver to solve the murder of a maid at a Solo Road hotel. He had stationed himself outside the hotel until he could pinpoint who among the establishment's frequent visitors and employees was the murderer. Because of Edy's renown, crime reporters befriended him to pick up the latest thrilling murder stories. One *Bernas* reporter said that the detective always began his investigations from one simple theory. According to Edy, the reporter had been told, two motives explained ninety-nine per cent of all crimes. People broke the law for rarely any other reasons than for love or for money. Among the reporters who had known Edy was Udin himself. The Bantul journalist had spent countless hours lounging with Edy on the porch outside the Bantul detectives' office. The detective often invited the reporter to accompany him on investigations. Now the police made him responsible for tracking down Udin's killer.

On 19 August 1996, Edy paid a visit to Udin's Trirenggo home while the family was still hosting prayers for the reporter. Udin's uncle Mardimin received the detective under a coconut tree in the front yard. The detective asked if the family still had the blood that Bethesda orderlies had collected from Udin's hemorrhaging brain. After the operation, the nurses had offered the blood to Udin's family, who brought it to Samalo. The blood sat for several days in a plastic bag in a refrigerator. After Udin's death, his family had decided to bury Udin's blood with his body. They entrusted Mardimin with the task of bringing the blood to the burial. Edy's request now reminded Mardimin that he had been remiss. He had forgotten to put the bag inside the journalist's coffin. Fortunately, Udin's family recovered the blood from a pile of garbage, where Udin's younger sister had thrown it during a fit of cleaning. They turned the liquid over to Edy, still in the cheap, crinkly plastic bag.

Some time after Edy had acquired Udin's blood, the two young *Bernas* reporters Moko and Ndari encountered the detective at Bantul police headquarters. Moko had a received a tip that police would be interviewing Sukrisno and Suwandi, Udin's visitors. The journalists arrived too late, however, to catch the councilor and the alleged election broker. But while they were waiting, Edy had introduced himself, and the three struck up a conversation. Edy told them he had known their fallen colleague well. When he heard what had happened to Udin, he said, the detective had dropped an out-of-town case to rush to Bethesda Hospital.

"I was close to him," the detective declared.

Edy boasted about the homicides he had solved, such as one that involved a body so mangled only a watch the corpse was wearing could be used to identify it. The detective spread out case files from his bag to show the reporters photographs of another case he was handling. Pointing to color shots of a blood-spattered woman, Edy bragged: "This is a murder case that I'm tracking. I already know the murderer. The only job left is to catch him."

The detective said he regularly consulted *dukun* in his work. "Believe it or not. I often solve these cases with the help of 'elders.'" Then Edy pulled out a cheap, black plastic bag and smiled. Something inside it weighed down the bag's bottom.

"You know what's in this?" he asked mischievously. "This is Udin's blood. This can be used to trace who killed him. If you want, you can later meet Udin's spirit through this blood."

When the two *Bernas* reporters declined the unusual offer, Edy brought other plainclothes officers who had gathered on the station's front porch into the game.

"Guess what this is?" the detective asked his colleagues.

"Liquid or solid?" one of them tried gamely.

"Liquid!"

"Can you drink it?" a detective asked.

"You can," Edy answered, smirking.

When his friends gave up, Edy revealed that the bag contained Udin's blood. An officer – the one who had asked if the bag's contents could be consumed – immediately protested.

"Well, blood can be drunk if you want to," Edy explained, with a snicker.

The two reporters left with vastly opposite impressions of the case's lead investigator. Moko believed he was sincere. Ndari, however, was skeptical. For someone who claimed Udin as a close friend, Edy seemed awfully cavalier about evidence of his murder. He seemed to treat other people's deaths just as insensitively. He had spread photographs of bodies out like pornography. He seemed arrogant, vain and slick – far too confident in his own reputation and his abilities. Ndari wondered: could this man be trusted with so sensitive an investigation?

CHAPTER 5

Puppeteers

IN JAVA, SOME BELIEVE that a person's spirit lingers on the material plane for up to seven days after death. The reason is that death dawns on the newly-deceased only slowly, especially to those who have passed away suddenly. Life, the believers might say, maintains a hold well beyond death. Even though a body might fail in a moment, a human soul has stronger attachments, if not to life itself then at least to the living.

Marsiyem had been at Udin's bedside when he died. Yet weeks after his burial, she continued to feel Udin's presence near her. At night, especially, she would dream of her husband. In those encounters, she thought she could see him from afar, and sense that he was speaking to her. He was close enough so she could see his lips move but too far for her to hear what he was saying. She wondered what pained her more: Udin's constant nearness or his unreachable distance.

While her husband was in the hospital, the reporter's wife had moved in with his family in Trirenggo, where she felt safer than at the Krisna Photo Studio in Samalo. After his death, she stayed on in the care of her in-laws. Nonetheless, an unceasing procession of visitors, mostly strangers, still found her. They contributions to support her now that her husband had passed, or at least expressed their condolences for her grief. Many were journalists seeking her time for lengthy interviews. Although talking about what had happened never helped dull the pain of her loss, she could not bring herself to close the door on her husband's old colleagues. *Bernas*, after all, had taken care of Udin's hospital bills, which had cost more than $2,300. Radio stations and newspapers from Jogja to Jakarta had also raised scholarship money for Yuli and Wikan, even though *Bernas* had already committed itself to funding their future education. In addition, Marsiyem received donations from the PWI, Information Minister Harmoko's wife, and even Suharto's grandson. She also received dozens of letters of sympathy, which mostly had one message. They told her to have faith in God that evil would be punished. One, however, urged her to invoke other forces. The writer advised her to sprinkle soil from her husband's grave around her house so his murderer might be quickly arrested.

The money and the attention only reminded her that being the nation's most prominent widow was a role she would have gladly surrendered. She would give it all back only to be back in Samalo that evening with Udin. This time, she would have left the ironing alone, turned off the lights, and locked the front door until morning. She tortured herself with questions about the night of the murder that were more biting than any detective or investigative journalist could have mustered. Why had she opened the door? It had been late at night. Why didn't she just send the young man away, or ask him to come on a more convenient occasion? The visitor had spoken so politely. Now, she feared for her own life, and the lives of her children. For she had seen the murderer's face and she knew his features. Perhaps now he would come after her.

Marsiyem ate little, and spent most of her time curled up in her bed. Her daughter, Yuli, had grasped her sadness. The eight-year-old tried in her own way to comfort her mother. "Why can't we move somewhere far away where no one can bother us?" Yuli often asked. Her daughter invited Marsiyem to visit Udin's grave in the Trirenggo cemetery, an activity that soon became a twice-weekly ritual. There, Marsiyem would stare at Udin's white marble headstone. The words engraved on it – "Fuad Muhammad Syafruddin. Born: 18 February 1963. Died:

16 August 1996" – reminded her of his passing with factual finality. Yet every time her son, Wikan, heard a Honda Tiger motorcycle purring down the road outside Wagiman's house, he would recognize it as the sound of his father's vehicle. Then he would shout, his voice melodious with hope, "That's papa coming!" and Marsiyem would burst into tears, and the pain would start all over.

On 22 August 1996, a week after the reporter's death, Udin's newspaper held its own remembrance for the fallen journalist. *Bernas* draped the front of its headquarters with a black cloth that reached from the roof to the ground. Inside the shrouded building, hundreds of guests attended Muslim prayers held traditionally seven days after a death. To an audience that spilled out into the newspaper's parking lot, several prominent Jogja figures delivered speeches honoring the reporter. One of those speakers, a young Muslim preacher and poet, further underlined Udin's secular canonization. He called Udin a *syuhada*. A martyr for his faith.

In the days since the burial, calls and notes of sympathy choked the newspaper's phone and facsimile lines. The mail also brought stacks of letters and cards. Most came from local and foreign news publications and press freedom organizations, although government officials, military commanders, student leaders, and ordinary citizens also sent in their sympathies. International activist groups backed up their letters of condolences to Jogja with missives of concern to high officials in Jakarta protesting the suspicious death of a working journalist. One note, above all, expressed how sorrow and solidarity combined to turn this one death into a cause that united the usually splintered members of a beleaguered profession. The editor-in-chief of the banned magazine *TEMPO* had written a seven-line poem to honor Udin. It read:

If I die today or tomorrow,
I wish to stand, if God
Allows, behind Udin's spirit
Who now stands before Him.

And I will be proud to do this.
Only a soul as unafraid as Udin's
Can remind us: We are not vile creatures.

"It is our duty to carry out a thorough investigation," the Central Java police chief had assured *Bernas* reporters and editors. "We will seek the perpetrator until we find him." On 20 August 1996, Central Java's chief detective had indicated how the police department would be focusing its search for the killer. "With this kind of assault," he had told reporters, "we conclude that the criminal was very professional." That word – "professional" – meant a hired gun, someone trained in the art of violence. In Indonesia, a professional could be a killer-for-hire or a petty criminal, even an off-duty policeman or an AWOL soldier. The entry requirements were low: All that the job needed was anyone who wanted money and had no qualms about taking the life of another. Approaching a house, knocking on the door, and beating a man required bravado. But the assailant had also committed his crime in a lighted yard, across the street from an open restaurant, a few steps from the victim's wife and sleeping family. What had emboldened him? Udin's colleagues wondered. Was it unbreakable nerve or a few muttered enchantments? Or did the criminal perhaps believe an earthly force more powerful than any *dukun*'s mantra protected him? Perhaps the crimson-clad youth could knock so calmly on Marsiyem's door because someone with influence had assured him that no matter how horribly he hurt Udin, he would never be punished. The reporters became convinced that it would not be enough for the police to locate the killer; the detectives also had to find the person who had paid or protected him.

Over the next few weeks, officers from the Central Java Police District and the national police visited Jogja in a constant parade of teams and task forces to investigate the killing. Police examined and reexamined the Krisna Photo Studio and its surrounding area, questioned and reinterviewed the couple's neighbors, and held frequent meetings to discuss their progress at the province's police headquarters. Once, when reporters visited the Jogjakarta chief detective's office, they glimpsed on a blackboard a list of five issues the investigators apparently thought might be connected to the reporter's murder. The list included Udin's coverage of the IDT corruption allegations, Sri Roso's "One-Billion Rupiah Promise," the *bupati*'s reelection, Sri Roso's Golkar campaign and land scandals in the villages. As the PWI team had done, detectives pored over stories Udin had written over the course of the preceding year. Officers were dispatched to Karangtengah to examine whether anyone had been offended by Udin's exposure of the IDT anomalies, while others were tasked to follow the journalist's exposure of local officials. Sukrisno, Suwandi, and Kuncung and his five friends were all questioned. "We didn't touch anything else," one detective would later recall. "There were indications that officials were displeased with the victim."

Yet although three of the five topics concerned Sri Roso directly, neither the police nor the journalists had any solid leads linking the *bupati* directly to Udin's death. In the past, local government officials had been known to kill to protect their careers. In 1981, for example, a police lieutenant colonel, soon to be appointed a *bupati* in East Java, asked a subordinate to help him murder his mistress. He feared she would become a liability to his professional advancement. The two, however, bungled the killing. Their victim survived and reported the two to the police. A court tried and convicted the perpetrators. But in the case of Udin, all the evidence that could be assembled was that Sri Roso had wanted to sue the journalist and that he had not attended Udin's funeral. Neither would suffice in a court of law to support a charge of conspiracy or murder.

Heru did meet a police contact who told him that the *bupati* had confessed privately to ordering a hit on the journalist. The officer revealed that a team from the state civilian intelligence agency had visited and interviewed Sri Roso. In that encounter, the *bupati* had supposedly broken down and admitted that he had never meant for Udin to die.

The journalist was only supposed to have been bullied into silence. "He wept," the officer told Heru and Ida. "He wept right there." Although the officer's position high in the local command persuaded the journalists that his information was credible, they had no other sources that would confirm his account.

The Jogjakarta newspapers took care to avoid fingering Sri Roso directly as a suspect in Udin's murder. But the fact that journalists dogged his steps and wrote about his movements was enough to telegraph to readers that the local media regarded the Bantul chief executive as their primary suspect. Finally even the aloof Sri Roso, in his splendid, teak-clad office complex, could no longer ignore the gossip and speculation swirling through his kingdom. To end the chattering, the *bupati* summoned a press conference, his first since Udin's death. Sri Roso's spokesman told the press to come to Bantul on 23 August, which happened to be a *Kliwon* Friday. A full panoply of the *kabupaten's* senior officials, from assembly chairman Kamil to Bantul Police Chief Adé, would accompany Sri Roso. The retinue was perhaps deemed necessary to demonstrate that Sri Roso had the full confidence of his government.

The room chosen turned out to be too small to fit the press. Cameramen and correspondents from all over Java had augmented Jogja's regular population of local reporters. Even a few pale-skinned foreign journalists peered out of the sea of brown faces. The main table bristled with microphones. Television cameras blocked the view of all but the tallest reporters. The crowded function room in this peripheral corner of Jogjakarta looked as packed as a national press conference in the capital. Most of the journalists had arrived as soon as Friday prayers had ended, as Sri Roso's spokesman had instructed. The *bupati*, however, kept them waiting for close to an hour before he made his appearance. When Sri Roso finally arrived, a chorus of boos accompanied his tardy entrance. This was not a good beginning for what was supposed to be the *bupati's* attempt to unlink his name from Udin's murder.

Sri Roso launched quickly into his defense. "The problem is that I am often at the receiving end of over-dramatization," he complained.

"The press has a big role. But we have to create something that is fair and within context. Something that isn't fair for you is fair for me. And what isn't fair for me is in the right for you. We must meet in the middle, so that the result will be tranquility. For what do we exert all our sweat and tears if the product is not tranquility?"

A reporter interrupted to ask if the corruption of the IDT funds had indeed happened as Udin had reported. Sri Roso answered calmly. "That's really a technical matter. There was no reduction of village development funds." Contrary to what Udin had reported, the *bupati* insisted, every intended recipient of the government subsidy had received his or her money.

"So there wasn't a meeting to bring Udin to court and stop him?" another journalist pressed.

"That isn't an indication we were panicking. We received news of questionable accuracy…the responsibility of the *kabupaten* government is to guide. Right? The press is guided. This was an abuse. If I may say, if you are from *Bernas*, then ensure mistakes like this don't happen. Often something shows up in *Bernas* that isn't in other papers…Bantul has three times won an award from the national government. We've won trophies. Recently, I got an agriculture award. This never made it to the papers. But I've never been offended. We've never felt there was a problem."

"Maybe his death was connected to his reporting," a third reporter ventured.

"I'm not going to guess or theorize," Sri Roso retorted. "That's the job of detectives. It's not my responsibility, and it's precisely this that I'm trying to avoid. So the police don't feel stepped on. Don't force me. If I am constantly asked to guess, I can't. I won't. Because there's a huge risk in guessing…It could have happened to anyone. Syafruddin was a journalist. Journalists are also people, right? He might have had problems that we don't understand. This might be different from what you think."

Until this point, the officials Sri Roso had assembled remained silent.

But Bantul Police Chief Adé now joined in to defend his superior. "I think what the honorable *bupati* has said is true," he said. "We, the Indonesian police, are really the ones involved. This starts from the crime scene. There are suspects, evidence, and witnesses. From there we can begin to investigate, maybe with some help from you who give information to the Bantul police. But not all this information will be correct. Whether it's right or wrong, leave it to us. Don't pass on information that attacks someone like the *bupati*. If the information is true, okay. But what if it's not? Don't allow someone to get hurt."

A journalist from Jakarta shot Adé a question: "Just be honest. Are there any 'obstacles' to solving this case?"

"I am being honest!" the police chief exclaimed. "At this moment there is no connection…all of us officers…maybe we're not well-trained, not diligent, or not careful. But obstacles from the outside, there aren't any. The suspect's characteristics are clear and complete: A body my size, but well-muscled. A thin mustache. Light brown skin. He was wearing jeans and a tight T-shirt. Pray that in two or three days we can catch him. I'm not saying one week, two weeks, or three weeks. But Monday night, Tuesday night, maybe. For the moment, let me, the police chief, speak. Leave the *bupati* out of this."

"Is there a 'puppeteer' behind this case?" one reporter shouted.

"At the right time, I'll reveal all. Let's not just arrest anybody. We need proper papers. Witnesses. A connection. Puppeteers are only in the shadow play. Give us two to three days. There is no 'puppeteer.' Period."

Even in the twenty-first century, people throughout Java will abandon their televisions and computer terminals to watch the *wayang*. West Java and Bali have their own forms of the shadow play, but it is in Central Java where the art has become the most magical. Traditionally, performances of the *wayang* last from dusk until dawn. Performed for weddings, births and other important rites of passage, the shadow play requires that a *dalang*, a puppeteer, sit behind a backlit cotton scrim and retell in Javanese an episode drawn from the Indian epics, either from the troubled romance of Rama and Sita or the world-ending war of the Mahabharata. As he flutters his flattened figures of princes and ogres against the sheer fabric, the orchestra behind him taps, on deep-voiced gongs and drums, melodies that envelop the listener from a place remote and ancient. The dark and chilly midnight hours, haunting music, and the assured voice of the puppeteer guiding the audience through an adventure conspire to transform each performance into a mystical experience.

The *dalang*'s puppets of stiffened leather are intricately detailed and brightly colored. But since he wields them behind a screen, most in his audience see only shadows. Thus in Indonesia, the shadow puppeteer has become a popular metaphor for a mastermind, someone who manipulates appearances to hide realities. It is an image that has long been attached to President Suharto. At the end of thirty years of rule, Suharto could argue that his country had become one of the most successful and stable countries of the developing world. In 1965, his country had been poorer than Nepal. But by 1995, Indonesia had the largest economy in Southeast Asia – worth over $107 billion. Much of that wealth had actually been accumulated in the 1980s and early 1990s. After the oil-price collapse that precipitated the *Petrus* murders, Suharto's economic advisers had advised him to open the economy so capital could flow into the manufacturing and service industries, and then into the infant stock market. The transition from a largely state-run oil-driven economy to one that thrived on trade, manufacturing, and capital worked wonders. Between 1987 and 1989, foreign investment jumped from $1.5 billion to $8.75 billion. In 1989, the economy returned to its pre-1980s pace of expansion of seven per cent a year, a trot it smartly maintained until 1995.

Yet behind the scrim of wealth and stability whirred what one of Suharto's biographers has called "a secret economy." The increasing prosperity gave only the appearance of expanding opportunities for the great mass of Indonesians. In reality, the money remained limited to a fortunate few, most of who had connections to Suharto's cronies in the business world or the army. In the military, Suharto had learned how well involvement in businesses and "charitable" foundations had helped guarantee his soldiers' loyalties. So when he became president, not only did he install soldiers throughout the administration, he also granted them vast economic privileges as a reward for their support and as a way to bind their fates to his own survival. He granted one barracksmate control of the state oil company, and made another general head of the government's rice purchase and distribution monopoly. Other soldiers had first grab at government contracts, appointments, and licenses. It was not long before military businesses had involved themselves in everything from automobile assembly to shoe factories, from banks to forestry companies – all mostly off-the-books operations that at one point were thought to account for as much as a third of the military's budget.

The bureaucracy and big business, dominated by established Chinese trading families who had cleverly forged mutually beneficial alliances with Suharto's soldiers or servants, also enjoyed the benefits of access to the new, purportedly "private" sources of wealth. As Indonesia gradually liberalized its economy, officials, their family members, and their friends went to the front of the line for lucrative government-assigned import and distribution monopolies in goods such as plastic, steel, plywood and even cloves, an important ingredient for the local cigarette industry. Because of these monopoly middlemen, a commodity like steel, for example, would cost the end consumer from a third to a half more than it would had the metal been bought on the open market. In 1995, ten large companies, many owned by Suharto cronies, were worth almost half of Indonesia's gross domestic product. The wealth became increasingly concentrated in an oligarchy, with monopolies and market niches passed down and along lines of family or official connections.

Children of well-placed military officers or civil servants turned easy and unsecured credit from state and private banks into business empires on the strength of their parents' connections. For example, one son of a Jakarta governor, with strong ties to the food distribution monopoly, managed in a few years to leverage a $7,500 loan into a company with assets worth thirty-two million dollars. Similarly, from 1985 to 1994, Suharto's eldest daughter, Siti Hardiyanti Rukmana, better known as "Tutut," had gone from running a stationery business with fifty thousand dollars in initial capital to managing a massive conglomerate worth an estimated four hundred million dollars. Her sixty subsidiaries were involved in industries from publishing and construction, from radio to manufacturing. Even more impressive were the achievements of Suharto's youngest child, Hutomo "Tommy" Mandala Putra, who started his own empire at the age of twenty-two with $300,000. Within a decade, he owned twenty-seven companies valued at one billion dollars, in businesses as varied as sea and air transport, petrochemicals, oil, toll-road operation, banking, property, communications, and automobile production. Although the government lauded these youngsters as natural business moguls, clearly their parents had given then more than just the genes for entrepreneurial talent.

These sinecures earned the New Order oligarchs so much money they could barely spend it at the same rate. They lavished their lucre on parties, clothes, mansions, and other trinkets of conspicuous consumption. Senior civil servants drooled over private jets like the Minister of Labor's BAC-11, with its gold-plated faucets. Generals adopted expensive hobbies, such as collecting Harley-Davidsons, big-game hunting, or sailing out into the Java Sea for deep-sea fishing. Their wives planned opulent weddings, where televisions and VCR's were handed out as door prizes as Suharto's brother had done when the president's niece had married. The children of the ultra-rich luxuriated in the care of nannies and played with less-fortunate children brought to entertain them as "contract playmates." The servants of the rich wore white gloves; their chauffeurs polished their sparkling automobiles with spittle.

The New Order elite's privileges were defended by military force. In order to construct her Beautiful Indonesia-in-Miniature theme park, for example, Tien had the military evict some three hundred families. When one group of young demonstrators protested at the park's secretariat, she hired a group of goons who stabbed one of the activists and shot another. In faraway Irian Jaya, arrows from the bows of resentful natives would whiz past guests finishing their rounds at a resort golf course. The hotel that housed them had been built on tribal land, seized and secured by military might.

To most Indonesians, the secret economy and the shadow state were invisible; their inner workings incomprehensible. They read how certain businessmen, generals, or politicians had become enormously wealthy. They saw the unqualified win coveted jobs with the help of recommendations, documents that were called, by virtue of their power, *surat sakti*, or "magical letters." They noticed how others received better treatment as long as they affixed decals with military logos on their windows or slipped policemen's business cards underneath their glass tabletops. They saw how certain people could be immune from arrest or prosecution while others, clearly innocent, went to prison.

This situation may explain a cultural phenomenon that seemed to contradict the country's progress: in this rapidly urbanizing and developing country, traditional beliefs in mysticism were finding even greater purchase among Indonesians. The *dukun* never seemed to have a shortage of clients. Perhaps their customers had, on some level, realized that hard work, good education, or a smart idea would not grant them admission into the rarefied realms of the elite. If they could do nothing on their own to change their own fates, then maybe, indeed, the only solution was to turn to magic.

※

The Bantul police chief had announced at the *bupati*'s press conference that Udin's killer would be arrested in days. But as those days passed, the Jogja journalists came to doubt the way the police were handling the case. First, Udin's colleagues wondered why the police had never cordoned off the crime scene. The area around the Krisna Photo Studio had been open for weeks to any journalist or curious onlooker to examine. The crowd on the night of the assault might have erased the most obvious traces of the youth with the red bandanna or his accomplice, but the absence of a police barrier or even yellow "crime scene" tape that indicated an ongoing investigation meant that any clues that did remain would have long been destroyed.

Only two weeks after the assault, on 27 August, did officers stretch yellow tape around Udin's house in Samalo. But so long after the crime, the tape's presence now seemed superfluous, not as much to keep the site pristine than to keep out the curious media and establish the area as police territory. In fact, fewer than twenty-four hours later, the police tape had inexplicably been taken down either by the police themselves or by pranksters. Bantul's Police Chief Adé had declared the police would start from the crime scene. But a total lack of oversight had virtually assured that little would be found there that would lead to the killer.

Law enforcement's tardiness in securing the crime scene might be ascribed to poor training or even a shortage of equipment, a real possibility in a country where police stations often lack the most basic crime scene kits. But the police's sidelining of Udin's colleagues, despite sincere attempts to help the investigation, seemed more intentional. From asking around Udin's neighborhood, Heru had discovered that on 13 August, the night of the attack, several people had seen two men on a motorcycle stop at a public telephone kiosk at an intersection north of Samalo. His sources had told him that one of the men had seemed agitated as he made a hurried phone call. Heru passed his information to the Bantul police, and made arrangements to accompany detectives to the kiosk to retrieve the call records from its attendants. But when Heru and other reporters showed up at the agreed time, they were told the police had reached the telephone kiosk first. When Heru tried to locate the officer who had taken the records, no one at Bantul police headquarters would reveal to him who now had possession of them.

Udin's family and colleagues also wondered what had happened to the evidence the detectives had already collected, especially the reporter's notebooks and his blood. Although Edy's men had taken Udin's papers, Adé's office said that the notebooks were no longer in the possession of the Bantul police. Neither the Bantul nor the Jogjakarta police had also questioned Sri Roso, which suggested that he was not considered a suspect, which ran counter to purported initial indications that Udin's stories had made the Bantul *kabupaten* government "displeased with the victim." In an interview with a foreign correspondent from Jakarta, Sri Roso declared he was ready to be questioned, as long as the police's request passed through the proper channels. Since Sri Roso was a public official, the investigators needed formal permission from the Interior Ministry to question him as part of a formal murder investigation. Until that time, Sri Roso declared, he would no longer comment on the case. "I will be silent for now," he declared. "Because if I talk too much then there will be a polemic that will never end."

During that same interview, Sri Roso wondered why the media had taken such an interest in Udin's death. "Actually, there are many cases like this one," he said. "Why is this case made out to be such a big matter?"

To a *Bernas* reporter, a local academic fretted that the police were delaying the investigation so they could devise a way to absolve Sri Roso and the Bantul government. He mused, "There could be a scenario to divert the cause of Udin's death from his journalism to something very different: perhaps a motive involving a family matter, or revenge."

Udin's colleagues came to believe that they took the investigation into Udin's death more seriously than the police. Since August, the PWI team had been assembling reams of data could about the crime. Masduki, its leader, and the rest of the team had gone to the Krisna Photo Studio to reconstruct the events of 13 August. They circled the yard where Udin had met the late-night visitor. They measured the distance from the front door to where Marsiyem had been ironing, and clocked the time required to traverse it in order to estimate how many seconds had elapsed between Udin's exit from his home and his collapse on the pavement. The PWI Fact-Finding Team asked Sujarah to show them where the reporter's body had lain in its pool of blood outside the studio.

The PWI team visited Marsiyem several times to secure solid descriptions of her husband's assailant and his weapon. On one occasion, they showed her several spare parts gathered from various machine shops around the city. They wanted her to identify what kind of metal bar the murderer had brought. Udin's widow looked at a handlebar, a muffler pipe, and a part of a shock breaker. But nothing resembled the gleaming length of metal the youth had flashed in front of her.

A few days after, the PWI journalists returned and brought with them an art student and his sketchbook. The team asked Marsiyem to describe the young man she met that evening. So once again, the widow had to fix her husband's murderer's image in her mind: his red button-down shirt, skin the color of a ripe *sawo* fruit, and his thin mustache. Once more, she could hear his three loud raps on her door, his voice speaking in that obsequious tone of respect, and her unsuspecting answers: "*Who is it?*" "*It's me, ma'am…Is Udin in? I want to leave my motorcycle with him.*" As the widow described her visitor, the student passed his stub of charcoal over the paper. Repeatedly, he erased and redrew chins, noses, ears, and other features, until finally the face of a hard-eyed, square-faced young man appeared in front of Marsiyem. When the sketch was complete, Asril, who was about as tall as the suspect stood up. He placed the paper in front of his face and asked Marsiyem: "Is this him?"

Marsiyem covered her face. "Yes…Yes…" She answered, her voice trembling. "Nothing needs to be added."

By early September, the PWI team had assembled a rough chronology of the crime. They had narrowed down possibilities for the murder weapon and produced a sketch of the suspected murderer, which *Bernas* and several other newspapers ran on their front page to see if a member of the public might be able to identify the suspect. For the PWI team, however, whatever exposure their work received was incidental. The information they had gathered was intended for a report to the union's Jakarta headquarters, which was to be confidential. Masduki had insisted that the team be scrupulously fair. Rather than release unconfirmed rumors, or give information to some journalists and shut out others, the PWI team eventually decided to release no information at all. After a while, the more facts they gathered from Udin's neighbors, family, and other Bantul sources, the less comfortable they felt revealing what they had found to their colleagues.

As his involvement in the PWI team engaged his colleague Putut, the responsibility for guiding *Bernas'* coverage of the Udin murder investigation fell increasingly to Heru. "I could not just sit on my hands in the office and wait for their reports," he would later explain. His friend had been killed. Could he stand by and do nothing? At the very least, his professional commitment to journalism required him to provide the newspaper's readers with some answers. Achadi, Moko, Ndari, and other idealistic junior journalists at *Bernas* joined Heru to help produce daily reports on the investigation. Although Heru's involvement in the case was personal, Udin's murder, for the younger reporters, had become a cause – a crusade, even. Achadi would later admit that he did not know Udin as well as the others. "He might have been an asshole," he would say. "But he did not deserve to die the way he did."

Since 1994, the Indonesian media had become characterized by ferment. That year's banning of three magazines had radicalized many journalists and caused demonstrations to roil Jakarta and other major cities. Reporters fed up with the Information Ministry's iron hand and the PWI's craven monopoly had formed their own journalists' union. They called it the Alliance of Independent Journalists, or AJI for short. AJI had just fifty-eight official members, compared to the hundreds of thousands forced to sign up with the PWI. Yet the official union seemed to fear what an alternative group represented: a challenge to the New Order's monopoly of meaning. The PWI's secretary-general called the tiny alliance's existence "an insult."

When AJI began publishing out of Jakarta an irregular, unlicensed bulletin packed with political gossip, investigative reporting, and rabble-rousing columns, the government struck back. Police arrested two AJI members and the office's teenage errand-boy. The prosecutor-general banned the AJI broadsheet for causing "concern and public distrust toward the government." The PWI dutifully followed suit by revoking the memberships of thirteen journalists who had publicly supported the independent union. Since government regulations disfavored publications that employed non-PWI members, the affected reporters either lost their jobs or were transferred to non-reporting positions. After accelerated trials, Jakarta courts slapped the arrested AJI members with prison sentences from twenty to thirty-two months in jail. In this context, the activist Jogja journalists thus had the sense that they were engaged in a struggle that went much further than the sultanate. They were in the middle of a nationwide effort to pull back the blindfold and gags the Suharto government had imposed on public discourse and civil society. Udin's murder presented these reporters far from the capital with an opportunity to take the struggle straight to the government.

For those same reasons, the story attracted many others outside *Bernas*. One of them, Lucia Nucke Idayanie, would become one of the group's most active members. At the time of the killing, she had been the Jogjakarta correspondent for the Jakarta crime-and-politics magazine *Detective & Romance*. But she had begun her career at the shuttered *TEMPO*. The short, motherly thirty-three-year-old, whom everyone fondly called "Ida," started working at *TEMPO* to support her mother and brothers instead of going to college. She had successfully made her way up from an office secretary to a full-fledged correspondent when the Information Ministry banned her magazine. For months, she wore black as a sign of mourning. She joined the street demonstrations, where in her own form of protest, she snapped pictures of the secret policemen who haunted the rallies. The spies tried to pass themselves off as activists or journalists, complete with multipocketed vests, cameras, and notebooks. But Ida could still pick them out from the crowd by the oily smirk beneath their straggly mustaches and their swagger, which betrayed their need, despite their disguises, to smugly show off their power. Whenever she spotted one, she raised her viewfinder to her eye and released her camera's shutter.

Ida had built up a large collection of photos of government agents by the time she started attending meetings at the *Bernas* office, joining the dozens of reporters from other media organizations who had gravitated to the newspaper's Solo Road office. The city's journalists had set aside their traditional, institutional rivalries to pool resources and share information about their colleague's murder. Every day, once enough reporters had appeared at the *Bernas* office, they would discuss the latest developments and decide what trails to follow. One favorite time to talk was late at night, when the newspaper had gone to press, or early in the morning, while most were still plotting what they needed to produce by that day's deadline.

Heru and the *Bernas* reporters kept one of the office cars on constant standby. It was a white Toyota van known locally as a "Kijang," a type of deer whose image the company had appropriated to brand its converted pickups. The Kijang ferried them and other reporters to Samalo, Bantul, police headquarters, and other locales throughout the province. At least eleven people could fit in the Kijang. *Bernas* may be paying for the gas and maintenance, but the newspaper's resources were assisting all of the local media.

In the first weeks after the murder, *Bernas* rarely ran short of tips and leads. The problem was distinguishing the crank calls from the ones worth pursuing. The newspaper's receptionist constantly received calls from strangers claiming to know the address of the killer. A couple of callers recklessly insisted that they themselves were the murderers. Stories about the night of the assault also floated freely around Samalo. To pick up on the village talk and rumors, the reporters frequently visited Marsiyem and Wagiman, or ate at Ponikem and Nur Sulaiman's noodle restaurant.

Many of these leads took them nowhere. Heru, for example, once attempted to confirm what some of Udin's neighbors had sworn they had seen the night of the killing: that the murderer's motorcycle had been tailed that night by a blue Honda sedan. With crime reporter

Herman's help, Heru discovered that the district chief of Imogiri, in which Karangtengah village was located, had owned a blue Honda. However, none of their sources could provide a license plate number, so their lead vanished in a puff of rumor and speculation. On another occasion, Heru met a man who claimed he had been Noto Suwito's assistant. The man provided Heru with copies of *surat sakti* letters signed by Suharto's half-brother recommending well-known figures to positions in the state-owned oil monopoly or to gubernatorial positions. The letters confirmed what Heru already knew about the Argomulyo headman – that he was very influential. But nothing Heru uncovered pinned responsibility for his friend's murder on Suharto's half-brother.

Heru, Ida, and a group of journalists tried tramping through the freshly-harvested paddies near Udin's home to search for the murder weapon. Under the hot, noontime sun, their figures painted a curious picture: well-educated men and women with rolled-up trousers scrabbling through dried rice stalks and clumps of clotted earth. When passers-by inquired why they were getting themselves so dirty, the embarrassed reporters came up with the excuse that they were looking for duck eggs. Their search was fruitless. Several farmers nearby had already told them they had recovered no strange objects dumped in their fields.

Some of the more enthusiastic young journalists even searched out *dukun*. One mystic claimed he could channel the dead reporter's spirit. The reporter who visited him said the *dukun* had intoned: "There is a connection to government...An official is angry, because his secret has been exposed." Another paranormal they consulted had declared optimistically: "Now is the *zaman edan*, the time of madness. Whoever commits something like this crime will certainly face tragedy. He will be caught."

It was not long before other journalists joked that the ragtag group led by Heru at *Bernas* was competing with the secretive PWI team. Heru and his colleagues began to be called the "White Kijang" team. The phrase's initials in Indonesian, TKP, had an additional connotation. They stood for *tempat kejadian perkara*, which was Indonesian police jargon for "scene of the crime." The differences between the two groups became marked. The White Kijang team included many supporters, sympathizers and underground members of the rebel reporters' union AJI, while the PWI Fact-Finding Team represented exclusively the government-backed journalist establishment. Many in the White Kijang team distrusted most the senior journalists loyal to the PWI, who they considered hopelessly tarred by the New Order's media culture. When Achadi passed by the PWI's Putut in the *Bernas* corridors, the two would not talk to each other – despite the fact that both worked for the same publication and on the same story.

On 31 August, the *Bernas* reporters took the white Kijang to see Sukrisno and Suwandi, the two men who had met the reporter in the newspaper's parking lot before his killing. Heru had at first been reluctant to visit Sukrisno because of the man's fearsome reputation. But after a *Kompas* reporter scooped *Bernas* by publishing an interview with the alleged election-broker, Heru prevailed on Bantul correspondent Djoko to arrange a meeting for his own paper. At Sukrisno's home in Bantul, Sukrisno and Suwandi explained that the real estate broker had not been the one who had met Udin that night. It turned out that Sukrisno's younger brother Hatta had used his elder sibling's name because he thought Djoko, who they had initially wanted to meet, would know his older brother better. The men had come to discuss some land Djoko was considering purchasing. When Suwandi and Hatta could not meet Djoko, they explained, they decided to speak to Udin about other lots that were available.

Both men denied that Suwandi and Hatta's encounter with Udin had any connection to the assault which occurred later that night in Samalo. Yet throughout the interview, Sukrisno played with a shiny Japanese sword which he would pass from one thick, bejeweled hand to the other. Nervous about the flashing blade in front of them, Heru asked anxiously if Sukrisno was trying to sell the sword, which was why he was exhibiting it.

"If you want to buy this, it's about four thousand dollars," Sukrisno answered with a smirk.

The reporters knew the murdered journalist had been offered a parcel of land but the deal had fizzled before it was completed. At the same time, the journalists also could not accept that Udin's meeting with people so closely connected to the *kabupaten* government – a Golkar representative and an alleged election-broker – the night he was attacked could be simply a coincidence. Suwandi and Hatta might have come to discuss land, as they claimed. But the journalists still could not shake their suspicion that what they really had done was to threaten the Bantul reporter to stop his negative coverage of Sukrisno's patron, the *bupati*.

"I wrote what they said," Heru would later say, "but I did not believe it." Sukrisno's brandishing of a weapon seemed to Heru a crude attempt at intimidation. The blade was a literal reminder, to use Achadi's words at Udin's burial, of the sword that hung a few centimeters from the throats of the local media. But the days were long past when such a pointed message would have worked on Heru and his associates. A friend had died; the least they owed him was their courage.

CHAPTER 6

A Finger's Breadth of Earth

ON 20 AUGUST 1996, two men appeared at the door of a twenty-four-year-old woman in Bantul named Tri Sumaryani. She was a fan of citizens band radio, or "breaker," as the locals called it. Yani spent hours chatting on her amateur radio apparatus to people across the villages and hamlets of Jogjakarta. She attended meetings of people who had met over the airwaves much like people in Internet chatrooms seek out one another's real-world incarnation. Her hobby had given her a wide circle of friends and acquaintances. That circle was wide enough, it seemed, that people she had never met had now heard about her.

The men at her door introduced themselves as fellow aficionados, and engaged her in a conversation about antennae, channels, and groups of other amateur radio fanatics. Then her visitors brought up Udin, the Bantul reporter whose murder the whole *kabupaten* kept discussing. Yani mentioned casually that she knew him. Earlier that year, perhaps in February or March – she could not quite remember – she had bumped into Udin at one breaker meeting. The accounting graduate had dated Udin's younger brother for two years. Although she had ended the relationship, Yani remained a friend of Udin's family. Since Yani lived not far from Samalo, the reporter offered to take her home on his motorcycle from the gathering. That was the last time she saw Udin before his murder.

The men now seemed far less interested in her amateur radio hobby than in her relationship with the reporter. They quizzed her about Udin, and how well she knew him and his family. When they had exhausted their questions about the murdered journalist, the two men left. Two weeks later, Yani received another visitor. This time, she knew him. He was Kuncung, Sri Roso's nephew and one of the youths who had brought Udin to the hospital. A mustachioed and stout twenty-nine-year-old with skin the color of butter, the smooth-talking Kuncung had, for the past three years, handled government affairs in Bakulan, a part of Patalan village just north of Udin's Samalo. Kuncung registered births and deaths in the hamlet. He monitored the arrivals and departures of residents and foreigners. He processed identity cards and handed out permits for meetings and parties. He wrote letters of "Good Behavior" and "Clean Environment." He registered transfers of land and managed the neighborhood night watches. His responsibilities had led the villagers to call him *Pak Aman*, or "Mr. Security." For them, Kuncung represented the security of being registered and counted, of being listed and licensed, of being watched and guided. He was security with a capital "S" – Bakulan's own representative from Suharto's state.

The visit of "Mr. Security" surprised Yani. Although they knew each other's names, neither moved in the other's social circles. When they passed each other in the village, Kuncung had never said a word to her. Now, as they talked in her living room, Yani had the creepy feeling that he was acting like a longtime friend. Like the two strange men before him, Kuncung seemed friendly only to probe her relationship with Udin. He wondered if she had ever made appointments to see Udin during his working hours. He asked her whether she had ever hitched a ride with the reporter on his motorcycle outside the Bantul courthouse? Yani had the impression that Kuncung was asking, in a sly and roundabout way, if Yani had been having an affair with Marsiyem's husband.

Yani grew uncomfortable with Kuncung's insinuations, which eventually became explicit. As she would later tell police and reporters, Kuncung urged her: "Yani, just admit to your affair. Whatever you want, I'll fulfill it."

"What do I have to admit?" Yani told him. "Even if you gave me a plane complete with runway, I wouldn't know what to say. I know nothing about this!"

Before he left, Yani would later relate, Kuncung said that if Yani knew anyone who could identify Udin's attacker, he would also give that person anything he wanted. She did not understand whether Kuncung's offer was supposed to be an offer for information or a bribe to keep silent. When Kuncung returned several days later, with a policeman in tow, he had dropped the friendly pretenses. The officer had an official summons for Yani to the Bantul police headquarters. There, Edy Wuryanto was waiting to question her officially about her relationship with Udin.

Yani did not know how to answer the detective's questions. Edy's questions poked and prodded deeper, as if he hoped to snag the admission Kuncung had unsuccessfully attempted to extract weeks earlier: that Udin was her lover. Yani was terrified: how could she admit to adultery if she had never committed it?

Both groups of investigating journalists – the PWI team and Heru's White Kijang team – had convinced themselves that Bantul officials worried about their reputations and positions had killed Udin. When the reporters heard about Yani's interrogation, they realized that the police had now long left behind that theory and were now looking exclusively at other, more personal motives. During her regular meetings with detectives, Marsiyem had noticed the shift in focus as well. When Bantul police had questioned her the day after Udin's burial, they had been sincerely interested in her husband's work. At the time, she told them what she knew about Udin's coverage of the IDT fund scandal. Her information, she had to admit, was very limited. She knew several officials had complained to Udin's editors about his story. She had asked her husband to solve the problem as quickly as possible. Udin had pledged he would meet Imogiri officials himself, but she did not know why the promised meeting never happened.

Yet in the questioning that followed, the police became more curious about their home life than about her husband's profession. The officers who sat across from her wondered to her face if her husband had been seeing another woman. They inquired into the couple's household finances. They asked her to confirm rumors that her husband had several enemies. On 24 August 1996, some two weeks after the assault, she complained to her husband's friends from *Bernas*: "These police always ask now about family matters. They even mentioned that Udin had tried to ask for a *dukun*'s help in exchange for five million rupiah." That amount was equivalent to about two thousand dollars. "Where would he get that kind of money?" she asked. "What's more, when it comes to religion, Udin was devout. To request something from a power other than God is *mushrik*. Blasphemy."

As September wore on, each time she went to the Bantul police station, detectives continued to ply her with oddly invasive questions. "Is it true that before this incident, your husband kept a knife close while sleeping?" she was once asked. "Did your husband ever tell you that he had borrowed money? If so, who lent the money, for what purpose and where is it now?" Her interrogators needled her about how Udin could afford a computer on a freelancer's salary, or to buy a Honda Tiger, which, at the time, cost more than $3,500. Marsiyem explained that the couple had bought the motorcycle secondhand from a neighbor. In fact, they had borrowed some money and sold their old bike to pay the $2,000 or so its previous owner had wanted.

The police seemed unsatisfied by her answers. On 25 September, they asked again about the Krisna Photo Studio, its employees, and those who had invested in the business. They inquired about whether her parents approved of their marriage. How much rent did she pay? Had they had any problems with their landlord? When her interrogators asked about pieces Udin had written, they invariably wanted to know about the minor, scandalous stories, such as the one about a village official's affair in Karangtengah or about the manipulation of land certificates in another village. Her husband's most controversial work, in her estimation, was his coverage of the Parangtritis megaproject, the *bupati*'s promise to buy his reelection, or Sri Roso's early campaigning for the ruling party, Golkar. All those stories now seemed to have been discarded.

The neighborhood of Samalo was not large. Gossip spreads up or down Parangtritis Road in a matter of minutes. If Udin's family had been hiding an affair, then the secret must have been buried deep. Or it had never existed. To check, the PWI team had asked the reporter's friends and neighbors whether he had ever experienced disputes over inheritance, unpaid debts, love affairs, or grudges – any possibility that Udin had had personal problems that could be related to his death. "The results were zero," Putut would later say. If her husband had been cheating on her, they concluded Marsiyem would have long known about it.

"It wasn't possible!" Marsiyem told Ndari when the young reporter asked if her husband had been seeing Yani. "What was in Udin's head was work, work, work." She knew that Udin had given Yani a ride home from an amateur radio meeting – he had told her himself. "All this time, the Bantul police have been dragging this case towards personal matters," she complained to her husband's friends. "The news that Udin wrote has never been touched. I've been harassed by personal questions…the police don't want to understand my feelings."

The reporters wondered how the police had obtained its information, since none of the couple's neighbors – not Sujarah and Sujarwati, or the noodle sellers across the street – had ever mentioned to them any stories that Udin had been unfaithful. The reporter's neighbors may have been loyal to him, but they would not have failed to mention such a key fact if it helped locate his murderer.

One expression in Javanese culture is *wangsit*, a word that might be translated as "message." A *wangsit* is a kind of supernatural communication, perhaps from a deity, a demon, or a spirit. It might come in the form of words whispered from the air or as phrases uttered by a complete stranger that have a meaning only to the intended listener. When Jogjakarta's sultans hear from Nyai Roro Kidul, for example, it is through *wangsit*. Borne on the wind like *wangsit*, talk that Udin had cheated on Marsiyem began to spread around Bantul, sourceless and insubstantial. None of the investigating journalists could understand what came first: the supposed affair itself or the rumors that surrounded it.

On 7 September 1996, a fat, dark man arrived at Wagiman's home while Heru, Ida, and several other *Bernas* reporters were visiting Udin's father. The man distributed his business card to the journalists sitting on Wagiman's cool floor. The card identified him as Thojib Djumadi, a correspondent for the Surabaya-based Javanese language weekly *Jayabaya*, read by about 55,000 people, mostly in East Java. The reporters invited Thojib to join them. The fat man first listened to his colleagues' questions before asking some of his own. The *Jayabaya* reporter asked Wagiman whether Udin's death might have been due to some private peccadillo, not to his work. "I've heard that Udin liked to fool around," he said glibly.

Thojib had asked the question with a smile. Wagiman did not return the visitor's friendly expression. "Rude!" the imam exploded. "Who do you think you are?"

As Wagiman's voice rose, the young *Bernas* reporters urged the *Jayabaya* journalist to leave. The fat man rushed out the door and mounted his motorcycle. "It seems as if journalists have been infected by cannibalistic tendencies," Thojib later complained in on article published later that month in his magazine. "If the victim of that cannibalism was someone who did something wrong, that's not a problem. But why is it that just for asking a question a reporter is considered a sinner?"

Thojib explained that he had just wanted to confirm what he had been hearing. He had heard that Udin frequently had affairs. "That's not right, is it? His father is an imam," Thojib's contact had told him. The reporter's antennae had picked up rumors that Udin had adopted his philandering from his father, Wagiman, and that Marsiyem had also been unfaithful – with, of all people, Sujarah. Thojib later revealed that his man source for these stories was Gunawan, a Golkar representative for the Bantul assembly who lived in Patalan. Gunawan also happened to be Sri Roso's older brother and Kuncung's father.

Both Gunawan and Kuncung lived near Parangtritis Road, on the other side of a bridge over Bakulan creek. That the *bupati*'s kin lived so near Udin's own tinged the meddling by one family in the affairs of the other with the intimate poison of a quarrel between neighbors. "Why is this family so busy?" Marsiyem would later say of the *bupati*'s relatives. The reporter's widow recalled the phrase she had heard someone say in the confusion of the Bantul hospital the night of the attack: "*Mas Udin nek nggawé berita kendel banget* – the stories Udin wrote were just too daring." Now that she thought about it, those words had come from a voice that had seemed a lot like Kuncung's.

On 14 September 1996, the PWI team confronted Gunawan about the rumors he was spreading. The team's leaders, Masduki, Putut, and Asril asked Sri Roso's older brother why he had been telling reporters that Udin had been cheating on Marsiyem. In the records Asril retained from the meeting, he noted that Gunawan had insisted to them that the reporter had been spotted with an unknown woman outside the Bantul courthouse a day before he was killed. A pity, the reporters were told, that police investigators had not looked earlier into the possibility that Udin had been killed by a jealous lover. If they had, Gunawan supposedly had said, perhaps the case would have been solved much earlier.

"*Sak dumuk bathuk sak nyari bumi*" is a Javanese proverb. The phrase means "An inch of forehead, a finger's breadth of earth." To speakers of English as well as Indonesian, the proverb's meaning is obscure and untranslatable. But its suggestion makes sense to many Javanese. The saying means that a man will battle to the death to defend his personal honor, even if over the smallest sliver of land or the slightest of touches. This was the likely motive behind Udin's death that Sri Roso's older brother was trying to explain to the reporters. "I can't tell you what to do," Gunawan told the PWI team. "Check on your own." He advised them to start by investigating Yani.

Shortly after the PWI team's encounter with Gunawan, the young *Bernas* reporters visited Kuncung. In the dailies and broadsheets of Jogja, editorials and articles had suggested that Kuncung's appearance at the scene so soon after the assault had to be investigated. The police did interview Kuncung and four of the five young men who had accompanied him that evening. Their names were Sigit Bambang Suryanto, Sigit Prasetyo Wibowo, Yunari, and Yanadi. The fifth youth, Akung Prastono, lived in Sumatra and had been in Bantul at the time for a quick visit. He had returned to his work in the port of Bengkulu. All were village youths who had gone to school in Bakulan and had grown up together in Bantul.

When the *Bernas* reporters arrived at his home, Kuncung immediately summoned the other young men who were available. His appearance in front of the Krisna Photo Studio, Kuncung explained to the journalists, had been pure chance, the end of a chain of events that had started on a volleyball field in Bantul. In no way had he heard that there would be an assault that night on Udin. Earlier that evening, he explained, Yunari had been working as an announcer in an intramural volleyball game between two local neighborhood associations. Yunari had spotted Akung on the field, who everyone thought was still working in Sumatra. Over the microphone, Yunari called Akung over to join him and a group that had gathered in the commentator's section, which included Sigit Bambang Suryanto and Yanadi. Sigit Prasetyo and Kuncung joined them shortly afterward.

Someone suggested that the group should have noodles at a stall about a kilometer south of the Krisna Photo Studio. Akung, who was doing well at his job in Sumatra, promised to buy everyone's supper if his old neighborhood team won the game. Even though the match ended with a humiliating defeat for their side, the group decided to go anyway. They left riding two vehicles: Kuncung and Sigit Prasetyo got on a black motorcycle, while the Sigit Bambang Suryanto drove his Jeep with Yunari, Akung, and Yanadi as his passengers. It was late at night when the convoy left Bantul town. On their way down Parangtritis Road,

Kuncung's friends told the reporters, they had not noticed anyone traveling towards Jogja. Only Yunari saw a vehicle heading north: one lone motorcycle, carrying a Patalan resident and his wife, both of whom he had recognized.

When the group passed through Samalo, Kuncung explained, he saw on his right-hand side a man sprinting northwards along the road's shoulder. He recognized the running figure as Sujarah, who at the time had been sprinting to find a car to take Udin to a hospital. At that moment, Kuncung told the reporters, two women stepped into the middle of the road and waved down his motorcycle. Later, he found out that they were the noodle restaurant owners Ponikem and Nur Sulaiman. One of the women grabbed his hand, and shouted: "Someone has been beaten up. The man ran – there!" She pointed north, toward the direction from where they had come and where Sujarah was running.

Kuncung let his passenger off and wheeled his bike around. Meanwhile, the Sigit Bambang Suryanto maneuvered his Jeep to follow Kuncung. Sigit thought there had been a hit-and-run accident, and that Kuncung had gone in pursuit of the fleeing vehicle. But at that moment, he heard someone crying: "Car! Car!" The Jeep's driver then saw a man, in his early thirties, lying on the ground. The blood-spattered woman cradling his head appeared to be his wife. From his seat, Sigit could see the man's wounds were serious. From a crack in the side of the victim's head, a pool of blood was spreading across the concrete yard.

In the hysterical cacophony of voices that greeted him as he stopped the car, Sigit could barely make out what the group wanted, which was that he put the unconscious, bloody man in his car and take him to a hospital. His friends grabbed the victim's legs, while a shirtless neighbor supported the man's back and arms. They stretched him out on the back seat of the Jeep. The shirtless man, clad only in a threadbare sarong, climbed in after them.

By that time, Kuncung had returned from his chase. He told his friends he had reached as far as the first intersection on Parangtritis north of Samalo. There, he found two food vendors standing on the northeast corner selling grilled corn. Both appeared to be in their late twenties, although he could not describe either of them later to police with any clarity. "Did someone go by here?" he said he had asked the pair. They had answered in the negative. The attacker, or attackers, had made a successful getaway.

When the young men had delivered the reporter to the Bantul hospital and watched Marsiyem head off to Bethesda in the ambulance, they returned to their vehicles and discussed whether they were still going to eat their noodles. They decided to continue the night's original plans, despite the traumatic interruption. At the noodle stall, Kuncung left the group briefly to see what had happened at the Krisna Photo Studio. After he had instructed Samalo's neighborhood watchman to report the crime to the police, he returned to his friends. Then the six young men ate their food as if nothing had happened. Akung still kept his promise and bought everyone dinner.

Kuncung explained that his uncle had not tipped him off that something might happen to Udin that evening at Parangtritis Road. Just as Sukrisno, Suwandi, and Hatta had before him, Kuncung explained that he was not involved in any crime, and that his appearance the night of the killing was purely by accident. As for his visit to Yani, he said that was a separate matter. The encounter had been part of his duty as supervisor of village security. Kuncung said Yani had long been under police surveillance. The two breaker fans who had visited her in late August had been police agents. Bantul detective Edy had asked his help as Bakulan's security officer to get more information from the girl, who at the time they suspected was Udin's lover. So whatever he or his father knew about Udin's alleged infidelities, they had first learned from the police.

Just as in their interview with Sukrisno and his associates, the reporters could not shake their doubts about Kuncung's story. During the entire time he was recounting his alibi, Kuncung frequently had to wipe away the rivulets of sweat that sheeted down his face. The reporters could not decide whether he was perspiring from the heat and humidity or from nervousness.

By late September, two distinct, divergent approaches to the Udin case had emerged. Despite their early scrutiny of possible connections between the reporter's coverage of local Bantul politics and his death, by the end of September, the Bantul police had apparently abandoned that line of inquiry. Detective Edy, who had his men and Kuncung investigate Yani, now seemed more interested in building a case of alleged adultery. But both rival teams of Jogja journalists could not accept that any motives for the killing existed other then official anger over Udin's reporting. All facts and inferences they had found pointed in the *kabupaten* government's direction. The divide was a deep one: Police detectives complained among themselves that the journalists were encroaching on their authority, while journalists had become cynical that the police were turning this investigation into another tragic farce as they had done to Sum Kuning and to poor Marsinah.

It was around this time that the *Bernas* office began receiving calls warning the paper to stop covering the Udin case so intently. The threats did not distinguish between PWI members and AJI supporters. To the callers, the targets were simply meddling journalists. Masduki recalled receiving call at his office. "If you get into an accident, that's the risk of being in the PWI team," the guttural voice on the other end of the line told him. "But if your wife and children get into an accident…well, that's a tragedy." The threat tainted the daily lives of the PWI and White Kijang teams with paranoia and anxiety. Some among them would swear they saw cars and figures tailing the journalists on their various errands. When one reporter was involved in an accident on Parangtritis Road after interviewing Kuncung, many local reporters worried that someone was trying to use violence, once again, to silence the local media.

The paranoia in particular affected the PWI's Putut, a strong believer in the paranormal. A woman once asked to use his home's bathroom while both he and his wife were out. The stranger had urged his young daughter to play outside with her. Putut was certain the woman had been trying to kidnap his daughter. When he came home one day to find his phone line cut, he could only believe that someone was trying to prevent him from speaking to his colleagues. The *Bernas* editor eventually enlisted a *dukun* for protection, who advised him to store the information he had collected for the PWI in a little-used location. When a thief broke into his house and stole his possessions, Putut felt that he had just dodged disaster. Although the burglar took a television and some videotapes, the *Bernas* editor was certain the culprit had really been looking for the PWI team's documents.

How deeply the police, police intelligence, or the military were involved at this time in harassing the reporters remains a matter of speculation. Some of the threats may have been pranks, but others seemed genuine. Was this how the police vented their frustration over the journalists' perceived interference in their investigation? But it was precisely the unknown that made the intimidation effective. A few incidents were enough to instill widespread fear among the journalists.

Law enforcement's persistent probing into Marsiyem's personal life seemed, to the journalists, like another form of pressure. If Udin's widow were to admit to some discord at home just to stop police from pestering her, Marsiyem would be handing the police just what they needed to bolster their gathering case for adultery. But if that had been the authorities' goal, the constant questioning backfired. Instead of wearing the widow down, the laden interrogations encouraged her to deny the adultery theory even more vehemently. To Marsiyem, the police seemed to have no idea how to conduct an efficient inquiry. Detectives would visit her at home at all hours to show her photos of suspects. One of Edy's assistants once brought her images of several men, including one he said came from Surabaya. "If that's the case," she said in exasperation, "bring him here so I can see him in person!" On one occasion, Marsiyem recalled Edy asking her: "Have you heard a *wangsit* telling you the identity of the murderer?" She was incredulous. The detective depended on supernatural messages his investigation?

The journalists encouraged Marsiyem to enlist a lawyer to accompany her on her trips to the police headquarters. At the very least, they thought, she should have an advocate who could defend and advise her during the questioning. At their urging, Marsiyem turned to another of her husband's contacts and associates: Budi Hartono, the forty-eight-year-old lawyer and director of operations for the Indonesian Legal Aid Foundation in Jogjakarta. A short, stocky man with perpetual bags under his eyes, the genial Budi had been with the pro bono legal assistance group for a decade.

Adnan Buyung Nasution, a civic-minded lawyer, had founded Indonesian Legal Aid, known locally by its initials "LBH," in Jakarta in 1971. He and his organization, a national association of legal advocates, had been concerned about the vast numbers of Indonesians embroiled in legal disputes without any legal representation. In one survey conducted in 2001 in the nation's major population centers, more than half of those questioned believed that the legal system does not protect them. More than half were convinced the justice system is corrupt. Most of their distrust was directed toward the police and the courts, which they called arrogant, unreliable, disrespectful, and partial to the wealthy.

Most of the cases Legal Aid handled were battles over property, labor, or human rights between ordinary citizens and the rapacious government, military, or Jakarta-based businesses. In Jogja, for example, Budi's office assisted poor people engaged in land disputes, such as the complaints lodged by farmers against the Kedung Ombo Dam, a structure built using a $166-million soft loan from the World Bank that had flooded over six thousand hectares in Central Java. More than thirty thousand people lost their lands and livelihood. The litigation that arose from the dam's construction occupied courts for more than a decade. Jogjakarta Legal Aid had also defended ex-convicts targeted by the *Petrus* operations. Residents around the ancient monument of Borobodur, at one point, also appealed to Legal Aid to defend them against the bureaucrats and Suharto family members who were trying to secure choice swathes of land near the temple to build hotels or restaurants.

Although he did not consider himself close to the murdered journalist, Budi knew Udin as the reporter who often parked his red Honda Tiger outside Budi's door when he visited Legal Aid to speak to the group's volunteers for stories. Because of the kind of cases that Legal Aid assumed, the group's office had long become familiar with police surveillance. After ten years with the Jogja branch, Budi could shrug off threatening phone calls or rocks thrown through the window of the Legal Aid office. "That's our risk," Budi would say to people who asked. "We're ready for everything. Our soul and effort are for the public interest."

Although Indonesian law required that defendants threatened with more than five years' imprisonment be assigned legal counsel, the government set aside no funds for legal assistance, leaving it to municipalities, courts, and local officials to decide how they would fund public defenders from their own budgets. Since 1980, a Justice Ministry regulation limits legal aid payments to a maximum of 100,000 rupiah (about forty-three dollars in 1996) per client per case through all appeals, motions and procedures, even though much litigation can take years. Intentionally or not, the limits on funding often left organizations that served indigent plaintiffs or defendants perpetually strapped for resources so they could barely continue delivering legal services. Jakarta, the most progressive of cities regarding legal assistance, gave legal aid bureaus the equivalent of fifteen dollars a month in funding. Jogja, on the other hand, gave its bureaus nothing. Groups like Legal Aid begged for money to fund their operations from foreign aid sources, or they took in private, paying clients to fund their public interest activities. At the beginning of September 1996, Marsiyem became one of Legal Aid's thousands of clients.

If police officials cared about Marsiyem's souring relationship with investigators or the distrust that had now opened up between themselves and the journalists, they did not show it. On 19 September, Jogjakarta's police chief said blithely that they were exhausting all possible avenues of investigation, including inquiry into the supernatural. "We don't sleep at regular hours. We've been going to various paranormals," he said. "All of this has one goal, which is to solve the case quickly." The police's fascination with Udin's supposed adultery frustrated his colleagues. If constant press coverage and, now, the involvement of Legal Aid could not pressure the authorities to investigate the murder impartially and Sri Roso to extend his full cooperation, the journalists thought, then perhaps another authority might be more effective. In Jogja, that alternative was the reigning sultan.

Under Suharto's rule, the sultanate's power and influence had been sadly diminished. The great Sultan Hamengkubuwono IX had served in Suharto's first cabinet, and in 1973, began a term as the former general's vice president. But as the New Order matured, the populist sultan had become disenchanted with his president. Sickened by the omnipresent security that restricted his movement and worried by the mounting repression and corruption, Hamengkubuwono IX decided to retreat back into his *kraton*. He abandoned Suharto just days before their scheduled reelection in 1978, leaving the president to scramble and find an alternative vice president that, by most accounts, later served a disappointing single term.

The Jogjakarta-born president never forgave the sultan for his last-minute betrayal. The general elevated his own role in the 1 March 1949 General Attack to eclipse the sultan's own influential role in planning the dramatic raid that helped bring about independence. In 1983, on the event's thirty-fourth anniversary, the president unveiled a monument celebrating the military's achievement in Jogjakarta, built on Malioboro Road in front of the *kraton*. After the sultan's death in 1989, Suharto inaugurated another, much more ambitious structure: a great, green cone rising out of the paddy fields at the city's northern edge. His "Jogja Returns" monument commemorating the General Attack encroached on the mystic axis connecting Mount Merapi with the sultan's palace and Nyai Roro Kidul's Southern Ocean. With the monument's construction, Suharto had clearly wanted to impress on the sultan's successors that he was now unquestionably the real boss over this corner of Java.

The sultan bequeathed his kingdom to his tall, well-groomed son, who assumed the title Hamengkubuwono X at his coronation. But where his father had been active running the province, the tenth sultan had to be content with an even more peripheral role in Jogjakarta's affairs. Suharto discontinued the practice that had been in place since independence of confirming the sultan as governor of the province. In another slap to the Jogjakarta royal family's face, Suharto made a member of rival minor noble family "acting" governor.

Shut out of active administration, Sultan Hamengkubuwono X decided to focus on the sultanate's business interests. During his rule, Jogja began to show the flashy development of other large Indonesian cities. It became crowded with motorcycles and mini-marts, finally casting out what old guardian spirits remained and putting its culture on show for the tourists. Malioboro, the ceremonial avenue that led north from the *kraton*, became wreathed in pollution from motorcycle traffic to and from the malls, shops, and hotels that had sprung up on it. In Jogja's usual way, its response to modernity was to turn to tradition. When Jogja's mayor threw up his hands in exasperation with his expanding and increasingly-chaotic town, the city elders suggested he might hold an exorcism with a performance of the *wayang*.

Hamengkubuwono X joined Golkar and participated in campaigns for the ruling party. But the young sultan, given his family's chilly relations with Suharto, was at best a lukewarm supporter of the New Order. To meet him, the journalists thought they would have to invoke a traditional formal rite, the *tata pepe*. In Jogjakarta tradition, the ritual to ask for an audience with the sultan required supplicants to clad themselves in white and stand between two great banyans in the northern square of the *kraton*. The *Bernas* photographer Tarko, who knew the sultan personally, chose an easier route. He dialed the palace's phone number.

"Just tell them to come!" was Hamengkubuwono X's cheery answer.

On 25 September at 9.00 p.m., the sultan received several dozen journalists inside the *kraton*. Wearing a shirt of glittering batik, he greeted them in a large room decorated with antique mirrors and portraits of his ancestors. Hamengkubuwono X listened to the reporters' grievances calmly. They related their frustration with the police and their suspicions about the Bantul government and its *bupati*. The journalists, however, left the meeting disappointed. The sultan told them what everyone already knew: that he had no official authority to compel the Bantul *bupati* to come forward to answer the accusations, or to ask the police why they had suddenly swerved from investigating Udin's reportage to examining his marriage. The sultan did reveal that he had suggested to the *bupati* to swear an oath at Jogja's Great Mosque to dispel the public speculation. The *bupati* had never responded.

"I will help as far as I am able" was all Hamengkubuwono X could promise. As October progressed, stories about the investigation dwindled in the pages of *Bernas*. It seemed as if the police had given up ever locating the murderer. Heru and his colleagues could only report the frequent, aborted attempts by the Bantul police to locate suspects, endeavors that seemed more and more as if the police were just going through the motions of an investigation that they had long ago abandoned. On 16 October, Marsiyem sighed to her friends: "I give up. Whether or not the killer's arrested, I leave it to God."

From the beginning, one *Bernas* reporter never trusted the authorities to conduct an honest investigation. The rebellious campus activist Achadi had long ago stopped attending the police press conferences, visiting the station, interviewing witnesses, or attending meetings with local dignitaries. If the reporters really wanted to get anywhere, he concluded, they had had to put aside their interviews and fact-checking and actually do some investigating. Achadi's goal was to bypass the police and search for information directly in Bantul's criminal culture.

He joined forces with another youthful activist, Angger Jati Wijaya, an irregular columnist for *Bernas* whose barbed pieces critiqued New Order politics and culture. Angger was also active in various cause-oriented groups based in the *kabupaten*. More importantly, the twenty-nine-year-old was an appropriate guide: Bantul-born and bred; he knew the *kabupaten*'s physical and social geography intimately. He and Achadi decided to enter the detective world themselves – the night-time demimonde of small-time gambling rackets and tinpot protection schemes, of petty thieves and budding gangsters.

Both men understood that when a criminal investigation commences, the authorities search first among local criminals and marginal citizens to locate the most likely suspects or those they could lean on to become informants. Achadi and Angger knew that the facts of the case, and the identity of Udin's killer, would never be found in a function hall or a newsroom but somewhere in Bantul's back streets and roads, at its kerosene lamp-lit food stalls or in the quiet, shuttered homes of its nervous residents. So the two began their reporting late at night, between 8:00 p.m. and the early morning, at a time when stallkeepers laid plastic mats on the sidewalks of Bantul town, or set up tent-covered tables and benches beside Parangtritis Road. There, in the glare of kerosene lamps, the *kabupaten*'s truckers, travelers, off-duty policemen, unemployed laborers, and other assorted lowlifes gathered to sip tea as rocks of pure sugar slowly dissolved in their glasses. And there, Achadi and Angger would fish, like midnight anglers, for rumors, whispers, and fragments of information.

So they could track the Bantul police's movements, the two men obtained a walkie-talkie that received the police frequency. The phrases and words in Indonesian police jargon that crackled out of the receiver were at first incomprehensible to the reporters. The police talked about "zebras," "tigers," and "horses." They spoke in codes, reciting letters and numbers such as "T.M." or "eighty-eight," or groups of Javanese cities: "Solo-Bandung" or "Pati-Rembang-Demak." Over time, the men learned to recognize that an "eighty-eight" meant an invitation to a meeting, "Solo-Bandung" was a request for the listener to "stand by," and that a "zebra" was a traffic cop, who in Indonesia usually stands at crossings and wears black-and-white cuffs to direct traffic. A "horse" meant the ordinary brown-uniformed patrolman. Detectives, tellingly, called themselves "tigers," while "rabbits" were their prey, which could be ex-convicts and suspects or activists and student demonstrators.

In their efforts to understand the Bantul underworld, they found allies among the beleaguered local branch of the PDI. In its panic to prevent any rival to Suharto and Golkar from emerging before the 1997 elections, the military had perhaps overreacted, creating a backlash that made its grip on Indonesians slightly more tenuous. In July 1996, a month before Udin's death, armed forces agents had manipulated the tiny Indonesian Democratic Party's internal elections to replace its leader, Megawati Sukarnoputri, with a more pliable politician. An otherwise unimpressive housewife-turned-politician, Megawati's one asset was her family name: She was Sukarno's daughter. To protest her dismissal from the PDI, her supporters occupied the party's Jakarta headquarters. On 27 July 1996, hundreds of pro-government goons, backed by riot police and the military, attacked the building. As rumors of a mass wounding of Megawati's supporters spread through the capital, several hundred people clashed with police and soldiers. Mobs burned down more than fifty buildings and set two hundred vehicles ablaze throughout the city.

The turmoil within the PDI affected its branches in the villages. After the destruction of its Jakarta headquarters, the red-clad PDI split even more clearly into pro-Megawati and pro-government camps. When pro-government members held a meeting of their PDI faction, their rivals would show up to frustrate it. Although the pro-government supporters were few, they were firmly supported by the military's firepower and had the official recognition of Suharto's government. Meanwhile, Megawati's loyalists endured regular calls by the local military command for questioning, as pro-government members steadily forced them out of party positions. If in Jogja, the Udin case was a way for local media to fight the New Order; for the perplexed PDI, the outgunned supporters of Sukarno's daughter, helping the reporters was a way for them to strike what blows they could against those that persecuted them.

The assistance was not always of value. The local Bantul PDI chair helpfully arranged a meeting for Achadi and Angger with a local psychic. The paranormal ordered the two men to meditate outside in his yard until midnight. When the appointed hour came, the mystic asked Achadi expectantly if the dead reporter had spoken to him. "Well, did you receive a message from your friend?" he said. Achadi, who had sat outside in the cold for hours, could only look at his host blankly. More helpful to the two activist journalists was one junior PDI member, Wijiyono Titet. With chocolate-colored skin, the massively built twenty-nine-year-old Javanese resembled nothing as much as the statues of carved ogres that guarded the gates to the *kraton*. Although he looked like a thug and happened to be a friend of Edy Wuryanto, whom he had met during a criminal case that had involved one of Titet's relatives, the big man and Megawati loyalist was staunchly on Achadi's side. He passed on whatever information he picked up from Edy to the two activists.

Titet recounted stories told to him by Edy's colleagues: that the detective dabbled extensively in black magic, that he slept in graveyards to augment his power, that he was not averse to the occasional macabre joke involving evidence in his cases. In one popular, perhaps apocryphal tale told in the precincts, Edy had supposedly presented a friend with a large black plastic bag, the kind used to bag fruits from the market. "I have a present for you," Edy had allegedly teased his compadre. "It's a durian," a strong-smelling fruit prized in Southeast Asia as a delicacy for the taste of its creamy core. When his friend eagerly opened the bag, the story goes, he found instead a man's freshly-severed head.

Titet said that Edy had seemed utterly fascinated by the adultery theory. The detective kept mentioning to Titet names of various women, including Yani, whom he suspected of having an affair with the murdered reporter. One day in October, Titet told them, he and Edy had been traveling around Bantul by car when Edy pointed out a man on the street apparently at random. "That's the one who got Marsiyem pregnant," Edy told Titet conspiratorially. The PDI member could not tell whether the detective was joking or was serious.

It turned out that Achadi and Angger's nighttime research had not gone unnoticed by Edy. The detective had heard two reporters were canvassing Bantul each night asking about the Udin murder, and that they were in contact with his associate Titet. Edy asked the PDI member to arrange a meeting. The two journalists were hesitant at first. Angger was not sure whether they could believe anything Edy might tell them. But after a long discussion, both men decided that they needed to discover for themselves just what kind of man was this Edy Wuryanto. And the best way to do that was to meet him in person.

Late in October 1996, Titet arranged for Edy to see the two at a house in Bantul. The detective arrived after midnight, and immediately treated Angger and Achadi like old acquaintances. He appeared eager to persuade the two reporters he was committed to solving the case. After all, he told them, hadn't he known the victim personally? He repeated the story he had told Moko and Ndari months before: that he had hurried back to Jogja, arriving at Bethesda Hospital even before it opened, just to visit the injured journalist. "Don't think of us as the police and you as the journalists," he urged. In this investigation, he explained, "We're all journalists."

Edy begged for their patience. The police cannot prejudge a case, he told them. The authorities had to start with the material evidence, so neither he nor his colleagues could declare definitively that the journalist's stories had been the reason behind his murder. But, he reassured them, "Everything I have traced outside of his reporting comes up negative. I believe there must be a connection to his profession."

He repeated what the Central Java chief detective had said so many weeks earlier: the murderer had to be a professional. From the way the crime had been committed, Edy explained, the perpetrator must have been a deserter, an ex-military man, or a member of the riot police. "Only the military has a tradition of wearing a headband when they execute a person," he said. In front of Angger, Achadi, and Titet, Edy demonstrated how a trained assailant could make two crippling blows in a single motion. With his right hand, Edy jabbed an imaginary metal pipe forward, into an imaginary stomach, and in one smooth movement pulled the pipe up so it slammed almost audibly into an invisible head.

"Are you serious in handling this case?" Angger, still unpersuaded by Edy's fluent patter, demanded.

"There is no effort to twist the facts!" the detective answered hotly, "Nobody can buy me!" He swore that "in God's name," he would find Udin's murderer. "Break my left leg, and cut off my right one if I'm lying," he added. "Seven generations of my descendants will not be safe if there is a setup."

The conversation between the detective and the journalists lasted from 1:00 a.m. until well past sunrise. When Edy had finished, Achadi and Angger felt more confident in the detective's sincerity. Perhaps all the talk of adultery was a tactic to make the real suspects in the case let down their guard. The men met again the following evening, at a noodle stand on the outskirts of Bantul town. This time, the detective asked Achadi to take several mug shots to show to Marsiyem. But Edy's tone had changed. Less than forty-eight hours earlier, he seemed convinced there was a link between Udin's death and his reporting. Now the detective was telling them that the connection looked tenuous. His team now had studied the reporter's articles, Edy said, but they decided the crime had been personal. "I've looked at various possibilities…maybe his news, but not one of them fits," he confessed to Achadi and Angger. "It seems to be – sorry, okay – maybe a woman problem. Whenever there's a murder, if it's not about a woman, then it's about money."

Achadi now thought that perhaps Angger had been right not to trust Edy. The final time Achadi and Angger saw the officer was 20 October 1996, on the street in Bantul town. He appeared to be in a hurry. "I have to go quickly to the police headquarters," he told them breathlessly. "Everyone is gathering there." A major development was about to happen in the Udin case, he told them, perhaps the announcement of an arrest. The detective suggested that Angger and his colleagues might personally witness him question a suspect.

"Let's do it this way," the detective promised. "I'm going to bring the suspects to one place, then I'll contact you."

Edy set a date: 21 October. The journalists wondered who the suspects might be. Titet had mentioned that the detective had been tailing various people. One of the names mentioned sounded like "Atmaji," who Achadi assumed was a petty thief in Bantul who went by that name. Achadi, excited, immediately contacted his friends at *Bernas* to ask if they wanted to join him to witness the promised interrogation, which would be a true scoop. His nighttime excursions now promised to pay off handsomely. On the afternoon of 21 October, about ten reporters gathered at the newspaper to wait for Edy's signal.

Achadi's colleagues on the White Kijang team waited at *Bernas* until the afternoon hours lengthened into the night. Street lamps sprang to life along Solo Road; the newsroom was emptying of staffers. Achadi anxiously paged Edy several times, but Edy never returned his messages. The assembled reporters kept looking to the college student, as if expecting him to make the detective and his promised suspect materialize right there in the office.

The detective had reneged on his promise. By late evening, most of the reporters gave up and went home. Then, the next day, Achadi, Angger, and the rest of the reporters were surprised to learn that the Jogjakarta police had, that very evening, arrested Udin's murderer.

CHAPTER 7

To Teach Him a Lesson

LATE ON 21 OCTOBER 1996, ten weeks after the murder in front of the Krisna Photo Studio, Edy Wuryanto had marched Fuad Muhammad Syafruddin's murderer straight into Jogjakarta's police headquarters. The suspect, a muscular Javanese in his mid-thirties, had a thin, scruffy mustache and a dazed look. He seemed subdued, even docile. To anyone, he appeared a milquetoast of a man who seemed incapable of committing so violent a murder.

But that night, according to the police record, in one of the many rooms that branched off the headquarters' long corridors, the man Edy had arrested delivered a long and detailed confession.

"Are you in good physical and mental condition and are you ready to be examined?" one of Edy's colleagues had supposedly asked him.

"Yes," the suspect had answered.

"Do you understand why you are being examined by the police?"

"It is in connection to my having assaulted someone."

"Where and when did you beat the said individual?"

"On Tuesday, 13 August 1996, at about 11:00 p.m., on Parangtritis Road."

"Whom did you assault?"

"Syafruddin from Samalo."

"With what weapon did you assault Syafruddin?"

"I hit Syafruddin with a metal water pipe, white in color and about forty centimeters long."

"How did you hit Syafruddin?"

"I came from the direction of Jogja on a blue Vespa. I stopped about one hundred meters north of Syafruddin's home. Then I walked south towards it. I knocked on the door. Syafruddin's wife came out. I asked "Is Syafruddin home?" His wife answered "Yes." A short while afterward, Syafruddin came out. I immediately struck him with the metal pipe once on his abdomen. Then Syafruddin grabbed his stomach. His body bent over. Then I hit the top of his head with the pipe. I saw Syafruddin stagger."

Afterwards, the suspect said, he got on his motorcycle and fled north alone. In the police record of this, the suspect's first interrogation, he described how he disposed of the weapon: "I put the piece of metal into the back of a company-owned truck I had brought home…then I threw the pipe into a pile of scrap iron where I work."

"Why did you assault Syafruddin?"

"Because I heard from people around Bantul that my wife was often being courted by Syafruddin. It seemed to me my wife was having an affair with Syafruddin, which made my heart hot with jealousy. I decided to assault Udin."

"What was your intention?"

"So he would not bother my wife any longer."

"After you discovered that Syafruddin had died, what was your reaction?"

"I was shocked and surprised because my intention was only to teach him a lesson. I never imagined Syafruddin would die."

A few weeks before the suspect's arrest, an important change had occurred for the Jogjakarta police. The national police, as part of a wide-ranging reorganization of the force, had detached Jogjakarta from the command of the Central Java Police District. Now an independent police district on its own, Jogjakarta qualified for its own police district chief, a job filled by Colonel Mulyono Sulaiman. A contemporary of the national police chief Dibyo Widodo, Mulyono had languished for years as head of a police training school in West Java before his appointment to the brand-new district. Leading Jogjakarta's police force was Mulyono's first field assignment in years. Naturally, he was keen to make the Udin case a signal success, and he made sure the entire headquarters realized it.

The day the Bantul detective had brought in the suspect, Mulyono's Chief Detective Suko Hariyanto had assigned as Jogjakarta Police District's lead investigator on the Udin case a bright, promising thirty-two-year-old police second lieutenant who had also been posted to the Jogjakarta force barely a month earlier. According to Indonesian police procedure, detective work had two distinct stages. The preliminary, field investigation stage, which Edy and the Bantul police had successfully completed, was to narrow down, from a plethora of likely suspects, the individual most likely to have committed the crime. The second stage was more cerebral. It required assembling the available evidence against that individual to form an airtight case that would secure a conviction. The latter would be this detective's task: to ensure that the Jogjakarta police's case would stick and that the Bantul court would convict Edy's suspect of Udin's murder.

Hadi Prayitno believed he could handle the high-pressure responsibility. Hadi had been born in Jogja, where his father had been police chief of a city precinct. His father's law enforcement background might have been what inspired the light-skinned, intelligent young man to be a detective. Although he knew the pay in the force was abysmally low – about sixty dollars for a patrolman and double for a detective – the job demanded both a quick wit and a strong will, a challenge that filled his heart with excitement. In this hot, humid, and crowded country, crime scenes never stay pristine. The pounding rain washes away blood stains and gunpowder traces, while insects and rot make short work of corpses. Extracting even the faintest of clues from the decay and corruption taxes even the best of investigators, who also have to deal with human interference. Neighbors and curious onlookers gather within seconds of a body's discovery. They trample over crime scenes, stash away souvenirs, and thoughtlessly contaminate the area with their food, footprints, and spit. Since most killings in Java are committed not with guns but with common sharp or blunt objects such as knives, rattan canes, or lead pipes, forensic analysis is particularly difficult. All this made criminal detection in the tropics a nearly impossible science to practice.

Yet to Hadi, the underlying theory for catching a criminal was so beautifully simple. Since he first learned it during training, the detective had become captivated by its poetic precision. According to the crime scene management handbook he had studied at the police academy, every violent crime involves four elements – the weapon, the criminal, the victim, and the crime scene, all of which were linked to one another. A single diagram could sum up their interrelationship:

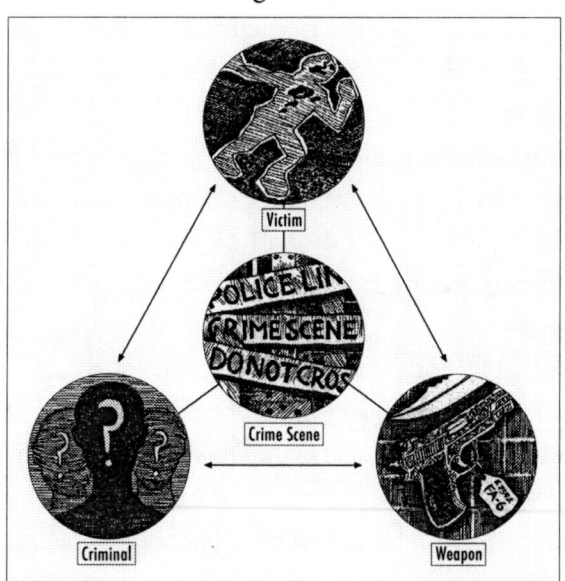

The Triangle of Evidence

Because a crime is such a catastrophic event, at the moment of its occurrence, victim, murderer, weapon, and crime scene come in mutual contact, with each leaving a trace on the other. In a hypothetical murder that Hadi's handbook had given as an illustration, a motorcyclist shoots a guard at a rice warehouse. The victim would, of course, be powdered with rice dust from the crime scene, and punctured by the bullet. But perhaps there might also be a trace of grease from the murderer's cycle on the scene near the victim. The killer could flee, but flecks of the victim's blood on his jacket, grains of rice on his shoes, or even his fingerprints on the weapon could still tie him to his crime. The killer might try to dispose of the murder weapon and of the victim's body, but he perhaps might not be able to extract the bullet remaining in the victim's body, or hide the burns on his arm, or sweep away the gunpowder scattered around the floor of the warehouse. In other words, the triangle of evidence dictated that no matter how hard a murderer tried to erase evidence of a crime, a good detective should be able to assemble from all these clues – the patterns of the dust on the warehouse floor, the bits of gunpowder on the sacks, the drops of blood on the floorboards – the nature of the catastrophe that had occurred, and catch the perpetrator.

The theory gave Hadi confidence that every crime, no matter how perfectly planned and executed, could always be unraveled. *Every crime leaves a clue*, the theory told him. It was a mantra, one which, if chanted long and often enough, made capturing the most accomplished criminal possible. To complete what Edy had started, Hadi had to apply the evidence and his knowledge of criminal detection to secure a conviction of this one suspect.

Before his assignment to his hometown, Hadi had earned a law degree and had taught criminal procedure to police cadets for four years. He knew what was required for a case that would stand up in a courtroom. Indonesia's laws gave precise, programmatic directions for what evidence was necessary for a criminal conviction. Once in court, judges will only convict a defendant if the prosecution has presented at least two out of five categories of evidence. These categories were: witness testimony, forensic evidence, expert analysis, documents, and a confession. Only when the Bantul public prosecutor concludes that the evidence presented in a suspect's dossier is complete would it ask the Bantul court to schedule a trial.

The young detective had been on the job long enough to realize that obtaining even two of these established categories of evidence was difficult. Obtaining witness accounts, which Hadi and his colleagues could collect themselves, was particularly taxing. It always seemed to detectives that the only people who feared the police as much as perpetrators were the witnesses to the crime. Locals will report crimes, but few will happily answer a police summons for questioning. They worry not just about the inconvenience but also about the risk that coming forward makes them targets for police officers on the hunt for easy suspects. "The people don't understand that giving information to the police is very valuable both for the interests of the court and for solving the case," Hadi would later complain. Early in his career, he had been a detective in a backwater East Java town. Once, his colleagues had caught a *dukun* accused of murdering babies to drink their blood in order to obtain some kind of magical power. The *dukun*'s fatal mistake had been to prey on his relatives' offspring. They turned the sorcerer over to the police. In many respects, witnesses are most enthusiastic to help the police when they themselves are victims.

As for forensic evidence and expert analysis, Hadi also had his work cut out for him. The national police had three overworked criminal laboratories in Jakarta, Semarang, and Surabaya to handle hundreds of cases across the nation. Forensic experts were rare and often difficult to schedule: for example, among a quarter of a billion Indonesians, only one individual had obtained advanced training in forensic DNA analysis. He lived in Jakarta.

Fortunately for the detective, Edy's suspect gifted Hadi with a complete and detailed confession. From the record of the first night's interrogation, Hadi knew that the murder weapon had been left at the suspect's workplace. The suspect had also described what he had been wearing the night of the murder. If Hadi could trust the triangle of evidence, then at least one item of the suspect's clothing would retain traces of the victim's blood. Hadi's first duty, then, was to seize immediately the evidence from the suspect's home and workplace and have the experts examine them. But although his superiors had already prepared the proper papers, the rookie detective had one more technical chore to perform before he could leave the Jogjakarta police headquarters. The suspect had to be first introduced to his lawyers.

༺༻

Three men in ties and stiff collars were waiting in Chief Detective Suko's office. One had the round face, mustache, and dark brown skin of a Javanese. The other two had the lighter complexions of transplanted Sumatrans. The younger of the two looked the part of a freshly-minted law graduate. He was earnest and energetic, not yet bored by the drab surroundings of a police station. The older one had similarly boyish features, but his casual bearing gave a far different impression: that of an established, confident, middle-aged country lawyer. He had long been a familiar face at the Jogjakarta police headquarters. His name was Triyandi Mulkan.

A lawyer for the past sixteen years, the forty-three-year-old ran his private practice, Triyandi Mulkan & Associates, out of a purple colonial bungalow on Pakuningratan Road, just north of the Tugu Monument on Solo Road. The same premises also housed a public interest firm that he ran called the Legal Defenders Agency, which took on most of its clients pro bono. Although the two firms were separate entities, they were essentially halves of the same practice. Triyandi, a transplant to Jogja from South Sumatra, staffed both offices with the same lawyers, associates, and administrative personnel. Most of his staff had graduated from his alma mater: the law school of Jogjakarta's Islamic University of Indonesia, or UII.

In the mid-1990s, Budi's Legal Aid, Triyandi's Legal Defenders, and UII's legal aid bureau were the only institutions in Jogjakarta offering free legal assistance. Since inexperienced law students largely staffed UII's bureau, Legal Aid and Legal Defenders took on the most difficult and neediest cases. Legal Defenders, however, assumed a vastly less-confrontational approach towards the authorities than the activist, crusading Legal Aid. Its relations with the police could almost be described as cozy. Legal Defenders could boast of long personal associations between its lawyers and the police apparatus. In the past, Triyandi had tutored police officers in martial arts. The associate he had placed in charge of Legal Defenders, the thirty-five-year-old Eko Widiyanto, was a friend of Chief Detective Suko. So when the Jogjakarta police handled potential death penalty cases, such as this homicide, for which the law required them to provide free legal representation to indigent suspects, they turned most often to Triyandi. That closeness to the authorities, however, gave Legal Defenders a reputation among the local media of being "police lawyers," who were more interested in banking favors by helping the authorities satisfy procedural formalities than mounting vigorous defenses for their clients. It was no surprise that for Jogja's most important case in decades, the new Jogjakarta Police District had chosen its old, trusted friend Triyandi Mulkan to represent Udin's alleged murderer.

That morning, 22 October 1996, Triyandi, Eko and the third lawyer, a twenty-six-year-old UII graduate named Djufri Taufik, had received a phone call summoning them to Suko's office. After they arrived, the chief of detectives described to the three attorneys their prospective client's details. Suko told them the suspect had willingly confessed, and that the arresting officer, Edy, had supplied additional details: the man was a cold-blooded killer, a former instructor for the Indonesian marines, an expert in self-defense, and a master of martial arts who had no rival. The three lawyers also learned the name of the man they were representing: Dwi Sumaji. He preferred to be called by his nickname, "Iwik."

When Hadi brought Iwik into Suko's office, the three men saw nothing that belied Edy's description. Hadi asked Iwik to remove his shirt. The alleged murderer revealed a sinewy torso, with skin stretched tight over compact muscles. His tightly-coiled arms looked like they could split wood, pulverize stone, or crush bone with a strong swing of a pipe or a hammer. Yet all three lawyers wondered why this supposed master of martial arts bore such a dull and confused expression. His frightened face showed none of the self-confidence or calculating intelligence they had expected from an expert in self-defense, especially a former marine instructor. When Iwik spoke, his voice was thick, slow, and uncertain. Triyandi's first reaction was that their client was a simpleton – not in the sense of being an idiot, but in the way of being a Javanese version of the country bumpkin.

Suko ushered the three lawyers to an empty office and left them alone with Udin's accused killer for about thirty minutes. Triyandi, Eko, and Djufri learned that Iwik was married, thirty-four years old, and a father of a six-year-old boy named Bimo. He earned a living as a driver for a billboard-construction firm named Dymas Advertising, which was located north of the city, off the main road leading from Jogja to Magelang in Central Java. He and his family rented a house in Panasan, a hamlet in Sleman *kabupaten*, sited even further north up Magelang Road, the main highway linking Jogjakarta with the north coast cities.

In their work, Triyandi and Eko had come to understand the difference between men used to violence and those surprised by it; between the calculating killers and the ones too blinded by rage, jealousy, or intoxication that they had realized too late that they had committed a murder. Oddly, this Iwik fell into neither of those categories. Despite his physique, he seemed incapable of violence. He told his lawyers he had never been in police custody before, and knew little about the legal system. He did not understand why he even needed lawyers. Triyandi, Eko and Djufri had to explain that, as his legal counsel, their role was to ensure that his rights were respected and protected throughout his criminal prosecution, and that they would defend him during the investigation and in court. Then they cautiously raised the most important topic: why had Iwik murdered the reporter?

"I didn't do it," Iwik answered.

"So you aren't Udin's murderer?" Triyandi asked in astonishment.

"Sir, I haven't killed anyone."

"But they say you already told the chief of police that you killed Udin!"

"I didn't kill him."

Many accused murderers deny their crime. Triyandi and Eko had known too many of these clients to believe this one's denial so easily. But before they could question Iwik further, an officer knocked on the door. It was the detective, Hadi. He and several other policemen, both plainclothed and uniformed, had prepared several cars parked behind the police headquarters. The officers wanted the lawyers and Iwik to join them so Hadi could search Iwik's home and office for evidence. As soon as the four men descended, the convoy of cars sped off towards Sleman.

Soon the city's sprawl of shop houses, signboards, and crowds thinned into a vista of lush rice fields and trees that blanketed the southern slope of Mount Merapi. The lawyers noticed they were on Magelang Road, which sloped gently upward as it navigated around the volcano that loomed over the city. Near the Jogjakarta headquarters of the Indonesian military police, the lead car in the convoy turned into an alley that led to an enclosed compound. This, the lawyers were told, was Dymas Advertising, Iwik's workplace.

Dymas looked more like a construction office than an advertising agency. Its business was to make and install roadside signage, so the office resembled a junkyard. Bits of scrap metal intended to buttress billboards littered the place in massive, decaying heaps. Painted wood planks, leftovers or rejects from old sign jobs, leaned on any available vertical surface. "REGISTRATION" read one; another announced: "OPEN TO THE PUBLIC." Some of the scrap metal came in the form of solid lengths of rusting pipe, the rest were thin strips of metal rebar bent at different angles. Dymas was a cemetery of signs, filled with billboard bones and signpost skeletons. The main workspace was a roofed cluster of cabinets and desks in the center of the mess, from which several people stared wide-eyed as a police convoy rolled into the parking area. As Iwik got out of a car, a few of his coworkers shouted: "What's going on, Iwik? What is it?" Iwik did not answer.

Hadi directed his team to locate the murder weapon Iwik had confessed to disposing somewhere in this area. Iwik and the police moved from one pile of iron to another, back and forth across the lot.

The suspect seemed unsure where he had stashed the pipe that he had used to batter Udin's abdomen and bash in his skull. The detectives rummaged through heaps of metal blooming with ferrous oxide, looking for one red-stained pipe among so many. One policeman tentatively picked up a piece: "Is this it, 'Wik?"

"No…" answered Iwik slowly.

"How about this?" another policeman motioned in another direction.

"No."

Finally, one detective thrust his hand into a pile and grabbed a length of metal. It was a thin length of piping, bent slightly at one rusty, serrated end, which at one time had been stuffed with cement, like a pastry, to give it ballast for some long-forgotten project. That end of the pipe looked heavier than the other. The metallic sheen had been dulled by long exposure to the elements.

"How about this? Yes or no?"

Iwik stayed silent.

"Isn't this it? Yes or no? Yes or no?" the policeman insisted.

The detective thrust the pipe into Iwik's hand. A photographer snapped a shot of the accused criminal and what was now, apparently, his supposed weapon. The picture recorded Iwik glumly holding the pipe, his body bent over, looking as if the light piece of metal were pulling his arm down to the ground.

As the lawyers returned with the policemen and their client to the cars, they looked puzzled. Something about this search they had just witnessed did not seem right. The suspect had confessed. So why was he so confused about where he had placed the weapon? Iwik had held that pipe as if he had never seen it before. And what was a former martial arts expert doing working for a dump like Dymas? The three men did not know what to do: Should they protest now, or wait to see what they would next encounter?

"For now, just follow along," Eko told his colleagues. "Just follow."

That morning, Sunarti awoke sick with worry. Her husband Iwik had not come home the night before. He had left no reason for his disappearance. The previous day, 21 October 1996, over their usual breakfast of rice and a fried egg, he told her that Dymas might need him to drive the company truck out for a job somewhere in East Java. "It looks like there might be overtime later," he had said. When Iwik did not stop home to confirm his out-of-town assignment, Sunarti assumed that the job had been postponed, and that he would be coming home at the usual time. So that evening she prepared a cup of hot ginger tea, Iwik's habitual after-work drink, and waited for him to come walking down their street from where the bus dropped him off on Magelang Road.

By 8:00 p.m., Iwik had not appeared. His drink had long gone cold. Sunarti drank the tea herself and left another cup for him before she fell asleep. When she woke the following morning, she was surprised to find herself and their son Bimo still alone in their bed. The ginger tea, untouched, had gone flat and cloudy. Perhaps Iwik had come home late in the Dymas company truck, she thought, and he had thoughtfully slept inside it because he did not want to wake his family. She slid open the front doors and peered out at the dewy morning, but neither the office motorcycle nor the truck was parked outside. The road was empty. She thought that maybe Iwik had been called away to that job in East Java after all, and he had no time to drop by and tell her.

It would be easier if they had owned a telephone. Sunarti cleaned up the kitchen and swept their bare cement floor before preparing her day's work. Iwik earned about sixty-four dollars a month. His salary barely supported them, even with the overtime pay for his jobs outside Jogja. In middle school, the thirty-one-year-old Sunarti had taught herself how to cut hair and apply cosmetics. Although most people her age believed differently, Sunarti never wanted to get a job in a private company or the government, which assured a steady, if small, income and the security of being part of a large organization. Her instincts told her it was better to be independent and to have her own business. "As long as we have something of our own, there is no need to apply for jobs or to beg," Sunarti would tell herself.

In 1991, she opened a beauty business in their one-room home in Sleman. She positioned a wardrobe to section off their bedroom and used the remaining space for a hair-cutting station, equipped with a chair, mirror, and a couple of fading posters of outdated hairstyles. She charged 750 rupiah per cut. By 1996, she had raised her price to two thousand rupiah but her services still cost the equivalent of less than a dollar. To make some extra money, Sunarti helped friends to prepare, dress, and make-up brides in exchange for a small fee and some of the food left over from the wedding reception. When she did not have customers for her hair salon, she worked as a seamstress. She sewed and mended clothes, which brought in a trickle of additional income. She and Iwik worked hard, but they still had not managed to raise themselves out of poverty.

On 22 October 1996, Sunarti was working on a cloth dyed a deep maroon and cut into a pattern for a bride's skirt. Her work did not calm her, however. She still did not know what had happened to her husband. At about 6.00 a.m., on the gradually lightening road outside, Sunarti spied her neighbor Betha Meirawan heading for work. Betha happened to work for Dymas as a signboard artist. She hollered: "Betha, my husband hasn't come home! Was there overtime?"

"I didn't see him." Betha answered. "But yesterday, they looked as if they were getting ready for something. Maybe there was a job outside the city. Doesn't he usually tell you?"

Betha explained to Sunarti that he had been at work for only half of the previous day. Since Iwik drove the company truck while Betha painted signs at the office, Betha at times did not encounter Sunarti's husband during office hours. Although something inside her continued to tremble with worry, she could do nothing but wait. Every few minutes, she looked up from her sewing to glance down the road, hoping that she might see Iwik's thin figure striding down it.

When the noonday sun had erased the dampness of the morning, Sunarti saw a convoy of cars come down the road from the Magelang artery. The vehicles halted in front of her home. A group of men emerged. Although many of them were not wearing a uniform, she could tell from the confident way they carried themselves that they were policemen.

Had there had been an accident? Was her husband hurt? At first, she could think of nothing but the worst. Then she spotted Iwik among the officers. He was still wearing the same clothes he had on a day earlier. The sense of relief she received from the sight of her husband, apparently healthy and unharmed, quickly evaporated. She noticed that the plainclothes officers surrounded Iwik in the alert, vigilant way reserved only for individuals who were in police custody.

As they approached her house, one of policemen pointed at her and Bimo as if they were zoo animals. "That's his wife, that's his kid!" he shouted.

A short, mustached man with carefully groomed hair approached. "Are you his wife?" Hadi asked. "Your husband is accused of committing a crime in Bantul." He showed her an arrest warrant. Fear and surprise gripped Sunarti, emotions that were drowned by her mounting hysteria.

"That can't be!" she shouted. She was still holding the cloth she had been sewing.

"Do you have his red shirt?" Hadi asked matter-of-factly.

Her husband did own a piece of clothing of that color, but she wondered: how did the police know Iwik had a red shirt? More importantly, why did they want it?

"That's not possible. My husband never leaves the house wearing that red shirt."

"How about his blue jeans?"

"What was his motive?" she asked the detective as she pulled Iwik's red shirt out of a pile of clothing. She took his jeans down from a clothesline across the road. Hadi's silence told her that Sunarti's position was not to request information, but only to give it. In place of an answer, the officer asked instead for Iwik's shoes. Sunarti took a pair of leather shoes from the rack. Another policeman snapped her picture.

Hadi demanded: "The metal pipe!"

"What pipe? He doesn't have any kind of pipe here." Sunarti argued.

"Then give us the cloth! The cloth!"

"What cloth?" Sunarti shrieked in confused desperation. The police gestured at the fabric she had been cutting. "Someone else owns this!" she answered. She pointed to scraps left over from the sewing that were headed for the garbage, and indicated the officers could have those if they insisted on seizing some cloth from her household. Then she handed the police officers a brown leather belt that Hadi also requested.

"Helmet!" the policemen ordered. "Helmet!" Sunarti raised her hands in bewilderment. Iwik no longer owned a motorcycle helmet. His friends kept borrowing his old helmet until one day someone failed to return it. Iwik never replaced it.

While Hadi was ordering her to collect his clothing, several policemen kept Iwik under guard. He did not have an opportunity to speak with Sunarti, much less to change his clothes in private. The police escorted him to the back of his bedroom, where he replaced his underwear with a fresh pair under their watchful eyes. Throughout the whole ordeal, Sunarti could see only his face, which looked pale and exhausted. His skin seemed smudged and oily, as if he had not showered or slept since she last saw him.

Officers found the family's battered, secondhand blue Vespa parked in the back. Iwik had bought it for $118 – more than it was worth, really. The aged model required several noisy attempts to start. The cycle had been in and out of the repair shop more often than Sunarti could remember. The police wheeled the Vespa onto the front porch so Iwik could sit on it while an officer took more photographs for his files. For each shot, a detective had him hold one of the articles seized from Sunarti: the rags of red cloth the police had pulled out of the garbage, the pair of light blue jeans, and the shoes she had taken from their closet.

Two men in clean shirts and ties detached themselves from the crowd and approached Sunarti. Their demeanor seemed different from the police and detectives. The two introduced themselves as Eko Widiyanto and Djufri Taufik, and explained that they, along with Triyandi Mulkan, would be her husband's legal advisers. She was informed, matter-of-factly, that Iwik had confessed to a murder, and that the police were conducting a homicide investigation. The three attorneys invited her to come back to the police headquarters with them. She accepted immediately, and bundled Bimo into one of the police vehicles with them.

"This can't be!" she kept telling the well-dressed strangers during the ride to the station. "How could it be that Iwik killed Udin? The man is a real coward. Please, this can't be true at all. This can't be possible. My husband can't be a murderer."

The three lawyers and Sunarti arrived at the Jogjakarta police headquarters first. Iwik's car had gone back to Dymas to retrieve one item on Hadi's list that they had forgotten: a denim jacket, which Iwik recalled that he had left at the office. Sunarti and the attorneys waited inside the detectives' office. When voices from the outside began murmuring "This is the murderer! This is the murderer!" Sunarti knew that her husband, the suspect, had arrived. Police brought Iwik into the room and then left the six of them alone for a few moments: the three lawyers, the couple, and Bimo.

"What kind of craziness of yours is this? Why did you confess to this crime?" Sunarti begged Iwik.

"But I was promised…that I could go home."

"This is a big deal," she shouted. "This isn't something small!"

Before the police came in to take him away, Iwik knelt on the floor and hugged his wife around her waist. He whimpered: "This is all because of your photo."

"What photo?" she asked in amazement.

"The one in Udin's wallet."

<hr />

Hadi, Iwik, and two of the lawyers went off to another room in the headquarters building. Although this was the second time Iwik would be interrogated, it was the first time under Hadi's direction. This would also be his lawyers Eko and Djufri's first opportunity to accompany their client at his questioning. Triyandi, Iwik's lead lawyer, decided to linger in the hallway to talk to Chief Detective Suko.

"Are you in good mental and physical health and ready to be questioned?" Hadi's interrogation began, according to the transcript.

"I am..."

"Have you ever been involved in a crime or convicted of a crime?"

"No."

"Are you accompanied by your lawyers?"

"Yes."

After a few more questions confirming Iwik's age, address, and background, Hadi asked: "Do you understand why you are being questioned today?"

"I have assaulted a man and caused the death of the said individual."

"What made you attack Syafruddin?" Hadi asked Iwik.

"I had heard news that my wife was often bothered by Syafruddin."

"What do you mean by saying your wife was often 'bothered?'"

"What I mean is that my wife, Sunarti, was often seduced by Syafruddin."

"What did you feel after you often heard that your wife was bothered or seduced by Syafruddin?"

"My emotion was hate. In my heart I felt bitter. I emerged with the intention to teach a lesson to Syafruddin so that he would no longer bother my wife."

Eko and Djufri would dispute the transcript Hadi would later prepare from this session. The lawyers would recall that Iwik had halted several times during the interrogation and refused to answer Hadi's questions. There was one point, they insisted, when Iwik fell silent for several minutes. Djufri then asked Hadi for some time so he and Eko could speak to their client in private. When Hadi left them, Iwik repeated what he had told the three lawyers earlier: "I didn't do it. I'm not Udin's murderer."

When the three lawyers emerged from the gloomy interior of police headquarters, they stumbled into a blaze of klieg lights, microphones, tape recorders and television cameras. Jogja reporters eavesdropping on the police radio frequency had first picked up the news that Udin's murderer had been arrested. Some had heard directly from their own police sources. A friend in the force had tipped off the PWI team's Asril the day before that a break in the Udin case was imminent. Ida had heard comparatively late. A friend had called her with the news just that afternoon. She had rushed to the police headquarters to find that dozens of reporters had arrived there before her.

Since the Jogjakarta police were restricting the media's access to the inside of the headquarters, reporters took naps on the grass as others discussed what they had gleaned from loitering police officers. Several patrolmen outside headquarters had helpfully revealed the suspect's name and biographical details. Apparently, the reporters were told, Iwik's wife Sunarti had been having an extramarital affair with Udin. Detectives found a photograph of her in the murdered reporter's wallet. And the day before the assault, several people had witnessed Sunarti hitch a ride on the back of Udin's motorcycle outside the Bantul courthouse. Iwik had also confessed that when he found out about his wife's infidelities, he took a metal pipe, mounted his Vespa, and went to Samalo to teach the journalist "a lesson."

In front of police headquarters, Ida spotted several officers taking a blue Vespa down from a truck. When she saw the motorcycle, her skepticism solidified. The motorcycle looked old and dusty, as if it had not been used in ages. It appeared incapable of producing the robust sound witnesses, such as noodle seller Nur Sulaiman's daughter Ayik, had heard on Parangtritis Road the night of the murder. Nearly everyone who had grown up in Jogja, this city buzzing with motorcycles, knew how to distinguish the confident whine of a Yamaha engine from the sputtering *put-put-put* of a Vespa. Ida thought: if the police were claiming that their suspect had traveled to and from the crime scene on *that* piece of junk, then this was not an arrest. It was clearly a setup.

The journalists sat on the grass with the lawyers for an impromptu press conference. A few reporters accused Triyandi and his associates of being the puppets of the police. The implication was that if the attorneys had any morals, they should decline the authorities' invitation to represent Iwik in what would inevitably be a show trial. The lawyer responded that whatever the Dymas chauffeur had done or not done, Iwik deserved representation. Other journalists wanted to know what had transpired during Iwik's questioning. "Dwi Sumaji said he does not know anything of what had happened," Triyandi replied. "He hunched over and held his forehead. Then he repeated that he did not know."

By the time the lawyers made it back to their office, darkness had blanketed the city and its palace. The day's events had exhausted them, but none could go home. They had to decide whether they should continue representing Iwik. The media had sent a message to the lawyers that if Legal Defenders continued to play a role in this case, their work would be scrutinized more than ever before, just as the journalists had scrutinized the police investigation. They realized that if they accepted the case, they would be caught in the middle, between journalists, who refused to believe Iwik had killed Udin, and the Jogjakarta police department, which seemed solidly behind the guilt of its suspect.

Triyandi asked a fourth lawyer, Adib Sujarwadi, to join their discussion of the firm's future. A short, rotund East Javanese in his forties, Adib was the firm's second most-senior lawyer after Triyandi. He had worked with Triyandi since the attorney had started practicing law in Jogja. In this meeting, Triyandi indicated that he needed Adib's experience and active participation in order to better represent Iwik. The Sumatran wanted to take the case, but he could not put his lawyers' careers on the line without their full assent and cooperation.

"Can we back out of this?" Triyandi asked his associates.

"But this is exactly our profession's challenge!" Djufri, the juniormost of the four, answered. A lawyer for fewer than three years, Djufri had been prominent at his law school in the predictable way of the smart and ambitious. A native of Padang in West Sumatra, Djufri had been elected to the UII law student council as one of its youngest representatives before becoming vice secretary-general of the All-Indonesia Law Student Senate. He had been active in campus politics and campaigns, and had been detained by security officials at least three times for joining and leading the protests. When he entered Triyandi's firm, he was made vice executive director of Legal Defenders. In his few short years in the firm, Djufri had represented clients in over twenty homicide cases.

With the naïve conviction of his years, Djufri argued that if the four of them allowed an innocent man to be found guilty, then there was not much use in them being lawyers. But the canny, ambitious, young associate also spotted the vast publicity this case might generate for the firm if they could successfully keep Iwik out of the cell that, it seemed, had already been prepared for him. "If we go forward, and if we are successful," Djufri said, "our name will be known all over."

The other two lawyers echoed the stand Djufri had taken. Then Triyandi concluded: "This is the situation. If we abandon him, we become one of the sinful. But if we defend him, we have to prepare to be destroyed because what we face is a wall that is very stubborn and strong. I'm asking you – are you going to be with me?"

No one refused. "In that case, we face whatever happens."

The four men turned immediately to their case. They discussed the evidence police officials said they had against their client: a photograph in the dead reporter's wallet, a witness who had spotted Sunarti with Udin on the back of his red Honda Tiger, and their client's confession, which was particularly problematic. During colonial rule, the Dutch had made the confession the most important piece of evidence in a criminal prosecution. On the basis of an admission alone, regardless of how it was extracted, a colonial judge would convict a defendant. Although a new criminal procedure code, introduced in 1981, required judges to rely on more than one category of evidence to enter a conviction, police, prosecutors, and courts still followed instinctively the colonial tradition: if the suspect himself had admitted guilt, who were they to argue?

A confession was convenient, practical and efficient. Gathering eyewitness testimony and material evidence can be time-consuming, but a confession can be obtained in minutes if the suspect is in police custody. Indonesian law has no equivalent of the U.S. Constitution's Fifth Amendment. The new criminal procedure code did give suspects similar protections from forced self-incrimination during interrogation and trial. It also prescribes a maximum jail sentence of four years to any officer of the law who uses violence to obtain a confession. But since the police are so infrequently prosecuted for failing to respect these code-granted rights, law enforcement personnel have naturally calculated that a violation has practically no consequences.

The very day of Iwik's arrest, a forty-two-year-old man in the custody of the West Java Police District died from beatings and wounds apparently received during questioning. The man was not even a suspect; he had been detained as a material witness, as he had the misfortune to be riding the same car as a businessman robbed and killed on a West Java highway. Because the thieves had left him and another passenger in the car unharmed, the police suspected that both survivors were possible accomplices to the robbery. Over the course of ten days, he was questioned at the police precinct and at local military police headquarters. When the man's wife came to visit, she was told her husband had died in custody. The police delivered his body wrapped in a burial shroud, and advised his family not to look at it. In the days that followed, a public outcry fanned by the victim's family and the media forced the West Java police chief to reveal that the witness had died from torture. The chief's explanation: "It was a technical and tactical mistake in the investigation."

In the past, judges demonstrated a reluctance to accept violations of procedure – even torture – as reasons to eliminate incriminating evidence from consideration in a judicial proceeding. Indonesian courts, for various reasons, including convenience and a preference for controlling crime, place greater value on completing the trial process rather than on ensuring that a suspect's rights are protected. Iwik's case did not appear to be a case of physical torture. As far as the lawyers could figure out, he had given his confession voluntarily. So before they could do anything to secure his freedom, they first needed to know why their client insisted on admitting a crime to police investigators while avowing innocence to his lawyers. Because as long as Iwik confessed, which he had done so far through two interrogations, he was helping secure his own conviction.

Djufri, Eko, and Adib volunteered to see Sunarti that evening. What they desperately needed from his wife was some kind of alibi.

CHAPTER 8

Political Business

THAT NIGHT, Achadi and Angger went searching for Edy. When the detective had last met them, he had insisted that he and the police had been honest in their investigation. He had assured Achadi that they had not excluded the possibility that the *bupati* might have been involved in the murder. But during his press conference in August, Sri Roso had said "journalists are also people," hinting that Udin might have had personal problems that had led to his murder. Conveniently, Edy had proven the *bupati* correct. When Edy had mentioned to Titet that he was tailing a certain "Atmaji," which Achadi had thought was some local hired muscle, Edy's main suspect was really this Dwi Sumaji, an indigent driver for some Sleman billboard company.

The two activist journalists asked Titet to find Edy at the Bantul police station. The PDI man returned with a message: the detective would meet the reporters at a tea stall near the police station. The three men sat on mats on the sidewalk and drank tea as they waited. Finally, near midnight, Edy appeared. He swaggered towards them.

"Thanks for all the help," he said. "The murderer of Udin has been caught."

"…If it isn't a setup," Achadi responded sarcastically. The young reporter tore into the veteran detective. "You really broke your promise. Two days ago you said that you would catch the suspect, that we could come along and watch you do it. Then you caught this guy on some cooked-up motive of adultery. That means you're just loyal to your superiors." Achadi spat out his words: "You're just someone who can be bought."

Edy's smile disappeared, as did his friendly demeanor. "You insult my institution, you insult the oath I took as a policeman," he said coldly. He reminded them of his own oath to them – that seven generations of his descendants would not be safe if this arrest was really a setup. Then Edy appeared to decide he would waste no more words explaining himself to Achadi and Angger. He removed a pistol from his belt, and laid it on the mat between himself and the reporters. He pointed his finger at Achadi and Angger, and threatened: "I can finish both of you off tonight!"

The Islamic college student recklessly shot back a response. "If you want to get rid of me, get rid of me tonight." Achadi replied. "But a lot of people know I'm here, and many know I'm on the Udin case. If I'm gone, all the newspapers will say the same thing: you will be the first to be investigated."

Edy then pulled out his walkie-talkie, and barked some words into it. Three cars and a motorcycle pulled up next to the stall. Suddenly, Edy's team and other policemen from the Bantul station surrounded Angger, Achadi, and Titet. Several officers came over to congratulate the detective on his arrest. One gushed: "Success and safety, commandant. Our work is done!"

Achadi and Angger, outnumbered by the police officers, kept quiet. Edy, satisfied that his intimidating show of force, if not his direct threats, had won the argument, paid for the journalists' drinks and left with his detectives. "A journalist, whatever – just blow them away," Achadi overheard one policeman tell Edy as they left. That was the last time Achadi spoke to the detective.

If Edy thought he could persuade the local media to swallow his suspect this way, he was mistaken. Almost from Iwik's arrest, local papers, especially *Bernas*, were skeptical. The following day, on 23 October 1996, *Bernas* reprinted the PWI's sketch of the murder suspect, which the paper had first published more than six weeks earlier. Under the graphic, the paper wrote: "CONFIRMED." Beside it, the paper ran a photo of Iwik. Under the driver's visage, *Bernas* printed the word: "REJECTED."

<hr />

When Sunarti was growing up in Bantul, her parents had lived in Sabdodadi, a group of houses a short distance from Samalo. She had gone to the local *madrasah*, or Muslim school, where a boy named Syafruddin had been in the class ahead of her. Sunarti had been in the natural sciences curriculum while Syafruddin studied social sciences. They shared few classes. But for a short while, they had both served on the student council, which is how she came to know him.

In 1986, when she was in her mid-twenties, Sunarti met Syafruddin again at a school reunion. He had been teasingly friendly, the way young men become when they reach the age when they start searching for a spouse. He had told her he had found a good job and showed her his business card. He made a small joke: did she want to "come back" to him? She and Syafruddin had been too young to have had a relationship so many years ago, and she did not want one now. But those were the kind of things people said at school reunions.

When she first heard about Udin's death on the radio, at first she did not recognize that the boy she had known was the same Fuad Muhammad Syafruddin, Bantul correspondent for *Bernas*. He had never used his first name in grammar school, and many did not know he sometimes shortened his last name to "Udin." But after she read the newspapers, she realized that young Syafruddin and the big-bodied reporter were the same person. As the daily paper brought in each development in the case, she and her husband wondered idly why he had been killed, and who had been behind it. Like hundreds of readers who followed the case with a similar mix of pity and fascination, she wondered if the killer would ever be caught. Apparently he had. And it was her husband.

On 22 October 1996, while Iwik was being questioned with his lawyers, an exhausted Sunarti took their son Bimo home. An officer from the Jogjakarta police, who was an old friend from Bantul, escorted them. On the way back to Sleman, Sunarti asked him: "How could this be? My husband does not even know the victim." Her companion shrugged, not knowing the answer.

When she reached her house, Sunarti found her front porch and house filled with neighbors and relatives. Most had seen the convoy of police cars earlier in the day, and had watched while Hadi ordered her to gather her husband's belongings. Those who had not been there in person had quickly heard about the arrest and were curious about her reaction. She noticed that many of her visitors were strangers. She would later learn they were reporters from *Bernas*, the *People's Sovereignty*, the *Jogja Post*, television and radio stations, and papers as far away as Jakarta and Surabaya. Later that evening, her lawyers joined the throng of bodies that occupied her home.

She sat in front of them as if she was before a firing squad. They peppered her with questions to which she herself wished she had an answer. They asked her if she had been outside the Bantul courthouse on 12 August 1996 to meet Syafruddin. They asked whether she had been having an affair with the reporter. They asked her to recall where her husband had been on 13 August 1996, the night of the murder. The lawyers Eko, Adib, and Djufri also pressed her to produce as detailed a memory as she could manage. They needed it, they said, to save her husband from a possible death sentence.

Sunarti had excellent recall. She could remember names of people she had met years before, even if the encounter had been in passing. She could recount the details of shows she had seen on television, or a story someone had once described to her. But her prodigious memory applied usually to people and to special occasions. The problem with 13 August, she thought, was that it had been an ordinary day. Three months had passed since that date, and every day that had come and gone since then had seemed the same as every other.

She could not remember where Iwik had been that evening. She guessed that date might have been a *Kliwon* Tuesday, and she recalled that one *Kliwon* Tuesday eve in August, Iwik had gone to sleep at about 6:00 p.m. so he could get up in the middle of the night with his neighbors to shoot bats with his air rifle. August was the month when the banyan trees produced tiny, blood-red berries the nocturnal creatures loved to nibble; berries that coated the ground with red splotches when they fell from the trees' tendriled canopies. On that *Kliwon* Tuesday eve, Sunarti recalled, Iwik and his friends took their air rifles to shoot down the beasts as they feasted on the ripening fruit. Her husband wanted to boil their carcasses to make a traditional remedy to ease his chronic asthma. But her neighbor, a policeman with the Sleman force, had insisted that he was certain her husband had not gone shooting bats that night of 13 August. The eve of *Kliwon* Tuesday was the night before, on 12 August.

Although the lawyers stayed with her until early the following morning, she could not get a precise fix on her memories. They might have gone to sleep early. They might have watched television with a neighbor. She just did not know. Eko, Adib, and Djufri jotted down notes about the couple's daily schedule, as well as whatever information her neighbors and relatives could offer. But when the journalists, lawyers, and neighbors finally departed, none of her guests had found the clarity they wanted.

Sunarti took several days to remember completely the events of 13 August. Although she was supposed to concentrate on establishing an alibi for her husband, she could not help but think about what the police were saying about her. They had accused her of having an affair with Udin, of having brazenly given the married reporter her photograph to slip into his wallet, of having snuggled into her lover's back as they sped away from the Bantul courthouse on his red motorcycle the day before her jealous husband killed him. She knew none of this could be true. But until she could provide a credible, alternate account of her whereabouts on 12 and 13 August, she had no hope of convincing the authorities to believe her more than their own detectives.

Her parents and family decided that they needed to keep watch over her, ostensibly for her peace of mind, but really for their own. A few relatives were deputized to keep her company, but a sound sleep eluded her. Sunarti tossed and turned in bed, while Bimo dozed fitfully nearby. She had explained to her son why his father would not be coming home right away – that he was in some kind of trouble that, God willing, could be resolved shortly. She wondered if she could ever tell Bimo when Iwik could come home. She dreaded the possibility that she might have to tell him he could only see his father through the bars of a prison.

After a restless night, she realized that she might have an answer. Every time a customer placed an order, Sunarti noted it down on a large wall calendar. After a while, the calendar had turned into a kind of diary, recording in its boxes deadlines for ordered dresses, wedding dates and haircut appointments – the progress of her and her family's unremarkable existence. She realized that this calendar still hung on their wall. She sprang up to examine it. There: on 12 August, the day the police had insisted she had been trysting with Udin, she had been dressing a bride until about 2:00 p.m., long after someone had supposedly spotted her riding on Udin's motorcycle near the Bantul courthouse at noon. On 13 August, she noticed, she had done a similar job that took up the entire day. In fact, she had been so busy with work at the time that she had asked her mother Pujiyati to come from Bantul to baby-sit Bimo. She realized she not only had an alibi for herself; she had at least one witness other than her husband and herself who could confirm it. "This was help from God," as she would later describe her thoughts at the time.

With the assistance of her family, Sunarti pieced together an accounting of her whereabouts in the days surrounding the reporter's murder. In her mind, the events of those days began to coalesce in sequence, as if she were watching a movie. On the morning of 13 August, the day of the murder, she had gotten up at 4:00 a.m. to make breakfast, as she did everyday. A friend who owned another beauty salon came by to lend Sunarti a motorcycle. Both women had been scheduled to assist at a wedding in a neighboring village, and Sunarti needed her own transportation to get there. At 7:00 a.m., Sunarti left for the wedding. She and her friend stayed there the whole day, since their customers, as always, insisted that they remain to remove the makeup of the bride and her entourage after the lengthy ceremonies.

Exhausted, Sunarti returned home at about 5:00 in the afternoon. When her friend stopped in to retrieve her motorcycle, she also gave Sunarti some leftover snacks and pastries from the wedding. About an hour later, as she heard the call to the early evening prayer from the Panasan mosque, Sunarti saw Iwik walking down the street from the direction of Magelang Road. After her husband changed his clothes and took off his shoes, they chatted while he sipped his evening drink. He fed his pet songbirds and sampled the food left over from the wedding. Iwik decided to go to bed early. Before he slept, her mother Pujiyati asked him if he was planning to see a show in a nearby village. The performance was one of the horse trance-dance, the *jatilan*, in which dancers, usually from a traveling troupe, invoke the spirits to possess their bodies as they ride bamboo hobbyhorses. In that state, they can chew on glass without shredding their tongues as well as spew fire across the heads of amazed spectators. A *jatilan* always drew large crowds from several villages. Iwik's mother-in-law wondered if Iwik was going to join them.

"No, I'm too tired," Iwik answered.

Pujiyati had unrolled a mat on the floor in front of the room nearest to the street, and tucked Bimo in beside her. As Sunarti closed the front door, she noticed that the time was 7:30 p.m. On the road outside, she spied her next-door neighbor, Heri Karyono, who peddled chicken-noodle soup from a cart, returning to his home. The wall separating his house from theirs was only the width of a single layer of bricks. When her neighbor chatted with his family, she could sometimes hear them as if they were in her own house.

She was so exhausted from working the wedding that she slept soundly. At about midnight, a couple of voices outside her door disturbed her. Heri was speaking to Gunarso Wibowo, another neighbor. The chatter had also disturbed her husband, who stirred from the bed and put on a thin blue jacket. He went outside for several minutes, and then returned.

"What is it?" she asked him, sleepily.

"A motorcycle has been stolen."

"Whose?"

"Some guest of Sajuri's. Why is it whenever there's a *jatilan* someone's motorcycle always goes missing?"

Sunarti was too exhausted to respond, and Iwik too tired to wait for her answer. The couple went back to sleep. The next time she saw her husband was the following morning before he went to work. As far as she could recall, that was what she and Iwik had done on 13 August, the day and night of the murder.

Once she and her family had fleshed out from a few scribbled lines on a calendar two days' worth of her alibi, her neighbors helped her pin down the details through their confirmations and revisions. Her neighbor Heri, for example, told her that he did remember talking with Gunarso until well past midnight about a theft of a motorcycle. At that time, Heri recalled, he remembered Iwik emerging from his house. The driver's eyes were ruddy, while his hair was uncombed and tousled, as if it had lain squashed on a pillow for several hours. Heri spoke to Iwik for about ten to fifteen minutes, after which time Iwik returned inside.

Heri assured Sunarti that he would be ready to confirm her husband's alibi. Iwik's wife then gathered other sworn statements to back up her memories. She went directly to the family of the bride she had dressed on 12 August. She had explained to them her situation, and had them sign a paper attesting that she had been present that whole day preparing their daughter to be wed. Anyone claiming to have seen her riding Udin's motorcycle that day must have given the police the wrong information.

A few days later, after Hadi returned some of the possessions he had seized on 22 October, Sunarti solved another nagging mystery: why her photograph had ended up in Udin's wallet. As she went through her husband's belongings, she found a picture of herself on her wedding day in her husband's wallet. The police said that they had located the same wedding photograph tucked into Udin's billfold. That was odd, she thought, because Sunarti had made only four copies of that particular photograph. She had given one to Iwik and the remaining three had been turned over to the Bantul religious affairs office in the marriage registration process.

Then she recalled a story her twenty-six-year-old brother Parjiyanto had told her weeks earlier. One night not long before Iwik's arrest, her brother, like many youths his age, had been whiling away the nighttime hours in a food stall in Bantul, when a man he had recognized as a Bantul detective took out several photographs to show to the stall's customers. Sunarti's brother had seen this braggart policeman around. He knew his name was Edy Wuryanto. When Parjiyanto glimpsed the photos, he realized that he recognized two of their subjects: one was a relative, the other was Sunarti.

"I know this person," he had told Edy. "She's my sister!"

The detective hurriedly stuffed the photos away and left the food stall. The next time he saw Sunarti, Parjiyanto asked why the police detective had her photograph. At the time, Sunarti had not taken her brother's story seriously. But after she showed him her wedding picture, he confirmed that he had seen the same photograph in Edy's possession. Since Sunarti was certain Iwik had not given the detective his copy before his arrest, she concluded that Edy must have obtained that photograph from the only other source: the Bantul religious affairs office.

When she told this to Iwik's lawyers, Triyandi dispatched an employee to check out her story in Bantul. The lawyers then learned that the photograph had never been in Udin's wallet. Police had indeed borrowed the photograph from the office as part of an investigation. Thanks to her memory and her brother's fortuitous encounter, Sunarti and her legal counsel had successfully exposed Edy and his team in their first blatant fabrication.

Sunarti realized with a shudder that she and her family must have been under police surveillance for several weeks. In October, she remembered, two sets of strangers had shown up at her salon asking about the Udin murder. The first encounter had been in early October. A greasy, unattractive dark man accompanied by a young girl in her twenties had requested a haircut. The man did not reveal his name, but he said the young girl was his daughter. As Sunarti snipped away at the girl's locks, the girl's "father" asked Sunarti where she had been born.

"Bantul," she answered.

The stranger claimed he had relatives from the area, and asked her what she thought about the Udin case. Sunarti mentioned that she and the murdered reporter had been *madrasah* classmates. She had last seen him at the school reunion, and recounted their playful little encounter, along with his teasing invitation to "come back" to him.

When she had finished cutting the girl's hair, the man told her to keep the change from the two dollars he paid her, and left. After their departure, Bimo asked naughtily: "If the father looks like *that*, how could the daughter be so pretty?"

Another evening not long after that, four people came to her salon. Two of the visitors were men, the other two women. One of the females wore a khaki-colored civil servant's uniform. She entered the salon with the two men, while the second sat waiting in the vehicle. The two men, just like the first man with his daughter, started chatting with her as the woman in the uniform received a haircut. They told her they were on their way to a wedding in the area. Like the other stranger, they asked her where she lived as a child.

"Parangtritis Road," she said.

"Near that journalist who was murdered?" one of them asked intently.

"Yes," she had answered. "What a pity! What a pity to be killed in that way. Especially since he was just becoming comfortable." She had seen all the details of his family's rising lifestyle and growing success in the papers. She knew Udin had recently purchased a new motorcycle, and had acquired other possessions, such as a computer. Clearly, he had a good job. "And he was a good man," she added.

"How do you know?" one man had asked, with the same unhealthy interest his companion had exhibited.

She replied that she and Udin had attended the same *madrasah*. They had known each other for years. Then, when Iwik came home from work, the three quickly departed.

Later she would learn that the first man who had visited her was none other than Edy Wuryanto himself. And one of the men in the second group was a member of Edy's team named Slamet Wijayanto. Like ill omens, the two strange visits and her photograph in the hands of a police detective should have tipped her off that something bad was heading toward her. But Sunarti had never tangled with the law before, nor had the family ever been involved in a police investigation. To be watched, investigated, and arrested were things that happened to *bad* people, not to the innocent.

People confess to crimes for any number of reasons: momentary weakness, severe psychological pressure, desire for attention or recognition, or perhaps a need to protect something or someone. Yet Iwik's insistence on confessing to a murder he told his lawyers that he did not commit puzzled his four attorneys. Despite his private protestations, the Dymas driver apparently could not stop confessing to detectives each time the lawyers accompanied him to an interrogation. His wife had found an alibi for him for the night of the murder, as well as corroborating witnesses. She had also enabled the lawyers to pick holes in the police case, especially Edy's claims that she had been seen with the reporter on 12 August and that Udin had kept her photo in his wallet. With those elements in doubt, how could the police maintain their story that she had been carrying on an affair with the reporter? Yet as long as the Jogjakarta Police District had Iwik's sworn admission, a court case against him could still be won despite the absence of a believable motive or a preponderance of corroborating evidence. Iwik was his own worst enemy.

In the three days after Iwik's arrest, on 22, 23, and 24 October, Hadi had questioned the suspect three times, and each time, Iwik had confessed to Udin's murder. On those occasions, Adib, Eko, or Djufri had accompanied Iwik. The only interview the lawyers had missed was the first, most detailed one: on 21 October, immediately after Edy had brought Iwik to the Jogjakarta Police District headquarters. Each of the interrogations the lawyers had witnessed followed a consistent pattern. Hadi asked Iwik questions about the crime. Iwik hesitated before answering, and shot frequent, nervous glances toward his lawyers. He broke the cycle of questions and answers with stretches of long, confused silence. At each of those sessions, Iwik would privately maintain his innocence to the lawyers. But when he returned to the table to speak to Hadi, he would continue confessing to the murder.

On 24 October, the lawyers received official records of each of Iwik's first four interrogations. The lawyers were not surprised to see that Hadi had cleaned up Iwik's long silences and confused hesitations in the transcripts. The criminal procedure code requires police to note down a suspect's words exactly as said. In practice, however, police officers edit and summarize a suspect's account to save time but also to instinctively shape the suspect's sentences to conform to their own theories. Indonesian police interview transcripts read like scripted dialogue. Suspects answer directly each of their interrogator's questions in full, coherent sentences. Regardless of the level of education, they are proficient in legal language and police terminology. They also thoughtfully include every detail requested by the police in their answers, including nearly exact measurements of objects and distances. In the transcripts, criminals sound so much like the police that questioner and questioned seem almost indistinguishable.

But even without the police's massaging of the confession records, the lawyers' client had at least once, on 21 October, clearly said he had committed the murder and described how he did it. Iwik seemed reluctant, even afraid, to contradict what he had admitted the night of his arrest. To his lawyers, Iwik pleaded for help. But as soon as he faced Hadi again, he continued to assert that he had planned and executed the assault on Udin, so that each interrogation solidified and made Iwik's admission more credible.

At least the lawyers could rule out one reason for Iwik's stubborn refusal to recant. The driver seemed of below-average intelligence, but he was not insane. A police psychologist who examined Iwik noted that the Dymas driver's "dynamism, self-confidence, self-control, resolution and ability to withstand stress are all among his shortcomings. The subject's emotional stability is unstable. He cannot act firmly (always shadowed by doubt)." The diagnosis confirmed what the lawyers had already concluded. Iwik could not decide whether he would hold fast to his innocence or allow himself to be tarred with guilt. He did the worst thing possible, which was to equivocate between both positions.

On 23 October, Hadi recorded Iwik adding more details to the events that led to the murder, such as how he heard about his wife's affair from gossip at the food stalls on Parangtritis Road. He said he could not identify the source of these whispers, these *wangsit*. Before he had left his home on the night of 13 August, Iwik told Hadi, the driver had thought through what he was going to do when he met the reporter.

"Syafruddin's body is larger than mine," the transcript of his interrogation that day reports him stating. "So I decided to find a tool in the form of a metal pipe."

The following day, 24 October, Hadi continued his questioning. Iwik obliged by explaining how he had investigated Udin's neighborhood on the night of 12 August. He had driven his Vespa down Parangtritis Road and parked it near a noodle stall across from Udin's house. He had spoken to an old woman standing there. He said that at the time, he had not yet developed a specific plan of attack. His only thought, he had said, was that "Syafruddin must be taught a lesson."

On 25 October, Djufri complained to a *Bernas* journalist: "When he meets the police, Dwi Sumaji confesses. But to us, he denies it. We tell him: 'You have to refuse to confess if it is true that you really didn't do it.'" To be fair, the driver also was confused whether the lawyers were there to help the police or to defend him. Triyandi and his associates felt they never had enough time with their client to convince him that they were truly on his side; that they were not police agents and thus could be trusted. Although Indonesian law permits lawyers "unlimited access" to their clients, in practice the authorities often conspire to limit the contact that criminal defense counsel have with their clients. One 1983 Justice Ministry regulation, for example, interpreted "unlimited access" to mean "unlimited access within office hours," which made it practically permissible for police to question suspects without counsel late at night or in the early morning, as in Iwik's case. During the moments Triyandi, Eko, and Djufri had with Iwik, they were rarely left alone. A detective or officer was always within earshot.

Only after Iwik's older brother, Eko Priyatno, who had rushed back to Jogja from the capital when he heard the news of his brother's arrest, and Sunarti successfully persuaded Iwik that his lawyers could be trusted did Triyandi and his colleagues finally get Iwik to describe fully what had really happened between the time he left Sunarti on 21 October and when they met him in police custody the following morning. Just as Sunarti had put together the couple's alibi over several days, the lawyers and Iwik's relatives assembled the Dymas driver's tale in several pieces, gathered during the minutes they had alone during interrogations or family visits.

Iwik's tale apparently began several weeks before his arrest. One evening, around quitting time, perhaps 5:00 in the afternoon, he had just emerged out of the alley that led to Dymas Advertising when a dark-skinned, greasy-haired man hailed him. The stranger sounded as if he was calling an old friend. "Eh, Iwik!" the man had said.

Iwik cautiously returned the greeting, uncertain if he had met this man before. Perhaps he had, because in the ensuing conversation, the man demonstrated a detailed knowledge of Iwik's family. He mentioned Iwik's father, a retired army officer, as well as Iwik's twin brothers, Eko Priyatno and Eko Prayitno. The man introduced himself as "Franky" and said that he wanted to do some business. He wanted to order a billboard advertising a new showroom for Yamaha motorcycles directly from Iwik. Franky said he preferred that the two men handle this deal without the knowledge of Iwik's bosses at Dymas. That way, he told

Iwik conspiratorially, the driver need not share his commission. "I profit, and you profit, too," Franky had told him. He explained that he would send Iwik the dimensions of the sign as well as a phone number where he could be reached.

Reassured by the man's easy familiarity, Iwik agreed to consider Franky's offer. About a week later, a note for Iwik arrived at Dymas. The paper, which was attached to a photograph of a motorcycle billboard, read:

> To Dwi Sumaji:
> Following our last conversation, I am sending a picture of the advertisement we mean. Like this, but wider by half a meter to the left and right and taller by about a meter and with a message that says "Honda Suzuki Motor." For further explanation, contact me by telephone no. 367-412 (Call to clarify).

The note was signed with Franky's name. Oddly, Franky had initially mentioned a billboard for Yamaha motorcycles. Now he wanted one for Honda and Suzuki. When Iwik called the number Franky had left to clarify the man's order, he received a recorded message from the telephone company stating that the number did not exist. His business lead had grown cold. Iwik wondered exactly whom it was he had encountered.

The next time he saw Franky was on 21 October 1996, the day of his arrest. After Iwik left his wife that morning, Iwik caught a minibus on Magelang Road so crowded with people that he had to hang off the vehicle's side to ride it. When the bus stopped at an intersection, Iwik felt a hand tugging at him. He turned around and saw Franky's face, grinning.

"Come on, get off. I've got a meeting for you with my boss," Franky said. "We can continue what we discussed the other day."

Surprised to see Franky again, Iwik followed him into a red minivan.

Three men sat inside. Franky introduced each of his companions as fellow employees of the company where he worked, which handled, among many other businesses, offshore drilling at Parangtritis. Franky explained that he was the foreman and the others were members of his team. Franky took the wheel of the minivan, started the engine, and maneuvered the car out into the southbound morning traffic towards Jogja.

Iwik felt the first twinge of worry when the minivan passed the Dymas office. He realized that he had not told anyone at the office that he would be late. Iwik had only been with Dymas for less than a year. Taking time off without informing his superiors could earn him a dressing-down from his boss. Franky and his companions assured Iwik that his employers would not mind, especially if Iwik brought back some business. Franky steered the car onto the highway circling the city, bypassing the motorcycle traffic that clogged the alleys and roads around the *kraton*. Soon, the minivan was rumbling down Parangtritis Road toward the Indian Ocean. The journey through Jogja and Bantul took up most of an hour. Some of the minivan's occupants dozed off, leaving Franky and Iwik to fill the time with conversation.

As they passed Bantul's paddies and cane fields, Franky asked something that seemed to come out of nowhere.

"'Wik, do you know the Udin case?"

"I don't know anything about it," Iwik replied. He and his wife had read about the murdered journalist in the newspapers and had heard reports on the radio. But the couple knew nothing more than what they heard from media reports.

The minivan entered the strip of flophouses, dormitories, and small restaurants that marked the tourist zone of Parangtritis. Franky stopped the car at a small West Sumatran eatery. He, Iwik, and their three companions sat down at a clean table. As the waiter set out bowls of stewed spiced beef, curried chicken, boiled vegetables, and fried fish, Franky gestured expansively at the spread, inviting the Dymas driver to partake of the bounty. Iwik turned down Franky's invitation, since he was not hungry. Franky persisted, and insisted on ordering a cup of coffee for Iwik to drink. As the Dymas driver waited for the three other occupants of the van to finish their food, Iwik thought he saw Franky get up from the table and go into the kitchen. When the coffee arrived and he drank it, Iwik began to feel unfocused and woozy. He found it difficult to concentrate. Later, Iwik would tell his lawyers, he came to believe that the coffee had been tainted with some kind of narcotic.

After eating, the five men got back into the car. "'Wik," Franky told him encouragingly, "Do you want to work with us? It'll be easy to arrange. The important thing is that you want it. My boss is very powerful."

Iwik listened with interest. Born in Sleman as the third of five children of a snakefruit farmer, Iwik had never finished high school. His family had been too poor to support him through his education, so Iwik dropped out during the second year of his technical high school to acquire more practical skills for making a living. He took courses on automobile and motorcycle repair, which helped land him a job fixing machinery for a year for a plywood company in Kalimantan. After he was laid off, he peddled food and housewares in South Sumatra for another year with his older brother. In 1987, his parents asked him to return to Java. With money borrowed from an uncle, Iwik opened a garage in his father's house in a village east of Panasan. But his place was just too far from Magelang Road for him to get much business.

The stops and starts in his life had so far disappointed him. But by then, he had met Sunarti, an aspiring hairdresser from Bantul. Iwik had chosen Sunarti because he knew that she was strong-willed and self-motivated. His guiding principle was: "Don't let it be that the wife depends entirely on her husband." All his life, he had been searching for a way to be independent, to make a life for himself. He needed an ally in that effort, and found the person whose brains would complement his brawn. They dated for two years. Their first date had been at the beach at Parangtritis. They wed in 1989, when he was twenty-seven and she was twenty-four. The following year, their son Bimo was born.

As soon as Iwik heard there was a house available for rent in nearby Panasan, the couple moved out of his father's place. Neither had a job to pay the twenty dollars a year the place cost them in rent. In their one-room house that measured a bit more than sixteen square meters, the couple started a cottage industry in deep-fried pastry dumplings, which Sunarti prepared by hand and Iwik sold at dawn to food stalls.

He and his wife lived a hand-to-mouth existence. But at least they ate, and for the first time, Iwik felt that life had some good in it. Soon, however, he grew embarrassed to be working at home. He felt a man should not be making a living in a kitchen. He searched for another job and found one in a place that sold scrap metal. Then his cousin told him that Dymas Advertising was looking for a driver, a job that paid almost double what Iwik was making at the scrapyard. Although he took the position, Iwik knew he wanted something better. As long as he was young and strong, Iwik could work in positions that required strength or endurance. But as he grew older, he had to find something else to sustain his family. His sixty-four-dollar-a-month salary at Dymas was not much to live on. If Franky was offering something better than the succession of marginal jobs that had devoured his life so far, the least Iwik felt he could do was give the man a hearing.

The minivan's destination was the posh Queen of the South Hotel. Perched on the cliffs that formed the eastern border of the beach at Parangtritis, the Queen of the South is the area's only luxury accommodation. Even though it is located on the south coast of Java, the hotel's décor mimics the lush landscaping of accommodations at the more popular tourist spots of Bali. With its thatched-roof lamps in the shape of small huts and its sarong-clad, flower-festooned statues, the Queen of the South, perhaps to justify the exorbitant resort prices, wanted to make its visitors feel they were at another beach that was sunnier and more charming than gray Parangtritis. While the car idled in the hotel's parking lot, Franky went into the lobby for a few minutes. When he returned, he told his companions that his boss had not yet checked in. They would have to wait somewhere else until his arrival.

The group descended from the cliffs to the seedy brick-and-cinderblock flophouses by the shore. Franky stopped the car at one joint called the Agung Inn, which resembled the many roadside boarding houses Iwik had often overnighted during out-of-town jobs for the billboard company. Iwik's companions ordered several bottles of beer, along with a couple of bottles of the Thai caffeine drink Kratingdaeng, also known as Red Bull. Once again, Franky disappeared. When he returned, he had a woman on each arm and sat them down near Iwik. One girl poured the men their beer, and mixed into each frosty glass generous draughts of Red Bull. Iwik tasted the syrupy sweet, head-clearing Red Bull mingled with the strong, bitter beer. The rough cocktail that was the color of a diabetic's urine left him, after a few sips, with a dull, throbbing headache.

"You have to drink," urged Franky. The driver had wanted to refuse, but Iwik drained the noxious stuff down anyway, since he worried that his new friends might interpret another refusal as a rejection of their burgeoning relationship. The strange-tasting coffee Iwik had taken at the West Sumatran restaurant, followed by the Red Bull-laced beer chaser, began to make him weak-willed and ill, especially since he had not eaten since breakfast. Iwik would later describe the feeling as "if he had become a water buffalo led by its nose."

Franky told Iwik to get some rest. He gave Iwik the equivalent of twenty-five dollars to use "if Iwik felt hungry." An Agung Inn employee brought Iwik to a room. One of the girls who had been at their table followed him inside.

<hr>

When Iwik woke, it was late afternoon. The girl, who had told him her name was "Retno," was gone. The driver splashed water on his face and straightened the clothes he was wearing. The dizziness he had felt since drinking the coffee and the cocktails had not left. He still felt ill when Franky arrived. The foreman announced that his boss had finally reached Parangtritis. He was waiting for them in a room at the Queen of the South.

When the men arrived at the hotel, Franky told Iwik to wait in the marble-floored foyer as he went to get his employer. Franky's three companions had left them alone; apparently they preferred to remain in the hotel's parking lot. Franky returned a short time later with a dark man wearing a plaid shirt and a pair of jeans. The man spoke Indonesian like a native, but his glossy, nearly black skin made Iwik think the man looked like a character from an Indian movie. When Franky introduced his boss, Iwik thought he heard the name "Jendra."

Jendra glanced at Iwik and said: "So they say you have a problem?"

Iwik thought that what the boss meant by a "problem" was Franky's order for a billboard. The driver asked what Jendra wanted to have on his advertisement.

The man waved the question aside. "Let Franky take care of it," he said, and walked back to his room at the end of a long, open-air corridor, the two other men trailing him. Franky followed his boss inside, as Iwik waited on the small terrace outside the room. The boss' room had the best view in the hotel. He could see the ocean and the beach below the cliffs. People, miniature at this distance, played in the surf or ran up and down the grey, wet sand.

When Franky emerged, he sat beside Iwik and told him to forget about the billboard. They had other, more profitable matters to discuss, he said. "These times are the age of political business," Franky declared. Again, he brought up the Udin case, but added the startling announcement that Iwik was the police's main suspect. "The police are looking for you," he told Iwik. "You've been accused of killing Udin." The police had found Sunarti's photo in Udin's wallet, he said. It would not be long before the investigators linked him to the crime. But there was a way out, Franky explained. If Iwik confessed immediately, he might be protected from prosecution. The proposition made no sense: confess to a crime to avoid capture?

"You must do it," Franky urged. "It's better than being another *Petrus* victim." Besides, in return for confessing to Udin's murder, Franky promised, a certain high official would pay Iwik money for his trouble.

The sum, he told Iwik, would not be insignificant.

This offer was too much for the Dymas driver to absorb. Iwik found himself faced with a befuddling combination of cajolery and intimidation. If the police were set on making him a suspect, then he was doomed anyway. He knew no one powerful enough to protect him from the authorities. But if he surrendered, confessed, and accepted a scheme in which a part had already been prepared for him, he would at least be paid. So there, before a garden gaily lit with Balinese lanterns, with the sound of the crashing surf in the middle distance, in a hotel where one night cost one month's salary, his muddled mind made the leap to thinking this tragedy might somehow lead to a better future. He might work forever and never come close to the security and success that seemed to come so easily to others. But if he gave in and confessed, as Franky had suggested, then he might earn something for his pain. At the very least, Franky and his friends might let him go home. Because all he wished was that the whole day would be over.

Iwik agreed. Yes, he told Franky. He would confess to a murder.

For over an hour, the two men sat on the room's terrace. Franky described Udin's neighborhood of Samalo. He mentioned the restaurant across the street from the Krisna Photo Studio, and how Udin's killer had come to "batik" the crime scene the night before. Franky also seemed to know quite a lot about Iwik's work at Dymas, and he wove them expertly into Iwik's narrative. Iwik was to say he had used a piece of scrap metal from work to attack the reporter, and then drove the company truck back to his office to hide the murder weapon in a pile of rusting rebar.

Franky asked Iwik to repeat his "confession" until the foreman was satisfied the details were fixed in the driver's mind. Then Franky instructed Iwik to tell Franky's boss, the man named Jendra, exactly what they had practiced.

"You must tell it this way, if you want to be safe" were Franky's final words to Iwik as he pushed Iwik in to see Jendra.

"This man is the Dwi Sumaji who has confessed to killing Udin,"

Franky announced to his boss. "He asks for protection. What about it, boss, if we keep him safe? We protect him so no one looks for him? Let's look for a place in Jakarta or in the offshore drilling business." Franky said. Iwik, the foreman explained, had a knack for repairing machinery.

Jendra looked at Iwik, and then repeated what he had told Iwik in the lobby: "If you have a problem, then just say you have a problem."

Franky wandered in and out of the hotel room as Iwik poured out his practiced tale. Throughout Iwik's account, Jendra nodded with approval. Then the man told him: "Don't worry, you will be protected. This is political business. I'll hide you. Don't worry about your family. You'll get a salary. What else do you want?" If Iwik wanted a car, pledged Jendra, all the driver had to do was choose what model he wanted. All the licenses and registration papers would be ready. A house? Iwik just had to ask for it. His ears ringing with Jendra's larger-than-life promises, Iwik heard Franky ask his boss if they could move on. Jendra nodded, and with that the interview ended.

As soon as they left Parangtritis, Iwik felt relieved. He was finally on his way home. Maybe all Franky had wanted was that one performance, which Iwik had dutifully delivered. But as they passed through Bantul town, Franky declared: "We're going to a second boss." He parked the minivan in front of a large house that seemed like the residence of a senior official. Iwik noticed it was a large compound, because the lot was large enough to fit several cars. It sat next to the Bantul police headquarters. The building reeked of some kind of power, perhaps not of a national kind, but certainly something that had potency in Bantul. "This, too, is the house of a boss," Franky told the driver. "Say what you said before. This man will also protect you."

He took Iwik into the house through a back door. In one of the rooms, the foreman introduced Iwik to a man in a uniform. The room's occupant looked at Iwik expectantly. Franky told Iwik to repeat his story one more time. When the driver finished, the man told him: "Yes, we'll protect you. Better you go home now."

After his second confession, Franky drove Iwik back the way they had come that morning. Iwik was wondering how to explain this strange, extraordinary day to his wife – why he had skipped work, why he was coming home so late, and why his breath smelled of rancid alcohol – when Franky took another detour. Instead of continuing along the highway to Magelang Road and north toward Panasan, Franky turned unexpectedly into the Jogjakarta Police District compound. He stopped in front of the main building's entrance. Franky nudged Iwik to get out of the car. As Iwik stepped down, policemen surrounded him. The Jogjakarta police seemed to recognize the foreman. They greeted him warmly. Franky, Iwik thought, must have many friends among the police. But, oddly, they were addressing him by a different name: "Edy," they called him.

The man named "Franky" or "Edy" – Iwik was no longer sure – led him up the stairs and through the police headquarters' long corridors. Franky/Edy navigated the building with ease, as if he knew exactly where to go. They reached a door. As he gestured for the driver to enter, Franky/Edy warned Iwik: "If you want to be safe, just repeat what you had said before."

By this time, Iwik had realized that his companion – whatever his name – was not just someone who knew the police well. He had to be a policeman. So too, it seemed, were the three men who had accompanied them since the morning. All the time he had thought he was on an outing to Parangtritis, he was actually surrounded by police officers. Edy saluted a man inside the office, the third "boss" Iwik would meet that evening. Iwik's confusion had now turned into terror, and the wooziness he had felt from the beer, the Red Bull, and the coffee sloshing around his empty stomach had now been replaced by a sickening nausea.

Later, he would learn that the second "boss" he had met in Bantul was Edy's immediate superior, Bantul Police Chief Adé Sudarban. And the person he would confess to at this moment was Adé's superior, Jogjakarta's demanding Police Chief Mulyono.

Iwik had placed his entire trust in Edy, and now Iwik was completely in the police detective's power. The detective had opened before Iwik a vision; by the time he had recognized the illusion, he was trapped by reality. The hapless driver repeated his halting and confused confession. At the end, he begged the man for the same "protection" Edy, Jendra, and the last man to whom he had confessed had promised.

"You can go home," Mulyono said to him. "You won't be jailed."

Edy steered Iwik downstairs. But instead of returning him to the minivan as Iwik had expected, Edy brought Iwik to another room where several police officers were waiting. For the fourth time that night, Edy told Iwik to confess to the murder of Udin. This time, an officer took down his words. During the interrogation, each time Iwik got a detail wrong, Edy would glare at him and warn: "If you want to be safe…" He left the threat unfinished, hanging in the air like a storm cloud. When Iwik finished, the officer typed up the interview notes which Iwik would later sign.

By the time Iwik was finally left alone, it was long past midnight. The police told him he would need to sleep at the police headquarters. The room they prepared for him measured four square meters and had no furniture except for large straw mats spread out on the floor. There were no windows, only slits near the ceiling to let in a bit of air. There was a single door, the only exit and entrance. Three people sat inside. For what seemed like the first time that day, Iwik had a clear and lucid thought. These men were not guests of the Jogjakarta police. Certainly, now neither was he. His roommates were accused criminals, and his room was a detention cell. Edy had disappeared, and Iwik was now a prisoner.

CHAPTER 9

A Worm Squirms

AFTER THEY HAD HEARD Iwik's account of his arrest, his attorneys realized that greed or bewilderment could have first pushed Iwik to confess. But it was fear and ignorance that made him continue. During the first few days after his arrest, Iwik told his lawyers, Jogjakarta Police Chief Mulyono would summon Iwik to his office and request him to repeat what the driver had said when they had first met on 21 October. The police chief, Iwik said, would become upset if the Dymas driver deviated from his story in any way. Iwik also recounted his experiences every evening, when gruff male voices shouted threats at him from outside his detention cell. People warned him that if he changed his confession, he would be shot, or his nails pried from his fingers. Police sometimes brought in suspects who had been tortured to illustrate his fate if he reneged on his commitment to Edy.

Even though in detention Iwik experienced severe pressure to stick to his story, Eko tried persuading his client that continuing to confess was far worse. It was like suicide. The assurances Iwik had received from Mulyono, Adé, Edy, and Jendra, his lawyers told him, were worthless. If the driver continued to insist, every time he spoke to an interrogating officer, that he had killed Udin, then he was only helping them seal his conviction and execution. "He still depended on that promise. A promise that can't be kept, can't be enforced," Triyandi would later describe his frustration with Iwik. "In the end, the process, from interrogation to interrogation, leads to the courtroom. Did he consider a sentence that would be several years long? Had he thought about that if he still wanted to depend on that promise?"

Iwik had not been the only victim that day of deception. Marsiyem, too, received a bewildering invitation to play a part in the same grand scheme that had ensnared Iwik. In the early afternoon of 21 October, three men in a sedan arrived at Wagiman's house to visit Udin's widow and father. After Udin's death, his family received visitors and reporters often enough that the arrival of the strangers at Trirenggo did not, at first, appear extraordinary. Two of the visitors introduced themselves as Achmad Nizar and Achmad Herlin Bashari, businessmen from the Jakarta suburb of Bogor. Bashari's business card bore the name of a gasoline distribution agency.

The men told Marsiyem they were relatives of Chief Mulyono, and that they were in Jogjakarta for business. They had just finished lunch at a West Sumatran restaurant near the Bantul police station, and had decided to visit Marsiyem to convey their respect and their condolence. One of them reassured her: "You must believe. The killer will be caught," he said. "The police have their man." Neither Wagiman nor Marsiyem realized that on that very day, Edy already had Iwik in his custody at Parangtritis.

The following day, 22 October, Nizar and Bashari returned, this time with a third companion. The group brought gifts for the family, in the form of fruits, sweets, toothpaste, and school supplies for Yuli and Wikan. They visited Udin's grave, and promised to return again. On their third visit, 23 October, the businessmen invited Marsiyem and Wagiman to visit police headquarters to see the man who had killed Udin. One of them said that he could take Marsiyem directly to see the police chief, without having to navigate the multiple cordons of aides, adjutants, and secretaries. If they wanted to see the police chief, he told Udin's widow, she and Wagiman should come immediately. "There's a 'souvenir' waiting for you," he said cryptically.

Marsiyem and Wagiman did not understand what he was offering.

But they cautiously agreed, on the condition that their lawyer, Budi, could accompany them. At the mention of the Legal Aid attorney, the businessmen abruptly changed their mind. They said they had to go, but would return the following day to bring some books on Islam for Wagiman. They never returned.

Udin's family noted down the license plate numbers of the visitors' vehicles. Then they reported the incident to their friends in the press. The PWI team, through its sources in the police department, discovered that the sedan the strangers had used to visit Marsiyem and Wagiman had been borrowed by the Jogjakarta police that very day from a prominent Jogja businessman. Nizar and Bashari's visit now seemed even more baffling. In a car borrowed from the police, they had wanted to bring Marsiyem to meet Mulyono. The reporters could think of one possible explanation: the Jogjakarta police needed Marsiyem to identify Iwik as the killer. So either on their own initiative or at the police's urging, these businessmen from out-of-town, probably friends of someone high up in the Jogjakarta Police District, had volunteered themselves, since Marsiyem no longer trusted uniformed policemen. Although Police Chief Mulyono would deny any connection with these men, Nizar later told a Jakarta television station that he and the police chief had a "business relationship." That business, it was said, was providing stationery and supplies to the West Java police academy Mulyono had headed.

Marsiyem's reluctance at the last minute to go along with the plan must have irritated the self-appointed go-betweens. Yet even without her cooperation, the police could still keep Iwik in custody. Indonesian law allowed the police to detain a suspect for up to sixty days. When that period expired, Mulyono could request the province's public prosecutor to extend Iwik's imprisonment for another two months. Then, should the police require more time to prepare their case, the local court might grant another sixty-day extension. These regulations meant that the police could hold Sunarti's husband for up to six months before a trial. In the past, if they could present their clients as neither dangerous nor flight risks, Triyandi, Eko, and Djufri could persuade the police to release them into their custody. Iwik's case was clearly not as simple as that.

To Sunarti, Iwik's arrest and incarceration made no sense. "How could he kill a person – when he doesn't even have the guts to cut the head off a chicken?" she asked journalists who visited her in Panasan. But if her husband did not have the courage to resist what the authorities had apparently planned for them without their knowledge, she certainly did.

"Even though we're poor, we will not allow ourselves to be victims," Sunarti would declare to reporters. "Even a worm squirms when it is stepped on!" But the only weapons she could use in her battle against the authorities happened to be the same ones the journalists themselves used, which was words and paper. Within a week of her husband's arrest, Sunarti had posted letters to Mulyono, Jogjakarta's governor, the armed forces commander, the National Commission on Human Rights, and even the fearsome and distant Suharto. Her missive to the Jogjakarta police chief begged:

> My husband does not know anything about the murder...
> I ask for the Chief's humble mercy...grant my request to release Iwik from his detention...My husband's health is of great concern because he has chronic asthma...My husband, if imprisoned, cannot support us...His child always asks about his father.

To her surprise, one of her letters received an answer. On 28 October 1996, the National Commission on Human Rights announced that three of its commissioners would look into the arrest and treatment of Iwik. For both Sunarti and Udin's colleagues, the Commission's involvement in the case was wonderful news. In Suharto's Indonesia, the existence of a National Commission on Human Rights was an anomaly. The Cold War had accelerated Sukarno's downfall and assisted his rise to power, but Suharto had lingered too long. In the more liberal international environment after the fall of the Berlin Wall, authoritarians like Suharto seemed like dinosaurs. They embarrassed their Western backers with their crude attempts at control and their frequent crackdowns on their populations. After the Indonesian military massacred hundreds of Timorese demonstrators in a dusty cemetery in East Timor's capital, Dili, Suharto's government was forced to form a human rights commission to deflect and assuage international criticism of his human rights record.

However, the Commission's initial composition – retired military officers, senior bureaucrats and government-salaried academics – augured poorly for its capability or independence. Yet to the surprise of most cynics, by the time of Udin's killing, the Commission had become one of the few Indonesian institutions to oppose the government's insistence on having the last word on describing the national reality. The Commission rejected the official military casualty list from the government-supported invasion of the PDI headquarters as to be so low as to be laughable. Many more people died in the violence, it declared, than the military had recorded. In the Marsinah case, the Commission strongly supported the nine suspects' statements that they had been tortured to confess to the watch-factory worker's rape and murder. The commissioners urged the courts to reject their forced confessions. Despite the Commission's identity as part of the Suharto government, its image of independence had given it and its commissioners a certain respectability.

That, however, was little more than an image. The Commission had no formal power to achieve its avowed mission of promoting human rights. Suharto knew his international critics well enough to understand that Western governments had neither the patience nor the attention to care whether his Commission was effective. Even as it paraded the Commission as a symbol of Suharto's commitment to human rights, his government systematically undercut the body's authority. The Commission had no legal power to compel officials or military personnel to testify or to turn over crucial information in human-rights abuse cases. Local police and military commanders would thus give commissioners the courtesy of a meeting, but would reveal no information about their activities. Perpetually understaffed and underfunded, the Commission also could not force any government agency or official to justify, explain, or change policies and actions. The limit of its authority was to issue "recommendations" on how Suharto's government could improve human-rights protections. Held on such a short leash, Indonesia's human-rights watchdog was all whine and no bite. Some of its commissioners used their position as a way to raise their public profile, so as to leverage themselves into positions in government that had real power. The Commission served a similar function as New Order parliamentary elections: a simulation of democratic values instead of a true manifestation.

But Iwik's lawyers hoped that the publicity that always accompanied the Commission's inspections could be put to use in Iwik's defense. "We will show them what we have," Djufri pledged *Bernas*. When the human-rights commissioners traveled to Jogja, the media unleashed a flood of front-page articles on the Iwik case, crowding out other provincial news from the front pages. The attention paid off. Once *Bernas* reported that the police claim that it had testimony from a parking attendant who had seen Udin giving a ride to a woman in front of the Bantul courthouse on the day before his beating, one of Udin's colleagues stepped forward to challenge it. Sumadiyono, a reporter for the *Jogja Post*, told *Bernas* that he had been Udin's passenger. He had made an appointment with Udin to travel together to research a story elsewhere in the *kabupaten*. The two men decided they would meet in front of the Bantul courthouse on 12 August around noon. He was certain of the time because he remembered hearing the town mosques sounding the call to noonday prayer as he rode away with Udin on the reporter's red Honda. The account directly contradicted the stories the police had circulated about Sunarti's supposed tryst with the journalist outside the courthouse. A credible defense case for Iwik was now building.

On 30 October, Heru, Ida, and others in the *Bernas* White Kijang team located the young prostitute who had been with Iwik the day of his arrest. They had traveled to Parangtritis to see if she would confirm what had happened the day Edy, Iwik, and the three Bantul detectives showed up at the Agung Inn. To the reporters, Retno spoke frankly about her profession. "I'm used to being with men, although I have just turned seventeen," she told them. With Iwik, she recalled, she had not been asked to offer her services. "Usually, my guests start seducing me right away and taking off their clothes," she said. But when she and Iwik entered the room that day, all he and Retno had shared was a genial conversation. "He told me his wife likes to sew," she said. "He also said that he wanted to open up a motorcycle dealership. If that plan succeeds, he promised he'd invite me to a celebration."

Emboldened by the Commission's presence, the Jogja journalists dared to approach the only man they had wanted to interview more than Sri Roso himself: the president's powerful kinsman, Noto Suwito. Despite Noto Suwito's role in the scandal surrounding Sri Roso's election, and the speculation about his possible involvement in the Udin killing, none of the Jogja journalists had yet succeeded in interviewing him. A few, such as Moko, had tried repeatedly to contact Noto Suwito but were always told by the Argomulyo village office that he was unavailable. Other reporters, including Heru himself, were simply afraid to approach such a potent individual. Questioning Noto Suwito seemed akin to interrogating Suharto. "He was a village chief, but he has the power of a president," was how Heru would describe the president's younger brother.

On 31 October, the fearless Ida and several reporters set off for Argomulyo. There, several villagers directed them to Noto Suwito's main house in his compound that covered several properties like a miniature *kraton*. The building appeared empty. When they went around to the back, they spotted a balding old man sanding down a wood chair.

"Is Noto Suwito here?" they asked the old man, who they assumed was a servant.

He looked up and stared at them intently for a moment.

"Oh, yes," he said. "But he still has a guest. Wait a bit. In a short while he should be done."

Then Ida noticed that the shabby-looking man had a huge, glittering ring on one finger. "Excuse me, sir," Ida ventured. "Are *you* Noto Suwito?"

The man answered: "Yes…I am."

The journalists unloaded their questions. They wanted Suharto's sibling to confirm that he had signed Sri Roso's promise to pay the Dharmais Foundation $428,000 in return for the *bupati*'s reelection.

"You could say it's my signature," Noto Suwito responded.

"Was that one billion rupiah ever paid?"

"What would the *bupati* use to pay it?" Noto Suwito explained. "These political problems are often made up," he continued. "They say things in the paper, but the reality is something different."

"The death of Udin was linked to this 'One Billion-Rupiah Promise.' Did *you* have any problems with him writing about it?"

"If I'm insulted in the papers, I let it be. My guide is this: rather than being judged by other people, I'm always followed by an angel who notes down what I do. Angels do that. Journalists…well, truth or lie, they just decide what they want to write."

"What's your hope for this Udin case?"

"I hope they quickly find the person who killed him."

The interview was interrupted by the departure of four men who seemed to be Noto Suwito's guests. The reporters recognized none of them, but each wore uniforms from one of the four branches of the Indonesian armed forces: the army, the navy, the air force, and the police. From the insignias on their shirts, all of the officers appeared to be of senior rank. Such was the power of the president's kin, the reporters marveled, that even generals and commanders sought him out in this rural, marginal area.

When the journalists took their leave, Noto Suwito called them back. "Here's a little something to buy something cold," he said as he drew a large wad of small bills out of his pocket.

"No, thank you," the young journalists replied. "We already have all that we need."

"Then be careful," he told them. "Be careful what you write."

※

The human rights commissioners left Jogja with a promise to present their report in a few days. By the end of October, however, Iwik's lawyers thought they had enough evidence on their own to persuade Chief Mulyono and the Jogjakarta police that pursuing Iwik would be pointless. The lawyers could present Sunarti's calendar and the signed statements that supported her alibi that she was nowhere near the Bantul courthouse on 12 August. Thanks to Udin's friends, a new witness, Sumadiyono, could also swear he had been the one riding with Udin on his motorcycle. Iwik's lawyers had also obtained a statement from the Bantul religious affairs office saying that a Bantul police detective had requested Sunarti's photo from them, which contradicted Edy's assertion that he had found the picture in Udin's wallet. One of Sunarti's childhood friends from Bantul told the police she had never seen Udin ever visit Sunarti. Iwik's neighbors in Panasan also told the police that the couple did not appear to have any marital problems. After one rare altercation, their next-door neighbor Heri recalled, Sunarti had told him: "I'm lucky to have Iwik for a husband." Even if the journalist had been having an affair – which Marsiyem continued to deny – Iwik's lawyers felt they could show police, prosecutors, and a Bantul court that the reporter was definitely not having an affair with Sunarti. So Iwik had no motive to kill Udin, whatever he had said to police in interrogation.

The lawyers explained that Iwik had been at home anyway in Sleman while Udin was being attacked in Bantul. The couple's neighbors could verify they had seen Iwik emerge from his home that night. Iwik's colleagues at Dymas also told the lawyers Iwik was one of the most introverted souls in the city. When he left the office, they said, he always went straight home. Although not many of his coworkers said they knew Iwik well – he kept mostly to himself, and spoke little – they knew for certain he could not be a martial arts expert nor could he have ever worked for the Indonesian marines.

Triyandi knew the police case was riddled with false and faulty information – mostly, the attorneys believed, from Detective Edy. The lawyers suggested that if the police sought a face-saving way out of the fiasco of arresting a wrong man, they could make Iwik a "witness" instead of the main suspect. After the lawyers had presented their research, Chief Detective Suko told them: "I don't have the authority to release him, but let me bring this information to my superiors." But Mulyono, the Jogjakarta Police Chief, had no intention of letting Edy's suspect go.

Mulyono's insistence on maintaining Iwik as the main and only suspect in the Udin murder fueled speculation among Jogja's journalists that continues to this day. The most popular explanation makes Mulyono part of the conspiracy behind Udin's death. But this theory's proponents base their conclusion solely on the fact that both Mulyono and Sri Roso are members of the armed forces, making the police chief guilty by association. Regardless of whatever relationship Mulyono may have had with the *bupati*, the Police District's newly-appointed police chief had staked his own honor when his department arrested Iwik. To admit error at this point and begin the investigation anew would be an unbearable embarrassment. In fact, pressure from the media and the lawyers made the proud police less and less likely to retreat. As coverage of the case and criticism of the police spilled onto Jogja's newspapers and airwaves daily, many officers resented the reporters' appropriation of the prerogatives of investigation. Instead of proceeding from the facts and the evidence, as they had been trained, some officers felt the prejudiced, anti-establishment press wanted to force on the department a suspect – Sri Roso – based primarily on their unsupported suspicions. "Everything was hearsay," one detective on the case would later complain.

The Jogjakarta investigator Hadi believed he had obtained decisive evidence of Iwik's guilt. The detective had sent several of the items seized from the driver's home for forensic analysis at the police laboratories. On 25 October 1996, the Semarang serology laboratory reported the result: that technicians had found traces of O-type blood on Iwik's brown leather belt, denim jacket and the metal pipe retrieved from Dymas. Iwik's own blood had tested as AB, while O had been Udin's blood type. On 26 October, Chief Detective Suko signed a second warrant for Hadi to search Iwik's house. The detective retrieved a watch and the wallet he had earlier returned to Sunarti. Two days later, a police forensic team announced they had located more traces of blood on the timepiece. Once again, the blood type was O, the same as the victim's.

The forensic evidence was at odds with Iwik's alibi. The Dymas driver said he had been fast asleep during the murder. But here was the evidence: blood of the same type as Udin's all over his belongings. With the forensic laboratory's report and Iwik's confession, Hadi had fulfilled the minimum that Indonesian criminal law required for a conviction – two of out of the five categories of evidence. His superior Suko informed the Jogjakarta public prosecutor's office that Iwik was now the only suspect in Udin's murder. "We have found the same blood as the victim's on the metal pipe and the belt. The suspect has also confessed," National Police Chief Dibyo told journalists in Jakarta. "I'm surprised. Why is the public making such a big issue of this?"

Dibyo might have forgotten that several months earlier, the Bantul police had in their possession a sample of Udin's blood, in the bag Edy had taken from the reporter's family. Two *Bernas* reporters, Moko and Ndari, had seen Edy with Udin's blood. Many police stations throughout Indonesia do not have special procedures for storing evidence. Each detective is expected to keep and protect the evidence obtained in his cases. That Edy – or someone else in the police – might have tainted Iwik's possessions with Udin's blood was a possibility that had not escaped the attention of Udin's colleagues or Iwik's defense team. In late October, Legal Aid's Budi Hartono wrote the police to say he was "seriously concerned that the blood had been misused." Triyandi eschewed any pretense at polite indirection. He thundered to *Bernas*:

"We suspect that the blood was intentionally spattered on the evidence."

Unrefrigerated, Udin's blood would have quickly decomposed in Indonesia's hot climate. Ten weeks after the reporter's death, when Iwik was arrested, not much of it could have been useful. Yet the bag of blood *had* been in Edy's possession. Its current whereabouts were unknown. Even if blood from that bag had not been used, O is a common blood type: Sunarti's blood is O, as is Triyandi's. Anyone could have been the source of the blood on Iwik's possessions. "I'm just an ordinary person, but I have a thought," Udin's father Wagiman speculated to reporters. "Is it possible that Udin's blood that the police once borrowed was spread onto the pipe and belt? If my guess is right, then what kind of fate do little people like me have? We will only be victims." In any case, the evidence did not make Marsiyem doubt what she had seen the night of the murder: a man in a red bandanna who looked nothing at all like Iwik. "At the beginning of this case, my hopes were high," she told *Bernas* reporters. "Especially since when he was alive, Udin was very close to the Bantul police."

Despite law enforcement's success in making a case for his prosecution, Iwik's lawyers still had given Iwik a credible defense. The once malleable suspect became more confident. On 26 October, Hadi questioned Iwik again to reconfirm details of his confession. For the first time, Iwik stopped saying that he had gone to Samalo "to teach Udin a lesson." He told the detective instead that on 13 August, he had gone home and went to bed. He rose in the middle of the night because his neighbors had been discussing a missing motorcycle.

"After sitting for a moment in front of my house, I went inside and slept with my wife," he recounted to Hadi. The record of his interrogation on that day ends shortly after that statement.

Although Iwik's answer did not yet amount to a complete retraction of his earlier admissions, it seemed a promising start. His lawyers felt they were finally getting the message through to their client: only if he told the police the truth, could they begin to help him. After that interrogation, Iwik met his family during one of their regular prison visits. Sunarti's eyes misted over as she hugged him. She congratulated and encouraged him.

"Just be patient," she said. "Endure. God will show the way to people who are true." Later, she would tell her friends, the reporters, "May God give us the most blessings, and punish those who have slandered us. I hope they go to hell."

⁓⁓

Iwik's retreat from his admission made the central pillar of the police case – his confession – unsteady. Mulyono and his deputies alternately blamed the news-hungry media, the uncooperative Marsiyem, or Iwik's crafty lawyers for sabotaging their investigation and influencing the suspect. Hadi found Udin's widow particularly frustrating. "At the beginning, the investigation went smoothly," he would later complain. "But after this witness said that he wasn't the murderer, there was a change in his attitude." He was convinced that Iwik had been sincere when he first confessed. "He told his story honestly and clearly," Hadi would say. "Not just in front of the police, but in front of his lawyers. He gave the truth fluently. Fluently. From the beginning, he regretted what he had done. He had no intention to kill. His intent was to teach a lesson."

The police were right in one respect. The lawyers and the media had indeed joined forces against the police. They had put aside their institutional or intergenerational conflicts and mutual suspicion to ensure that an innocent man would not go to jail for Udin's murder while the real killer roamed free. In November, the PWI team, Legal Aid, Legal Defenders, and several of the anti-establishment *Bernas* White Kijang reporters gathered at Triyandi's office to attempt to dismember even further the police case. The PWI's Asril had suggested that the journalists and lawyers clock the time a Vespa took to travel the twenty kilometers between Iwik's home in Sleman and the Krisna Photo Studio in Bantul. Asril and several of Triyandi's staff drove six different makes of motorcycle through several routes between the two hamlets. They found that even the fastest motorcycle took a full hour for the round trip. A Vespa needed at least two hours to complete the journey. If Iwik had used his 1977 Italian-made motorcycle to travel to Udin's home on 13 August, he could not have returned home earlier than 1:00 a.m. the following morning, long after the time his neighbors said they had seen him emerge from his house. Iwik would also have had trouble starting the motorcycle without waking up his wife, mother-in-law, and son. The last two had also been sleeping on the floor beside the front door. They would have remembered had the Dymas driver tried to wheel the Vespa out of the house on top of them.

Both the lawyers and the reporters continued to query the identities of Marsiyem's suspicious visitors. Triyandi wondered whether one of the two businessmen might actually have been the "Jendra" Iwik had met at the Queen of the South. When the lawyer showed Iwik a magazine with Nizar's photo, Iwik had nodded and identified the subject as Franky's "boss." Triyandi became convinced that at the trial, the police would present a different "Jendra" to protect Mulyono's business associate. "They'll say it wasn't Nizar, but someone else," Triyandi told a *Bernas* reporter. "I feel there's an effort in that direction." When reporters contacted Nizar's companion for his reactions to Triyandi's speculation, Bashari insisted: "That's a lie – a big lie." Nonetheless, the controversy over the true identity of "Jendra" dogged the case all the way to the trial.

Relations between the lawyers and the police became brittle and icy. If Triyandi's lawyers had clients who had civil complaints, police officials would drag their feet on signing the police reports necessary before the firm could file a claim. In the past, when Legal Defenders handled criminal cases, the firm could usually persuade the Jogjakarta police to lift their clients' pretrial detentions quickly. Now, their requests for clemency went unanswered, even in cases pending in other police districts, such as Central Java. Such was the loyalty in the corps that the enemy of one police department was the adversary of all. Triyandi did little to relieve the tension when he demanded publicly that National Police Chief Dibyo fire Mulyono. For a while, reporters feared that the

Jogjakarta police would make Iwik's lawyers suspects themselves for slander, a criminal offense under Indonesian law.

Both Marsiyem's and Iwik's lawyers sensed that police surveillance and harassment of their homes and offices had increased to more intrusive levels. Both Legal Aid and Legal Defenders received threatening phone calls daily from strangers. Unknown men loitered in front of their offices, mixing in with the regular crowd of indigent clients and journalists. Budi told *Bernas* that some one would call his home to ask: "Are you bored of living?" Budi, inured to these scare tactics, would just laugh in response. Djufri, however, grew concerned enough about his safety to send his wife to live with her parents. His prediction had come true: the firm had become famous, but perhaps too well-known for his security or comfort. Still, the lawyers received dozens of letters of support from the public, and the firm was becoming known nationally. During this period, Triyandi visited his home island of Sumatra and found that many people there knew him as the lead defense counsel for Udin's suspected killer.

But within the police force, the arrest of Iwik had opened an unacknowledged rift. Although the entire hierarchy was careful to preserve the outward appearance of unity, within the corps the case had caused fractures: over the legality of Iwik's arrest, over the conduct of the investigation, and over the proper handling of the press. Some of the detectives assigned to the case confessed their unease about their suspect to Iwik's lawyers. "This is the Bantul precinct's mistake. Our mistake is that we accepted it," one detective complained to Djufri. Rusdihardjo, the chief detective of the national police in Jakarta, publicly criticized Edy's handling of the arrest, especially his plying Iwik with alcohol and prostitutes. Rusdihardjo called Edy's tactics "not exactly unprofessional, but less than ethical."

The disagreements came to a head in November, when Edy's superior, Bantul Police Chief Adé Sudarban, who had so strenuously defended Sri Roso in August, received an unexpected transfer to a position in remote Irian Jaya, the Indonesian half of New Guinea. Adé had just assumed the Bantul posting in May 1996, so his tour of duty had lasted barely six months. The reassignment shocked Adé, who, as witnesses told *Bernas*, had received the order while visiting Jogjakarta police headquarters to report on the progress of the Iwik investigation. At the hastily arranged ceremony marking the transfer of office to his successor, *Bernas* photographer Tarko snapped a picture of Adé's eyes watering with tears.

Initially, the transfer perplexed the local media. The national police's official explanation that Adé was due for a routine rotation was unconvincing. One senior police officer told a journalist that Adé had been "overenthusiastic" in prosecuting the investigation against Iwik. When Adé's successor was sworn in, the fog began to clear. The new Bantul Police Chief was Yotje Mende, a good-looking officer friendly with Jogja journalists. In a previous stint at Jogjakarta police headquarters, Yotje had earned high marks from local journalists for being particularly accessible and helpful to crime reporters. The local branch of the PWI had even awarded him the title "Most Sympathetic Police Officer." Before he received his transfer back to Java, Yotje had been working for police intelligence on his home island, at the Sulawesi port of Ujung Pandang, before its name-change back to Makassar. The Jogja media now believed that the police bigwigs in Jakarta had replaced the inexpert Adé with the slicker Yotje to help bridge the gap of perception between the police and the media and dampen the raging public criticism and skepticism about the authorities' intentions in the Udin murder investigation.

Despite the new Bantul police chief's excellent reputation with the press, the case had simply become too great a crisis for Yotje to exercise effective damage control. His superior Mulyono continued to reject any suggestion that Edy had arrested the wrong man, even after 5 November, when the secretary-general of the National Commission on Human Rights declared that they had concluded the police's refusal to investigate other leads and suspects had violated Iwik's rights. The authorities' insistent rejection of any facts that challenged their theory, the commissioner said, constituted "actions against the principle of equality before the law and a fair trial."

Mulyono's response was swift and curt. Chain-smoking through his own press conference in Jogja the following day, the police chief dismissed the commission's opinion. He was personally convinced of the suspect's guilt. He had heard Iwik's confession, and the case his men had assembled was based on incontrovertible scientific evidence. The police had over a dozen witnesses to support its case. The controversies stirred by the journalists had only managed to set back his target date for submitting Iwik's dossier to the public prosecutor for a time, but had not halted his department's efforts. "We are continuing our investigation," he declared. "The only thing that can stop it is a judge's order."

Yet at that same conference, Mulyono launched a new scandal. The police chief had staunchly defended Edy's tactics from the detective's detractors, insisting that the arrest of Iwik had been consistent with proper police techniques. But when a reporter asked if he knew what had really happened to the blood Edy had borrowed from Udin's family, Mulyono replied that as far as he knew, Edy's men had disposed of the blood long before Iwik's arrest. Apparently, he recounted, Edy and his team had thrown half the reporter's blood into the sea at Parangtritis as part of some kind of ritual, and then disposed of the rest at the Bantul police station. "If the blood of a victim is thrown into the Southern Ocean," the police chief explained nonchalantly, "it speeds up the process of solving the crime. That's what people say around here."

Mulyono gave the Jogja press another reason to doubt the credibility of the police. Detectives had disposed of possible evidence in an ongoing murder inquiry in a way that had clearly crossed a professional boundary. *Bernas* ran a critical editorial cartoon showing a petulant Nyai Roro Kidul rising out of the sea and shouting at police officers on the shore carrying a bottle labeled "Udin's blood." "What is this? A blood offering?" the caption read. "Just send it to the forensic laboratory!" Local *dukun* even criticized the police for performing the wrong ritual. "If you want to find the murderer, you throw in the clothes of the victim, not his blood," one explained to *Bernas*. "Only people who want to get rid of something throw items into the Southern Ocean." When Edy hurled Udin's blood into the waters, this *dukun* concluded, "the effect...was either to hide whoever committed the crime, or to curse the victim." A better place for Udin's blood, *Bernas*' own mystical advice columnist Suryanto would later explain, was the peak of Mount Merapi. To bring an object of some importance up the mountain means to ask for enlightenment. To plunge it into the sea's depths is to lose the truth in darkness.

Mulyono's revelation had other repercussions. Udin's family felt offended at the way the reporter's blood had been handled. In August, they had turned it over to Edy for safekeeping even though Wagiman insisted that his son's remains should have been respectfully put to rest in his grave. Marsiyem wondered what this Parangtritis ritual had to do with this murder. On 7 November 1996, the day after Mulyono's revelation, the family's lawyer, Budi, announced that the family would sue the Jogjakarta police. A threatened lawsuit did not intimidate the Jogjakarta police chief the slightest bit. On 14 November, Mulyono told journalists: "The investigation has been completed. There are no other suspects. All the evidence leads to Dwi Sumaji's involvement. All the police have to do is submit him to the public prosecutor."

But the publicity surrounding Iwik's arrest had made the public prosecutor's office cautious. Five days after Hadi submitted Iwik's thick dossier, which contained transcripts of Iwik's confessions, witness accounts and the forensic laboratory reports, the prosecutor's office sent the package back, with instructions that the detective had to supply not just the minimum required by law – the confession and forensic evidence – but clearer identifications of Iwik from key witnesses, expert testimony to support the forensic reports, and a staged reconstruction of the crime with the suspect's participation. In other words, Hadi had to obtain all the feasible evidence. The public prosecutors wanted to take no chances at trial.

To secure the expert testimony the prosecutors had requested, Hadi's superiors decided to pay for a technique rarely used in Indonesia and never before in Jogjakarta: DNA fingerprinting. Even in developed countries, the process at the time was only little more than a decade old. In 1984, a British geneticist had noted that in many spots on a strand of human genetic code, the same DNA base pair would repeat itself. These "tandem repeats" seem to have no apparent function except as filler, and might have been considered genetic static, had the scientist not noticed that the length of these repeats varies from person to person. By isolating these chemical stutters and locating where they occur on a ribbon of DNA, all DNA strands could be assigned unique identities. With the help of studies of how often those stuttering strands appeared in the general population, a technician could calculate the probability that more than one individual would have the same markers in the same locations. So a sample of blood, saliva, semen, or any human by-product recovered from a crime scene could be matched to a specific individual within a calculable degree of certainty.

The national police sent Udin's brown trousers, Iwik's denim jacket, leather belt and wristwatch, and scrapings from the metal pipe, to Strathclyde University in Glasgow, Scotland, where the Semarang laboratory's chief serology expert had been educated. The police intended the technique to settle any questions the lawyers might present at trial on whether any of the blood on the wristwatch, belt, jacket and metal pipe had indeed come from the victim. But on 15 November 1996, Indonesia's sole Japanese-trained forensic DNA expert, Djaya Suryaatmadja, told *Bernas* in an interview that even if the tests all turned out positive for Udin's blood and DNA type, then "all we know that on this metal instrument there is Udin's blood. However, we cannot say whether this pipe was used to kill Udin."

Hadi scheduled Iwik to participate in a police lineup on 25 November. By then, the driver had been in detention for over one month. Iwik, who had never been cited for even a traffic violation, now had intimate knowledge of the world inside the lockup. In Jogjakarta's police headquarters, his companions in jail were accused thieves, swindlers, brawlers, and burglars. Like the Palembang pickpocket Hari Raga, many were repeat residents. Hari had been accused of crimes in two jurisdictions and was awaiting trial in one of them. When he had been arrested, Hari told Iwik, the police took him out of his cell and put a bullet into his leg. His fellow inmates told Iwik this sort of thing happened all the time in incarceration.

One of the more colorful characters Iwik met in his cell was a stick-thin confidence artist named Supriyadi. "Yadi" had been arrested for an old scam: borrowing friends' motorcycles to duplicate their keys so he and an accomplice could later steal the cycles. In the holding cell, Yadi entertained his fellow detainees with feats of minor illusions. He could wrap a matchbox in paper and turn it into a tasty snack. Yadi could also turn the shiny paper lining inside cigarette boxes into a crisp ten-thousand rupiah note, an illusion that would last about fifteen minutes. Once, Yadi asked the detective Hadi to hold an egg while Yadi swallowed a needle. When the detective cracked the egg and opened it, the needle lay inside. "In Java, what is impossible can be possible," Iwik would later marvel.

One boring afternoon in the cell, Yadi drew Iwik into a game of prediction. The swindler sketched a star and two other symbols. One of the symbols, he told Iwik, meant that the driver would go to jail. The other signified that he would be released. A star symbolized both possibilities: that Iwik would be imprisoned for a time, but would ultimately win his freedom. But Yadi could not tell him how long this wait in jail might be – it might be months, years, perhaps even decades. The confidence artist murmured some incantations and broke the egg. Inside the shell, drawn in a fine outline, was a star, the symbol of Iwik's uncertain future.

On the day of the lineup, officers asked Yadi, Hari, and two other inmates to stand with Iwik against a wall and face a glass panel. Behind the glass stood Marsiyem, Sujarah, Budi, and Iwik's three lawyers, who had only learned that their client was to be placed in a lineup when journalists called them. The police had placed Iwik, the tallest and the lightest-skinned of the five men, in the middle of the line. Although each of the detainees wore the same clothing, Iwik stood out like the main pole of a circus tent. Yet after staring at the lineup for a quarter of an hour, both Marsiyem and Sujarah shook their heads. In the statement Udin's widow signed after the exercise, she attested: "Of the five, not one looks like that man who came on 13 August to my house."

That day also coincided with one of Sunarti's regular visits to Iwik in detention. This became the first occasion when the two women in the saga of Udin's murder had met each other in person. On her way into the police headquarters for the lineup, Udin's widow bumped into Iwik's wife. Upon seeing each other's faces for the first time in person, both women burst into tears, and ran to put their arms around each other. They embraced for several minutes, before police officers, visibly discomfited by the outburst of emotion, led them into separate rooms. "Marsiyem was thinking: how did I become a victim like this?" Sunarti would later explain their spontaneous outpouring of their mutual frustration. "I was also thinking: how did I come to be in this place?"

Hadi scheduled a reconstruction of the murder, starring his suspect. In most murder cases in Indonesia, police customarily ask suspects and witnesses to reenact their actions at the crime scene. With the suspected murderer under close guard, police officials take him through the steps that led to the fatal act, as witnesses play the same role they had at the time of the crime. Although a reconstruction is not always required, a reenactment also helps police confirm their theories about how the crime was committed, fixes and clarifies witness recollections, and gives the prosecution additional material to present at trial. Bantul detectives had first tried reconstructing the Udin murder all by themselves. Police officers played all the roles, except for those of the noodle sellers and Sujarah, who were on hand to reenact their activities on the night before and the night of the murder. But the prosecutors had deemed that in-house effort insufficient. They demanded Iwik's actual participation.

So another reconstruction was scheduled on 29 November 1996, which would involve the suspect, the victim's family and the key witnesses. It was to happen at night, at the same time the assault had occurred many months earlier. But that day, the tip-off that Udin's murder would be reenacted drew observers and onlookers from all over the country. "A sea of walking people filled Parangtritis Road," *Bernas* reported. "Traffic could only crawl, because the right and left shoulders of the street were filled with people, cars, and motorcycles…from Bandung, Jogjakarta, Wonosobo, Jakarta, and Semarang." So many people had gathered to watch the show that police could not enter the area. The authorities had to call off the reconstruction.

By early December, Hadi was running out of time. On 2 December, the public prosecutor's office had given him two weeks to revise the evidence dossier. But Hadi's suspect would no longer confess, and his forensic evidence was still being evaluated in Scotland. The stubborn Marsiyem continued to reject Iwik as the killer, and the public spotlight prevented police from putting together a proper reconstruction. On 3 December, Iwik's lawyers sent another request for the investigation to be dropped. The attorneys' position had grown significantly stronger. The two-month period during which the police could hold Iwik was soon to expire, and without a proper dossier, the police would have a hard time persuading the public prosecutor to extend Iwik's detention.

On 4 December, without informing either Iwik's or Marsiyem's lawyers, Hadi summoned the three noodle-sellers Nur Sulaiman, Ponikem, and Ayik to see Iwik in a lineup. This time, Iwik wore a white helmet like the one the noodle-sellers had seen their peculiar visitor wear the night before the murder. He stood not among his fellow detainees, but with other police officers also wearing white motorcycle helmets.

The two older ladies were a lot more accommodating of the police than Marsiyem. They readily picked Iwik out of the lineup as the man they had met on 12 August. When detectives showed them the metal pipe they had taken from Dymas, Ponikem and Nur Sulaiman agreed it was very similar to the pipe they had seen that same evening. Only Nur

Sulaiman's schoolteacher daughter Ayik refused to play along with the police. She kept telling the detectives that she had only seen the back of the killer's head on the night of 13 August. When reporters learned what the two noodle sellers had done, they demanded an explanation from the old women. "The police said that man was the killer," Nur Sulaiman said helplessly to a *Bernas* reporter. "What do you do? How can I say something different?" With their help, Hadi had secured his witness confirmation.

Iwik faced Hadi on 6 December, for his sixth round of interrogation. Hadi, who knew he had only a week left before he might have to release his suspect, was under particular pressure to reconfirm Iwik's confession for the prosecutor. At the time, Iwik's passions were running high. The Jogjakarta police had strictly curtailed his meetings with his family. Sunarti's previous visits had already been limited to periods of five minutes. Now, she was told, she could not see her husband at all. Iwik decided to stop answering Hadi's questions.

"During the 21 October questioning you explained that you beat Syafruddin using a piece of iron pipe," Hadi asked, hoping to encourage Iwik to recall his earlier confessions. "How many times did you hit him in the stomach and head?"

"I will not explain or answer," Iwik responded.

"How did you beat or assault Syafruddin? Please explain."

"I don't want to explain."

Djufri, who was accompanying his client that day, saw the detective stand up to halt the questioning. "That's it, Iwik," Hadi said. "You're making this difficult. You, Djufri!" He addressed the lawyer. "You're influencing him." The detective told Iwik to stand and recite the phrase: *Astagfirullah*. In Arabic, the phrase meant: "God forgive me."

"Hadi..." Djufri interrupted.

"Don't get involved, Djufri," the lawyer later would recall the detective's response. "Your function here is to accompany the suspect. You cannot answer his questions or influence his answers."

"Hadi, I'm not only here to listen," Djufri responded. "My function is to defend my client. If he does not want to answer, just write down that he does not want to answer!"

The tinder in the two men's voices caught fire. Hadi had Iwik returned to his cell before taking Djufri behind the station. Curious officers poked their heads out of office windows to see the commotion. Djufri was taller and heavier than the short detective. But Hadi was on his home turf. The detective would have a different recollection of this incident. Instead of an argument, he would explain, "We spoke like adults. I wasn't angry. In the end, he was insulted. I was used to the ways of East Java, which are different from Jogja. There, you say something and it's over. In Central Java, it's over but there are repercussions…I didn't yet know how the Jogja police did things, I didn't yet know Djufri. We didn't yet know each other." Before anything could happen, however, the evening call to prayer sounded, and the confrontation hastily ended. After that day, Hadi would never get another confession out of Iwik.

The Jogjakarta police informed Iwik's lawyers that there would be another reconstruction on 9 December 1996. This time, the police prepared for the crowds by having patrolmen cordon off an area in front of the Krisna Photo Studio. Growling officers forced journalists back some thirty meters from the scene. When a few reporters tried to sidle their way in, police officers threatened to hit them or break their cameras. Ida and *Bernas* photographer Tarko argued with the police before retreating to the roof of a parked car to observe the reconstruction. Below them, the atmosphere in Samalo was like an all-night village fair. Peddlers spread their wares along the ground and snack sellers pulled their carts through the crowds. Self-appointed parking attendants had appeared to herd the motorcycles and cars in exchange for coins to guard the vehicles. The throng of people spilled onto the damp fields. The day after, the paddies were littered with abandoned rubber slippers.

That morning, police had instructed Iwik and the witnesses on what they were expected to do during the reconstruction. First, the group had to reenact the events of 12 August, when the suspect supposedly first came to Samalo. Then the police would direct a reconstruction of the night of the murder itself. During that second part of the exercise, Dymas driver Iwik was told he would have to knock on the door of the Krisna Photo Studio. A policewoman would answer the door instead of Marsiyem. (Udin's widow, through her lawyers, had declined to participate.) Iwik's attorneys were concerned about the whole operation. "The reconstruction would finalize the dossier," Djufri fretted. If the reconstruction went well, it would give the public prosecutor more ammunition to expend in court. But because their client was still in police custody, the lawyers could not refuse to allow Iwik's involvement, as Marsiyem had refused to participate.

At 10:30 p.m., a convoy of cars from the police station snaked into Samalo. When the attorney's car reached the front of Udin's home, Eko and Djufri descended with Iwik. As Triyandi surveyed the gathered hundreds, he noticed several men clutching large stones. They seemed prepared for trouble. The façade of gaiety, he realized, could quickly turn ugly. Triyandi moved to the side to speak to the Bantul Police Chief Yotje about the security situation, as several police officers took places beside and behind Iwik to prepare for the reenactment. They pushed Dymas' hapless driver towards Udin's front door. Iwik had to knock on the door just like the man in the red bandanna had done the night he killed the journalist.

As three officers nudged him, Iwik heard his name screamed by the crowd. Someone shrieked at the police: "How could you arrest someone who didn't do anything?" The weeks of detention, the midnight threats, Edy's broken promises, and his own stupidity had led him to this point, a point where Iwik, who had never hurt anyone in his life, was now playing the role of a murderer before hundreds of people.

Iwik heard a shout from Eko. "Iwik, were you really here?"

"No!" Iwik answered, in a long, moaning cry. The driver struggled free of the cordon of officers. Eko grabbed him to fend off the approaching police. When the police started to move on the lawyer, Eko pushed his client toward Djufri, who clutched Iwik's arm and pulled him toward their car. The police ran after them onto the road. "No, you can't do this! It can't be done!" Djufri shouted as officers tried to grab his client. Iwik, it seemed, had found a dramatic time to show he could no longer accept the role he had been lured into playing. In October, Edy had promised that he and his family would be protected and that Iwik would receive a reward from a high Bantul official. Edy's boss, "Jendra," had also promised him a job, a car, and a house. Edy's other boss, Mulyono, had told him he could go home. Then they threw him in prison for two months, where had been threatened, bullied, and manipulated. He had had enough.

His lawyers thrust the hysterical Iwik back into the car. Triyandi slapped him on the cheek and told him to repeat God's name several times to calm him. No amount of threats or cajoling from the police could now persuade Iwik to emerge and rejoin the reconstruction. So, just as they had during their first reconstruction, police officers had to assume all the roles once again, with Sujarah and the noodle sellers helpfully reprising theirs once more. Now, since neither Iwik nor Marsiyem were involved, the reconstruction had become another farcical failure.

In Jakarta, National Police Chief Dibyo blamed Iwik's lawyers for sabotaging the operation. Yet despite the botched reconstruction, the police received some good news. The Scottish academic who had tested the samples of Iwik's belongings reported he had found DNA bearing the same markers on Udin's trousers, the metal pipe, and Iwik's watch and belt buckle. He could not say, however, if all four blood traces came from the same individual because no DNA database existed for Indonesians. If the crime had occurred among Caucasians, the expert said, he could declare that it was ninety-three times more likely the DNA on all four items came from a single source than from several. But if the crime had happened in Japan, it would only be twenty-eight times more likely. So without an appropriate database describing how often such DNA markers appear in the Indonesian population, the DNA fingerprinting results were ambiguous at best.

But the cautious conclusions were enough for the Indonesian police.

The blood placed Iwik at the murder scene. On 12 December, Dibyo announced happily: "The blood came back with positive results." The following day, Hadi resubmitted Iwik's dossier to the public prosecutors. The reconstruction may have failed, and Marsiyem still a stubborn non-participant, but the police now had, in addition to Iwik's earlier confessions, forensic evidence strengthened by foreign expert analysis as well as positive identifications of Iwik by the two noodle sellers Nur Sulaiman and Ponikem. All this meant the police could now present prosecutors with four of the five required categories of evidence. This should be enough for a conviction.

The formal fulfillment of the prosecutors' requirements relaxed the need to hold Iwik in detention. By mid-December, Iwik's fellow detainees were telling him that he would soon be allowed to leave his prison. If the public prosecutor had not extended Iwik's incarceration by then, they informed him, the police would soon release him. One night, Iwik dreamed he was signing stacks of papers. Sure enough, on 17 December, nearly two months after his arrest, a policeman escorted Iwik out of his cell to see Triyandi, Eko, and Djufri to sign some documents. When Iwik asked what these papers meant, his lawyers explained that these were the permits lifting his detention. One of them said: "Iwik, it's time to go home."

CHAPTER 10

Sorcerers and Mystics

ON THE DAY of Iwik's release, 17 December 1996, Sunarti felt she had a premonition as well. When she woke that morning, she started tidying up their tiny house in Panasan. She swept the bare cement floor, dusted their few pieces of furniture, and ironed Iwik's clothes. She had this feeling, she would later explain, that everything needed to be neat and clean in case her husband returned, even though she herself did not know when that would happen.

At noontime, a man showed his face at her door. He told her, in a secretive tone: "Come with me. Bring Bimo, too." Sunarti reassured her family that she knew this person, an employee of Iwik's lawyers. Once she reached Triyandi's office, the lawyers' staff ushered her and Bimo into a back room. As she passed through the building, she spotted several dozen waiting journalists. Then she saw her husband emerge from a back hallway. This was the first time since October she had seen him outside the prison. Sunarti immediately burst into tears. She rushed over and hugged Iwik tightly. The Dymas driver went pale and began to sob quietly. Bimo approached him and shyly tugged at his sleeve. "Don't go away again, okay," his son told him.

The assembled reporters clapped and cheered at the sight of the family's reunion. Sunarti asked the lawyers if she could call her neighbors. As she held the receiver close so she could reveal the surprise she had found waiting for her at Triyandi's office, she could hear her neighbors sobbing and shouting on the other end of the line. While his wife shared the news of his release, Iwik answered the reporters' questions. The journalists wanted to know how he felt about his regained freedom. He told them he was still overwhelmed. His mind, it seemed, was still in prison, wondering what had happened to the food he had just ordered not long before his lawyers appeared with his release. At the moment, he told them, he was only looking forward to a good rest. For two months, his back had not felt the pillowed embrace of a mattress.

There was a reason Iwik had met reporters at his lawyers' office instead of outside the Jogjakarta police headquarters. Triyandi and the lawyers had made a deal with the police. Journalists were savvy enough to know that Iwik's pretrial detention was nearing its natural expiration. Many had flocked to the headquarters to catch what they hoped would be the suspect's triumphant exit from two months of imprisonment. But Chief Mulyono did not want pictures of his suspect, with hands raised high in victory on the front steps of police headquarters, emblazoned across the city's papers.

The police had enough worries that day without the added embarrassment of a media circus. That very morning, the public prosecutor's office had returned Iwik's dossier to Hadi. The assembled case, although much more substantial, still left the prosecutors dissatisfied. The key witness Marsiyem had still not identified Iwik as the killer, and Iwik had still not taken part in a proper reconstruction. This was the second time the prosecutor's office had sent back the case file to the detective. To avoid further loss of face, Mulyono had asked Triyandi and his lawyers to be discreet in removing Iwik from the police premises.

Triyandi, Eko, and Djufri agreed. To divert the media's attention, the police called a press conference elsewhere in the headquarters. As the lawyers and their freed client left the building, Djufri tucked Iwik's head under his jacket and strode swiftly into a car. The two drove out of the police compound through a back exit, while Triyandi and Eko left in their own vehicle, which the journalists followed. Once the lawyers had shaken the media, they met up with Djufri and Iwik.

Some of the reporters felt betrayed by the lawyers' face-saving deal with Mulyono. "Why did they have to sneak around?" Heru would later wonder. But other conditions of the agreement the lawyers had forged with the police would turn out to be far more controversial. In exchange for the police dropping any future requests to the prosecutors or the courts to renew Iwik's detention, the lawyers pledged not to sue the police for wrongful arrest. Under the criminal procedure code, Iwik's lawyers had the right, before their case went to trial, to take the Jogjakarta police force to court for violating arrest procedures. Once they had submitted such a pretrial motion, the court would have fixed a hearing date within three days and decided the matter within a week. If the attorneys successfully persuaded the court that Edy had not followed regulations when he arrested Iwik, the court could have revoked the driver's arrest as illegal. The question of why the lawyers surrendered one of their strongest weapons against the police would frustrate and baffle their allies among the local media.

Triyandi would later explain that he did not believe he and his associates could marshal an adequate case to win a pretrial motion. The rules for a pretrial motion are perversely restrictive. All the court could do was to examine if the formal requirements of an arrest had been followed. The police could maintain they had followed the law to the letter. An arrest warrant had been issued, which had been shown to Iwik's family. A judge could not consider Edy's alleged entrapment of Iwik, because complaints of police misconduct or maltreatment were considered a separate matter. In order to bring these conditions of Iwik's arrest to a court, Iwik's lawyers would need to file a separate complaint of their own alleging police misconduct. The police could then investigate Edy and prepare a dossier. Triyandi felt he could not expect the Jogjakarta police, at that time, to go after their trusted detective.

Triyandi had also been a lawyer long enough to know that such pretrial motions rarely succeed. Even though the courts are required to dispose of pretrial motions speedily, police and government officials do not feel bound to the same schedule. In some cases, authorities summoned to confirm the validity of an arrest have delayed their court appearances for so long that the main criminal trial had begun, rendering the pretrial motion useless. Also, compared to the United States, where courts struggle over whether to exclude evidence obtained illegally or to set a clearly guilty suspect free, Indonesian judges seem to have an established aversion to letting suspects go for "technical" violations. Since the establishment of the country's new criminal procedure code, according to one estimate, fewer than ten pretrial motions have succeeded. Triyandi believed a pretrial motion in Iwik's case would have ended in failure. So, in his calculations, to give up that privilege in exchange for a promise by the police not to revoke Iwik's freedom seemed to him the best of bargains.

Triyandi had promised the authorities that he would be Iwik's guardian until the driver's trial. His responsibility was to ensure that the accused did not leave the jurisdiction, but Triyandi's larger concern was the driver's own safety. Given the harassment the attorneys and their friends in the local media had experienced, Triyandi and his colleagues deemed their office more secure than the couple's home from the furtive forces that had gathered against them. So beginning the day of his release, Iwik and Sunarti had to spend nearly all their time at Triyandi's office on Pakuningratan Road. The couple planned to sleep in a converted storeroom at the back of the office for as long as necessary.

Iwik did return occasionally to Panasan. After visiting a neighboring village to attend an organized prayer of thanksgiving for his release, Iwik visited his home for the first time since his arrest. At the sight of his bare room, he felt a surge of joy and sadness. He took one of his beloved songbirds back to Pakuningratan to keep him company. Iwik perhaps understood he was still in a cage, like his pet. Until a judge formally returned his freedom to him, all that had happened was that his cell had become bigger.

Although Iwik's neighbors and many journalists knew that Iwik had moved temporarily to Pakuningratan Road, the press loyally refrained from revealing his whereabouts. In their reports, journalists referred vaguely to Iwik's location as the couple's "hiding place." There, Iwik and

Sunarti adopted a routine. Udin's accused killer received well-wishers and journalists during the day, while Sunarti helped with chores around the office, such as cooking for the firm's staff. Triyandi urged Iwik to read through his shelves of law books, which Iwik did, both to familiarize himself with Indonesian law as well as to figure out whether he had a claim to a small inheritance from a distant relative. The attorney also encouraged his client to accept invitations from student organizations to speak at local campuses. Aside from his desire to drum up more public sympathy for Iwik before the trial, Triyandi wanted his client, through addressing small groups of students, to develop the confidence required to face large audiences, such as the one he would see at his own trial. The plan was a moderate success. The constant exposure to enthusiastic and idealistic youngsters reduced some of Iwik's innocent introversion. "Before this, I was quiet," he would later explain. "Now, speaking in front of hundreds is something I'm used to."

Iwik, however, never became accustomed to his notoriety as Central Java's most famous scapegoat. On the narrow back streets of Jogja, people he had never met somehow knew him by name. A short trip to the city mosque meant enduring some stranger hollering his name from the other side of the street, while a stroll to a nearby store brought on a flock of curious stares and knowing grins. Iwik dearly missed his anonymity, those days when he was no one in particular, any one of the millions of nobodies that pass through this city. But he desired his former innocence more than his old obscurity. For weeks after his release, the driver's lawyers had continued their attempts to have the police ditch the investigation. In many petty criminal cases, the case is practically over when police release a suspect from pretrial detention. Often, the police will forget to follow up on freed suspects. But Iwik was too famous to slip fortuitously through the cracks of a sloppy system. If he was to be freed of the suspicion, his lawyers had to find a way to have the police release Iwik formally. Over the next few months, Triyandi, Eko, and Djufri sent a stream of letters. On 25 January 1997, they wrote directly to the armed forces commander, the nominal superior of the national police chief, to remind him that both Marsiyem and Sujarah had not identified Iwik, and that the Jogja police had no case against their client. All in all, Iwik's lawyers would formally ask the police to drop the case five times. None of their requests were granted. "Poor Dwi Sumaji," Marsiyem told Heru, when the journalist first came to inform her of Iwik's release from detention. "Why don't the police just let him go?"

But the resistance did not bother Iwik. Iwik wanted his day in court. The Dymas driver felt that the best way to validate that his arrest was unjustified was to demonstrate to the public that he was not Udin's killer. This was something that could only be accomplished in a courtroom. "With a trial, when you're declared free, you're really free," Iwik would say. He understood that without a formal verdict, his name would never be cleared of suspicion. Somewhere in those letters which his village chief would one day write for him, somewhere on a piece of paper in some detective's office, somewhere in those files that shadowed every Indonesian citizen, something would say that Dwi Sumaji, also known as Iwik, had been a suspect in a murder and had never been cleared of the charges. Iwik would not be satisfied with a pretrial motion that made his arrest illegal or an official abandonment of the investigation. Now he wanted only one thing: vindication at trial. And he was confident, perhaps more so than his own counsel, that he and his wife would emerge victorious. After all, since he was a child, he had watched the tales played out on the *wayang*'s shadow-specked screen. In those stories, there was a simple lesson, he would later explain: "Those who do evil will eventually be caught."

After Iwik's release, Hadi summoned the driver at least three more times for more questionings. But the detective obtained no more confessions from Iwik. At one interview, on 30 December 1996, Hadi asked why the driver had changed his story.

"Because I did not do it," Iwik answered him.

"On 6 December, you answered that you 'did not want to explain, can not explain, did not know or did not want to answer.' Please explain," Hadi pressed.

"Because I did not assault Udin."

"During the reconstruction on 9 December, you did not want to participate. Please explain."

"Because I did not know this play-acting and because I did not assault Udin."

Since his arrest in October, Iwik's ordeal had pushed the Udin case and the personalities involved in it off the front page. Bantul *Bupati* Sri Roso's name appeared less frequently in the media. But the colonel's lowered profile did not mean that journalists had given up trying to pierce his confidence and extract an admission. Sri Roso had made himself increasingly unreachable. When reporters approached him at official Bantul ceremonies, the *bupati* refused to entertain questions related to the *Bernas* correspondent's murder. He considered the matter, if not altogether closed, then at least outside his concern or authority. Sri Roso's air of cool detachment did not discourage Ida, who had been particularly persistent in hounding Sri Roso. Throughout the last months of 1996, the former *TEMPO* reporter made it a routine to appear almost every other day at Sri Roso's office to pester the reticent *bupati* to answer her questions.

Sri Roso's bodyguards now maintained an impassable cordon around him. As soon as they spotted a group of reporters approaching, his men would whisk him into a waiting automobile or into some office deep in his complex. When Ida and her colleagues did manage to catch the *bupati* at an unguarded moment, Sri Roso rarely appeared pleased to be questioned. His expression would be sour, as if he had been presented with a piece of garbage. In November, Ida managed to ask him if the Udin investigation kept him awake at night.

"I sleep soundly," the *bupati* answered coldly.

On 6 December, Ida and other reporters cornered Sri Roso after Friday prayers at Bantul's main mosque. They told him that they had obtained information that Sri Roso had admitted to the civilian intelligence agency that he had ordered the assault on Udin.

"I don't have a comment. I don't have an explanation," Sri Roso responded irritably. "You have an unclear source. Then you ask me about it. That's the same thing as inciting me to say something."

Support for Sri Roso seemed to stretch far into the stratospheric heights of Indonesia's hierarchy of power. After Sri Roso's encounter with the reporters, the armed forces commander in Jakarta himself came out to deny that intelligence agents had interrogated the *bupati*. When *Bernas*, shortly after, quoted sources who confirmed that the police had questioned Sri Roso, the Interior Minister announced: "If anyone says the Bantul *bupati* has been questioned, it's not true." If the police had spoken to the colonel, the minister explained, they had done so in an informal, unofficial capacity. A formal interrogation was still impossible without permission from the Interior Ministry. That request had not yet been granted.

But Sri Roso's superiors had a more difficult time dismissing the furor over Sri Roso's promise to pay Suharto's foundation $428,000 in exchange for reelection. In that case, there was evidence in black and white – the *bupati*'s own signature looping on the bottom of an incriminating letter. The Interior Ministry promised the press it would conduct an inquiry into the "One-Billion Rupiah Promise." In early December, a team of bureaucrats traveled to Bantul to question the *bupati* about why his signature had appeared on the document. A week and a half later, a senior Interior Ministry official held a press conference to announce that no further questioning of the colonel would be necessary. The *bupati*, the press was told, had given a satisfactory explanation to the ministry. Apparently, or so his story went, Sri Roso had been pressured to affix his name to the letter. A group of people, led by a certain *dukun*, had approached Sri Roso's aides with an offer to secure his reelection in exchange for a sizable payout. The *bupati* had claimed to the Interior Ministry that he did not believe the group, but he had acquiesced to the *dukun*'s request to sign a letter.

Sri Roso explained that he had done so in order to secure written evidence he could later use to bring the supposed swindlers to justice. But, the Interior Ministry explained, the mystic later snared Sri Roso in the *bupati*'s own trap. "When this sum wasn't paid by the *bupati*, this paranormal leaked the document to journalists. It became news," the official recounted. So instead of exposing the would-be bribers, Sri Roso became portrayed as a briber himself. But, the ministry said, its internal investigation had found no evidence that the *bupati* had engaged in corruption in the management of IDT anti-poverty funds or in public works appropriations. Therefore, the ministry reasoned, he could not have the money he promised in the letter. According to this reasoning, the pledge was a false one, and thus no fault lay with the *bupati*. Shortly after the Interior Ministry's announcement, the Dharmais Foundation also said that the organization had never been informed of Sri Roso's planned one-billion-rupiah donation.

Once the Interior Ministry publicized Sri Roso's explanation for his signature on the damning letter, the Bantul *kabupaten* assembly's chairman Kamil felt it safe to reveal that Sri Roso and Noto Suwito had told him the same tale many months earlier before the *bupati*'s reelection. That May, Sri Roso and Suharto's half-brother had said that several men, one of whom was a *dukun*, had indeed approached Sri Roso with the offer. The *bupati* asked Noto Suwito for advice on how to respond to these purported election-brokers. The village chief told him to sign the letter the men wanted so that the *bupati* would have some hard evidence of the attempted extortion. The two men had explained to Kamil what the Interior Ministry later heard – the letter, which within its four corners appeared to be an attempt at bribery, was really meant to trap a gang of would-be extortionists. Noto Suwito's involvement indicated something else as well. Sri Roso had done what he did on the advice and implicit approval of Suharto's half-brother.

In late December, Ida managed to button-hole the *bupati* and asked him to explain his position. Sri Roso replied: "In principle, it was extortion. This man came. He said he could help. But I'd have to 'help,' too. So I contacted Noto Suwito. He said just sign it, so we would know who is extorting. That was the spirit. But because it was revealed, well, now it's like this."

Toward the end of December, the Interior Ministry announced that a written reprimand would be Sri Roso's punishment for allowing himself to be entangled in the embarrassing affair. A week later, Jogjakarta's provincial government promised that Noto Suwito would also be sanctioned. "But it would be lighter," the provincial secretary explained. "He's the lowest official, after all." So two weeks after, an emissary from the governor's office went to Argomulyo to deliver an oral reprimand to Suharto's half-brother. With the letter to the *bupati* and the warning to Noto Suwito, both the Jakarta and Jogjakarta authorities deemed the matter of the *bupati*'s letter a closed matter.

In the media, however, the affair was far from settled. Sri Roso's tale seemed intricate and unbelievable. Columnists in *Bernas* and other papers questioned how an itinerant mystic and his accomplices could cow a *bupati*, a twenty-year veteran of the military. They wondered why Sri Roso approached Noto Suwito for help instead of going directly to the police. Most importantly, they asked why both Suharto's half-brother and Sri Roso would even think of signing a document that implicated them far more than it did any alleged swindlers. On 27 December, *Bernas* ran an editorial cartoon depicting a shady, bearded character seated in a pavilion wreathed with incense from smoking braziers. A sign hung outside the *dukun*'s "office." It read:

Menu
To Finish University – Rp 0.25 billion
To Get a Project – Rp 0.5 billion
To Be a Village Head – Rp 0.2 billion
To Be a *Bupati* – Rp 1.0 billion

But once again, in the absence of contrary evidence, anything reporters might say about Sri Roso's story, in print or otherwise, still remained mere supposition. The official explanation of the "One-Billion Rupiah

Promise," supported by the unassailable word of Noto Suwito, had become the frame on which authorities had stretched a canvas of impenetrable silence. Yet well before Sri Roso's public explanation, some reporters as well as Iwik's lawyers had heard an alternate justification for the letter. Many elements in this alternate version are clearly false. Others are clearly fable. But the story, ironically, rang truer to the lawyers and journalists than Sri Roso's own far-fetched defense.

This information had been contained in a long, anonymous letter which Iwik's lawyers had received. The letter purported to explain the entire story behind Udin's murder. The note, dated 28 October 1996, ran to seven typewritten pages. Its author was unknown; the last page had an illegible signature. According to the letter-writer, Sri Roso, desperate as he approached the end of his first term, had instructed his closest aides to visit a *dukun* for advice on how best to secure reelection. The spiritualist, a man named Djuwadi, had been making a name for himself in the sultanate. Djumadi had supposedly earned close connections with the court of Nyai Roro Kidul. The goddess' patronage gave him an insight and power well beyond that of mere paranormals.

Sri Roso asked his employees to approach Djuwadi to intercede on the *bupati*'s behalf with Nyai Roro Kidul. After several nights of intense meditation on the sands of Parangtritis, the anonymous tipster explained, Djuwadi supposedly received a *wangsit*, in which the dreaded queen, most mysteriously, told him to seek answers for Sri Roso from another mystic on the opposite end of Java. This man was another, more powerful *dukun* by the name of Eyang Soma Wijaya. He lived near the north coast town of Cirebon.

Sri Roso's aides duly followed Djuwadi's advice, and visited Soma Wijaya. In that meeting, the *dukun* had apparently agreed to assist the *bupati*. The rationale behind Nyai Roro Kidul's order became evident. This wizened old Cirebon mystic wielded the powers necessary to secure Sri Roso's reelection. Soma Wijaya supposedly could live under the ocean for days or enter a locked room by passing through air vents, a keyhole or even cracks in the ceiling. Between 10:30 p.m. and midnight on 26 April 1996, the letter-writer wrote, Soma Wijaya used his powers to deliver Sri Roso's letter directly to Suharto. The *dukun* bypassed Suharto's own guardian jinni to arrive straight into the president's private quarters. The ex-general, terrified by this demonstration, quickly caved to Sri Roso's request brought by his mystic messenger. That same evening, the letter's author recounted, the First Lady Tien Suharto had also encountered Soma Wijaya as he was passing through her bedchamber. The *dukun*'s terrifying visage had left her heart beating furiously. The following morning, she supported her husband's order to the interior minister to reinstate Sri Roso as the leading candidate for Bantul *bupati* as soon as possible. The letter-writer pointed out that, although Tien spent that day relaxing while her husband went fishing, her heart, as a result of Soma Wijaya's visit, "was not calm, but full of anxiety and nervousness." That was why, he said, Tien Suharto had a heart attack and died two days later.

    The letter-writer claimed that Sri Roso had found himself in the position of having to hire a *dukun* to ensure his reelection because too much negative news out of Bantul had besmirched his image as an effective New Order administrator. When his scheme with Soma Wijaya ended in a successful reappointment, Sri Roso decided to declare revenge on those who had almost torpedoed his career. In August, the *bupati*'s henchmen Suwandi and Hatta came to the *Bernas* office to find out who was responsible for the bad publicity. They learned that Udin had written most of the unflattering coverage. Two hours later, the reporter was beaten. The *bupati*'s men, the letter said, had wanted to teach the journalist "a lesson." But the lesson "ended up killing him." The man hired to deal Udin his punishment was a member of the armed forces.

    Like many of the letters and anonymous tips the journalists and lawyers had received over the course of the long investigation, this one was a mixture of the impossible and the probable. The letter's unknown author blamed Sri Roso not just for Udin's death, but also that of the First Lady – an incredible claim. Yet his sentiments rang true. "Was there no other way for these bureaucrats to act?" he asked. "It was so crude…Let our wealth be one million billion, but if it is unclean, then our conscience will not be tranquil. We will always be seeking sorcerers and mystics to soothe feelings that are always restless…Believe in the power of God…Everything that is not rightfully yours will be exposed, and the dirt will be visible to the eyes of the public."

The letter-writer's tale somehow made more sense than the version Sri Roso, the military, and the Interior Ministry expected the public to swallow. In the years that followed Udin's murder, Sri Roso's bribery attempt finally was tried before a military tribunal. Several details of the anonymous note were confirmed, including Sri Roso's appeal to Djuwadi and Djuwadi's visit to Soma Wijaya.

Two of Sri Roso's aides explained to police and a military court that they had indeed visited the paranormal, who directed them to another mystic on the advice of Nyai Roro Kidul. In March 1996, they had journeyed to Cirebon and met Soma Wijaya, who requested the equivalent of $1,300 in exchange for his "prayers." To the police and the courts, the aides explained that their visit had been on their own initiative, not on the *bupati*'s orders, since they were worried about their own professional futures should Sri Roso fail in securing a second term.

When they were at Soma Wijaya's home, they told investigators, one of the *dukun*'s apprentices had sidled up to say that the mystic's prayers would not be enough. This man advised them to attempt more mundane means, but which promised a greater chance of success. The *bupati* should offer Suharto's charity, the Dharmais Foundation, an outright bribe. Between half a million to a million dollars would be reasonable. The apprentice, whose name – Anggoro Wicaksono – later appeared as a signed witness on the *bupati*'s "One-Billion Rupiah Promise," had offered himself as a contact with the foundation. He insisted, however, that he needed a deposit to show his contacts at Dharmais that Sri Roso's men were serious. The *bupati*'s aides, claiming that they had felt pressured, signed a note promising an initial $107,000 as a good-faith deposit.

On 2 April 1996, the Bantul *bupati* would later say in his own testimony, Soma Wijaya, Anggoro, and the Cirebon *dukun*'s son Suwarno – the second witness who signed the letter — visited Sri Roso. According to the *bupati*, they revealed themselves to be in the employ of a Jakarta matron named Atiek Hadiningrat, a supposed relative of Tien Suharto. She sold herself as an experienced election-broker. The *bupati* claimed the group had pressured him to sign a letter promising money in exchange for his reelection. Since he was unsure what to do, Sri Roso explained, he naturally asked for the advice of Noto Suwito, who, he assumed, knew the intimate affairs of the Suharto family. The Argomulyo village chief advised him to play along with the visitors.

After signing the promise, Sri Roso claimed that he received an angry fax from Atiek. "I am very insulted," she wrote at the top of her missive, which berated him for memorializing his pledge in such incriminating writing. "If you are successfully installed," she warned, his letter would be "a big 'abnormality' that makes it seem as if public positions could be *bought*...this is *very dangerous*." But at the same time she admonished him for his indiscretion, she also boasted that she had been successful in getting the authorities in Jakarta to reverse their support for Supardji and breathe life back into Sri Roso's candidacy. The police received a copy of Atiek's fax. To support Sri Roso's explanations, Noto Suwito also presented to police and military court a letter he claimed he had written to Suharto right after he had heard about this "Atiek Hadiningrat." In it, he reported that Atiek had been misusing the president and the First Lady's names to persuade people into believing that she had the influence to grant public office.

Yet that same facsimile from Atiek that Sri Roso and Noto Suwito would present to substantiate their claims is open to more than one interpretation. The Jakarta matron and supposed relative of the First Lady did complain – presciently, it would turn out – about the danger of a written "One-Billion Rupiah Promise." But the main subject of her letter appears less to be about her annoyance at the *bupati*'s stupidity than about her anger at Sri Roso for dumping her as an influence-broker in favor of Noto Suwito. She quoted the *bupati* as telling her that "Noto Suwito has already received a note from President Suharto, so could Madame please keep quiet, and let this other thing go forward?" She responded sharply that for several days she had gone to armed forces headquarters to argue his case. His reelection was now assured, Atiek claimed, and it was due to *her* efforts, not those of Suharto's half-brother, that he was back in the running. "When I succeed," she sniffed, "you say that it's someone else's work." The fax, on its face, appeared to be nothing more than one corrupt election-broker complaining that another had stolen her client.

The letter-writer's identity would never be discovered. The *dukun* Djuwadi would tell reporters that he knew nothing about the supposed extortion. In military court, Atiek would maintain that despite what the facsimile said, she had been uninvolved in any of Sri Roso's maneuvering. Both Sri Roso and Noto Suwito never abandoned their explanation that they were victims drawn into attempted bribery, despite the evidence that indicates that *they* were the ones attempting the bribery. Indeed, setting aside the mystics, magic, and whispers from the deep, deep ocean, what the anonymous letter, Sri Roso's aides' testimony, and Atiek's own words really provide a voyeur's glimpse into the treacherous market for public office in Indonesia. To secure a top spot, apparently one needed to enlist both magic and money. It is not hard to believe that Sri Roso or his men, who saw early on that the colonel would have problems, had tried several channels, both material and miraculous, to secure a victory. They consulted a mystic and retained the services of an influence-peddler like Atiek. Yet when neither Soma Wijaya's supposed powers nor Atiek's claimed connections appeared to be working, the *bupati* turned to someone he realized he should have approached in the first place: Noto Suwito, the only man in Bantul who had both powerful magic *and* the requisite connections.

Whatever really happened, a few facts are certain. The date on the "One-Billion Rupiah Promise" is barely a week after the Bantul *kabupaten* council had chosen three other people as potential replacements for Sri Roso. Within days of the letter, that decision was overturned and Sri Roso's name was reintroduced as a candidate. Perhaps it is easier to believe a man can enter a keyhole, or that a mystic can terrify a president, than to accept that Sri Roso's written promise was not exactly what its words baldly indicated: a pledge of cash in exchange for reelection.

In Indonesia, as in much of the developing world, the truth is like an onion: Peeling away the layers of lies, errors, and misunderstandings results in little but a big stink and cloudy vision. Perhaps the most important reason why the government had been so reluctant to judge and punish Sri Roso – to admit the possibility, in Atiek's words, that he had "bought his office" – was that to do so would confirm what everyone already knew. Public office in Indonesia is for trade in a shady underworld populated by thugs, mystics, and society matrons. Success in leadership – indeed, in almost anything – depends not on one's native virtues but on those that one knows, or, at least, how much one is willing to pay to those in power. If the government punished the *bupati* for buying his reelection, the New Order would have to reveal the corrupt guts of its rotten administrative system.

Soma Wijaya, an old man fond of wearing a *peci*, lives in a run-down house with broken windows beside a stretch of paddy fields some distance from downtown Cirebon. If you visit him, he will confirm that the *dukun* Djuwadi had indeed appeared at his door with the *bupati*'s men in 1996. He will say that at the time he was offered money to secure Sri Roso's victory. But Soma Wijaya denies that he is a *dukun*. He will say that the Bantul delegation's request "didn't make any sense."

He had tried to discourage the *bupati*'s people: "I couldn't guarantee a second term. I don't have that kind of power." But in the end, he will explain, he had accepted their request just to stop them from bothering him. His stout, garrulous wife might then intrude and scoff at the legends of her husband's great powers.

"People were saying he could enter locked rooms! They even said he takes care of jinni," she will say.

And Soma Wijaya, the great mystic who could breathe at the bottom of the sea, sneak through cracks into locked rooms, and frighten presidents and their spouses, will add, quietly: "I take care of chickens."

Despite Sri Roso's absolution and Mulyono's face-saving deal with Iwik's lawyers, 1997 still started out badly for the Bantul government and the Jogjakarta police. By late January, Sri Roso's Parangtritis megaproject had become increasingly unlikely to see realization. The sultan had finally fulfilled the promise he made to journalists in November: that he would do whatever he was able. It turned out that at least part of those two hundred hectares of beachfront Sri Roso had pledged to the Jakarta conglomerate encroached on land managed by the *kraton*. Any development in the area thus required the approval of the sultan. In late January, the sultan revealed his intentions. He declared that he would "allow Parangtritis to remain a public beach to be enjoyed by all people." The megaproject was finished.

Meanwhile, the police felt it had reached the limit of what it could do to satisfy the prosecutor's office. Chief Mulyono announced that the reconstruction they had conducted would have to be enough. "We can only do as far as that. It's not a dead end, but we've done as much as we can," he pleaded. Several days after, the chief public prosecutor corrected him. To reporters, he said that the reconstruction would have to be repeated if Iwik were to be formally charged. The reconstruction had to include the participation of the suspect and the main witnesses.

The request was an impossible one. Udin's widow had grown so estranged from the police she had plainly stopped responding to police summonses. She had come to despise the irrelevant questions that were asked. "Your husband has a computer – where did he buy it and with whose money?" she mimicked a detective's questions to one reporter. "Where did he get his motorcycle? Who are your husband's woman friends? Who are your male friends? I answered all these questions. But after I answered, I'd be asked more questions like them, which had no relation at all to the assault on my husband. It's as if he was an extortionist, and our household was in turmoil."

The depression that had set in since her husband's death had hardened and solidified. Her sadness seemed to have no opposite shore. In November, she had dreamed that Udin was calling her. The next day, a tall, heavyset man whose chin bristled with a beard just like her husband's appeared at her door. "Father is home!" her son Wikan had cried as he ran to him. The apparition turned out not to be Udin, but a television cameraman from Jakarta who bore an eerie resemblance to her departed husband. In mid-December, rumors circulated in the capital that Marsiyem had died of her grief. *Bernas* promptly printed a photo of her playing with her children to dismiss the gossip. Still, Udin's mother admitted to the paper that her daughter-in-law was falling apart physically from the loss of her husband and the stress of the murder investigation. Marsiyem had become prone to fits of vomiting. She had trouble sleeping and spent most of her time laying on the floor on a mattress.

In late January, Marsiyem came in for one last questioning. When Hadi asked his first question, she answered curtly: "At this moment, I am not in good health and do not want to be questioned." She ended the interview and left. Hadi attempted to summon her several weeks later, in early March. Her lawyer, Budi, replied on her behalf. "She has already been asked for her testimony seven times with the same questions," the attorney told the police. "This is just going to keep going back and forth." Hadi then approached Marsiyem's personal physician to cajole him into coaxing the widow to cooperate with the authorities. He refused.

Twice in two months the police had submitted Iwik's dossier, and twice the prosecutor's office had returned it. On 5 January 1997, Hadi was to submit the case file a third time. Instead, he turned it in late. Five days later, the public prosecutor returned it to Hadi, with the same complaints he had voiced earlier about the case's defects. The detective missed the next deadline the prosecutor gave him – 3 February 1997 – by two weeks. A week after the detective turned in the newest version, the dossier was back on his desk again. The instructions sent by the public prosecutor were the same as those that had accompanied the dossier the three previous times it was rejected: Marsiyem had not identified Iwik. After one of the rejections, an assistant public prosecutor had explained to *Bernas* why his office was so reluctant to accept the case: "If the file the investigators send us isn't perfect, how are we going to bring it to court?"

In late March, the public prosecutors were waiting for Hadi to submit the case file a fifth time. But any hope for Hadi to extract a positive identification from Marsiyem had evaporated completely. That month, hearings in her lawsuit against the police had begun. In early January, her lawyers at Legal Aid had filed their complaint with the Bantul court. In her complaint, Marsiyem was suing the Indonesian government, the chiefs of the national, Jogjakarta, and Bantul police, and Detective Edy Wuryanto for misusing her husband's blood. She was demanding the equivalent of $36,400 in damages. Most of that sum – about one million rupiah – was deemed restitution for "moral damages," while the rest was to compensate her for the cost of telephone calls, transportation between Jogja and Bantul, and the bill for her husband's care at Bethesda Hospital. Her lawyers asked the court to rule that the Indonesian police had broken the law, and to place a lien on the Bantul police headquarters to guarantee payment of the damages. Marsiyem's lawyers would probably not have requested any damages at all had civil tort suits not required plaintiffs to show some compensable harm or risk dismissal. Before launching the case, their legal strategist, Artidjo Alkostar, wondered whether he should ask for zero damages or just a single rupiah to satisfy the procedural conditions, but eventually Legal Aid and Udin's family settled on a final figure.

Although Marsiyem was the plaintiff, and her lawyer Budi her main counsel, Artidjo was the real mastermind behind the lawsuit. Based in Jogja, Artidjo had helped found both Triyandi's Legal Defenders and the Jogjakarta branch of Legal Aid, which he led personally for six years. He knew both Triyandi and Budi well. So even as Udin's case bifurcated into a civil suit involving Marsiyem and criminal trial involving Iwik, both sets of lawyers approached Artidjo for advice and ideas. In late 1996, Artidjo had suggested to Budi that Legal Aid take up Marsiyem's complaint about the misuse of her husband's blood and file it in a civil court. As Iwik's lawyers knew well, the problem with a criminal complaint was that only the Jogjakarta police could begin a criminal investigation – even if the complaint concerned the police itself. Some civil cases, however, could go to court without a police report, thus providing a way for Legal Aid to circumvent police resistance to exposing the machinations behind Iwik's arrest for Udin's murder. When they decided on the approach, Artidjo and Budi had to go to Wagiman's house several times to persuade Udin's widow and family that a civil suit was their best option. "My intention in suing the police was to get some transparency," Artidjo would later explain. "to expose facts at trial, so the public knows: ah, so that's how it works."

Marsiyem's lawyers and Udin's relatives realized that the odds were not in their favor. The jury system does not exist in Indonesia – a reflection of the legal system's heritage in Dutch law. The three judges that decide a case exercise absolute power; they alone decide which evidence to admit, which witnesses are credible, and what law to apply in a particular context. In many Indonesian trials, the judges participate actively in the cross-examination of witnesses. In the Indonesian justice system, the judiciary was supposed to provide an unassailable check on the executive or the legislature. But like everything else, it has been corrupted by politics and poverty. Since the 1970s, the Indonesian judiciary has lost much of its independence and integrity. Although its decline had begun under Sukarno, the trend had accelerated under Suharto, who made judges a badly-trained and poorly-paid part of the government bureaucracy, treated on the same level as school teachers or patrolmen. The courts were a part of the Ministry of Justice, so the president and his aides had ultimate control over court budgets as well as over judges' transfers and promotions. These tools were wielded to keep judges docile. The executive branch denied promotions to "activist" judges and rewarded those who ruled in favor of the government. Since Indonesia requires that prospective judges only have law degrees and be graduates of a three-month training program, Suharto also packed the judiciary with soldiers and ex-soldiers. In the mid-1980s, current or retired military men made up as many as one-third of the Indonesian Supreme Court's members.

At the local level, the ties between the courts and the local government became particularly tight. A *kabupaten* or provincial chief justice was required to attend regular "coordination" meetings with the police chief, the local military commander, and the public prosecutor. The *bupati* or provincial governor chairs this conference, in which matters of law, order, and security are decided by consensus. In fact it was at just such a meeting in Bantul that Sri Roso had discussed his intention to sue Udin with the very parties who would investigate, prosecute, and try the planned lawsuit. In the United States, such collaboration would constitute a violation of a defendant's right to due process. Indonesia has no such restrictions. But a higher court that is not bound by such local allegiances can sometimes make a fairer ruling than a lower one. In 1995, for example, an appellate court overturned a Surabaya court's convictions of the plotters behind Marsinah's murder. The Indonesian Supreme Court affirmed that ruling and also reversed eight other convictions connected to the case on the basis of insufficient evidence.

However, in cases where the central government's interests are directly implicated, the highest court still buckles. Although the Indonesian Supreme Court has the authority to review laws, presidential decrees, or ministerial regulations, it has never once ruled against the national government. Once, when the Supreme Court decided that the government should pay more money in compensation to farmers who lost their land to the Kedung Ombo Dam project, Suharto called the chief justice to meet with him personally. Shortly after that encounter, the Supreme Court reversed its decision. When a Jakarta administrative court ruled in favor of *TEMPO* after the magazine challenged its shuttering by the Information Ministry, the Supreme Court overturned both that decision and an appellate court's opinion ruling in favor of *TEMPO*'s position.

Embedded in this restrictive system, a judge's ideology and sympathies are often immaterial. What has come to matter most to lawyers and clients is not whether a judge can be persuaded, but whether he or she can be pressured or paid off. Although the government doubled judges' salaries in 1995, a typical judge with some experience and seniority in a local court was still receiving a salary of about $130 a month. A judge might work for three decades and earn only twice as much as he or she did during his or her first year on the bench. To make ends meet, honest judges chose to engage in part-time work, such as writing law books or teaching law. Often, however, judges succumbed to the temptation to extract the true value of their authority from litigants and their lawyers. They sold their decisions.

In Central Java in the mid-1990s, a favorable decision might be bought for as little as two hundred dollars. Indonesian judges and their assistants came to treat lawyers, plaintiffs and defendants as customers: they granted the best service to those who could afford it. Many judges saw their work as less like a profession and more like a business. They lobbied for transfers from small towns or rural areas to major cities, so they could enjoy the wider opportunities for graft offered by more lucrative commercial cases. Payoffs by lawyers and their clients to judges came in many forms: loans that were never expected to be repaid, gifts of cars or houses, or favors for children or relatives. Services that judges and the staff members offered in return ranged from scheduling speedy trials, to ensuring cases go to favorable judges, to writing letters to prevent sentencing, to outright forgery of court decisions. One corruption watchdog noted that all of these kinds of graft had occurred in one court alone. That court happened to be the Indonesian Supreme Court.

"You can have good judges but bad laws, or good laws but bad judges," one judge explains. "We don't have that choice. The laws are bad, and the people who implement the laws are also bad." For a country of its size, few cases are filed in Indonesian courts. The majority of disputes are settled informally, outside the court system, or simply abandoned, so as to avoid the hassle and peril of the Indonesian justice system. In the lawsuit over Udin's blood, Artidjo idealistically hoped that the risk the Bantul court would rule against them might be outweighed by the potential for a satisfying political triumph. "Under an authoritarian government, the courtroom has to be used as a place for political education," he would later insist.

So it seemed a bad omen that the day before Marsiyem's trial opened, one of the judges, a sixteen-year veteran well-known for his honesty, recused himself from the three-judge panel scheduled to try the case. Judge Syahlan Said, an occasional columnist for *Bernas* and a frequent source for the Jogja media on matters of law, said that he had known Udin personally and thus could not judge Marsiyem's lawsuit objectively. But the real reason for his decision was that a few days before, Bantul police representatives had complained to the Bantul chief judge that Judge Syahlan had been openly critical of the law enforcement's approach to the Udin investigation. The judge, they insisted, could not be expected to be impartial.

Fortunately for Marsiyem's lawyers, the panel's lead judge, Mikaela Warsito, had a sterling reputation. Judge Mikaela, who had been a jurist for thirty years, was known to accept neither money nor gifts, not even presents for the post-Ramadan holidays. When she had started out as a judge in a provincial Javanese town in the 1960s, she would return the presents of produce given by farmers involved in cases before her. So although Judge Syahlan had stepped down, Judge Mikaela's presence assured Artidjo and Budi that they were going into their courtroom battle with more than a slim chance of winning.

Before the trial, Legal Aid and the Bantul police department's in-house lawyers, who were police officers themselves, had exchanged a hostile salvo of written complaints and answers. Indonesia, unlike the United States, does not have a developed system of factual discovery prior to trial. Litigants do not send each other interrogatories, no witnesses are deposed, no documents are requested, and no experts are hired to produce reports that can later be introduced at trial. While the American system has been often criticized, the process of discovery does allow both parties to uncover and present far more evidence than they could have at the initiation of the suit. In Indonesia, without a formal discovery process, judges often have very little to base their decisions on other than the facts that surface during the trial itself and the arguments presented by the parties.

In their answer to Marsiyem's initial complaint, the police lawyers had responded ferociously. In a memo to the Bantul court that ran several pages, they argued that since the relationship between Edy and Udin's relatives "was like family," Udin's relatives had turned over the reporter's blood voluntarily. The blood was a gift, they argued, so Edy was under no obligation to return it to Udin's family. Edy, their client, also claimed that he had never shown the blood to any reporters. What he had dangled in front of Moko and Ndari so many months earlier was something else entirely: perfume and the photos of several suspects in a plastic bag, which some detectives had gathered as part of a good-luck ritual to assist their investigation. The police attorneys accused Marsiyem of demonstrating "poor etiquette" and of "commercializing the situation to seek material reward." By demanding the seizure of the Bantul police headquarters, they wrote, she demonstrated that she "could live without the service and protection of the members of the Indonesian police."

To the Bantul police force and its lawyers, Marsiyem's lawsuit represented an attack on their honor. Not only had Marsiyem blocked their prosecution of Iwik, she and her activist allies were now attempting to shame them in public. She had teamed up with Legal Aid, their long-standing rival, in a frontal assault on the way things had always been done in Indonesia, which was to let the authorities do their job in whatever way they deemed necessary. Nasty caricatures of Marsiyem appeared on bulletin boards at the Jogjakarta police headquarters.

Among themselves and their friends, officers intimated that the only person to blame for the failure of the investigation into her husband's murder was Marsiyem herself.

Marsiyem's lawyers responded just as aggressively to the answer. Legal Aid railed against the "arrogance of an institution that can never admit being wrong." Any criticism the government received, Budi and his colleagues wrote in their response, was always "squinted out of the eye, or blown out of the belly." The police lawyers then responded by accusing Marsiyem of similar arrogance: "It is as if the plaintiff is also someone who has never done wrong; one who is always right." Before the trial had commenced, the positions of both the plaintiffs and defendants had each hardened into fortresses of mutual resistance. For either side, there could be no settlement of this dispute. There would be no closed-door meetings, no face-saving agreements, no private handshakes followed by public smiles. There could be only battle. "We wanted the police to admit they were wrong. They wouldn't just admit it," Artidjo would later recall.

On 22 January 1997, riot police guarded the first session of what would become known as the "Blood Trial." The hearing lasted only twenty minutes, during which time Judge Mikaela asked the two sides to attempt to reach an amicable settlement. The Bantul police lawyer told her that he was under strict orders from his superiors to try the case. Chief Yotje, seated near the police lawyers, shook his head slowly, perhaps to indicate that he would not be able to fulfill Judge Mikaela's request. Although Yotje was a progressive officer, he was still a member of the police hierarchy. Personally, Yotje might be willing to admit there had been mistakes made in handling the case, which was what Marsiyem's family wanted. But headquarters in Jakarta would not allow the Jogjakarta or Bantul police to lose face in public. When both sides, after one more fruitless meeting, reported to the court their failure to reach a settlement, Judge Mikaela continued the trial. It began with a public reading of Marsiyem's complaint and the two sides' hostile memos.

Throughout the trial, dozens of people, many of them plainclothed detectives, crammed themselves into the stuffy Bantul courtroom. Reporters covering the Blood Trial sometimes even spotted Edy himself. He was once seen peeking in from a window that opened onto the front lawn of the courthouse. The witnesses began testifying on 19 February 1997. These first testimonies usually ran to two and one-half hours. Each witness took his or her place before a microphone that faced the three judges, who sat behind a large table cloaked in green cloth.

The first to face the court were members of Udin's family. They confirmed the fact that the detective had taken the reporter's blood six months earlier. The next group of witnesses comprised several journalists, including Moko and Ndari. Before Moko appeared in court, his mother and fiancée had warned him against assisting Artidjo's hopeless campaign. "Don't get too involved in this," they told him. "This is a case for powerful people." But Moko would not be dissuaded. The day he testified, police supporters thronged the court and shouted abuse at the reporters. As Moko walked up to the microphone, his friends yelled: "Don't pay attention! Go forward!" In court, Moko and Ndari recounted Edy's macabre guessing game at the Bantul police station. After them, PWI team members Masduki and Putut recounted to the judge what Mulyono had told them at his press conference: that Edy had thrown part of Udin's blood into the ocean and the rest into the garbage.

The court did not permit Edy to testify, since he was also a defendant. So the police lawyers brought forward several police officers to face the panel of judges. Their version differed from the one Udin's family had presented. On 19 August 1996 at 8:00 p.m., they said, Edy and two police officers had indeed visited Udin's family. But it had been Udin's uncle Mardimin, not Edy, who had first mentioned the existence of a bag containing the murdered reporter's blood. Then, according to the detectives, Udin's uncle had told them that Edy was welcome to use the blood "in accordance with his beliefs." A police officer who had accompanied Edy testified that not once did he hear the words "borrow" or "return" uttered during the meeting.

After taking the dead reporter's blood, the policemen, led by Edy, drove to the local cemetery, where they prayed at Udin's grave before placing three handfuls of soil from the grave into the same bag as the blood. Edy then stored the bag in his car's trunk until the next *Kliwon* Friday eve, on 22 August 1996. That night, he and six other Bantul policemen went to Parangtritis. Edy meditated alone on the beach while his companions watched. After praying, the detective hurled the bag into the crashing surf. Several police witness at the Blood Trial said that enlisting supernatural forces in their investigations was not standard police practice. Edy, however, explained in a special "advisory" testimony to the court that these "non-technical" habits are often permitted in accordance with officers' "personal beliefs."

The problem the plaintiff's lawyers faced was that Indonesian courts – as anywhere else – have a limited set of tools to compel witnesses to be honest. Each time Judge Mikaela swore in a witness, she mouthed the court's stock warning: "If you lie, aside from God's punishment, there will also be one from the court." The former surely was something to fear, but the latter was altogether an empty threat. If a court suspects a witness of perjury, the police often must launch an inquiry before the public prosecutor can charge a witness with the crime. So witnesses who are police officers or who are testifying on behalf of law enforcement naturally come protected by the force's unwillingness to prove they are lying.

The police maintained Edy had treated the blood as respectfully as any Javanese who believed in magic. Moreover, he had not kept any blood from the bag; everything had gone into the garbage or into the ocean. This additional point was made, perhaps, to contradict any claim Iwik's lawyers might later raise in the criminal suit that the blood had been used to taint the evidence against Iwik. The police thus set out to establish one version of reality, which was as vivid and unyielding as the one presented by Udin's family and their lawyers. In the picture they painted for the judges, Edy and Udin were old friends. Udin's family trusted the detective with the reporter's blood to dispose of as he wished.

So what appeared to be misuse of evidence was simply part of colorful local tradition, and what had later seemed to Moko and Ndari to be a bag containing the dead man's blood was really a strange assortment of charms: perfume, pins and needles. Just like Sri Roso's explanation of his reelection, the Bantul police department's story flew in the face of common sense, yet the public was supposed to believe it. Marsiyem's lawyers knew the flaws of the Indonesian civil procedure led to this result: without any firm evidence extracted from the defendants during the trial, the decision in this case would rest on whether the judges found the word of Udin's family more credible than that of its opponents.

On 7 April 1997, the three judges read their opinion aloud to a packed courtroom. First, the jurists rejected Legal Aid's motion to strike from the record the testimony of Edy's colleagues, the police witnesses. The judges explained that an evidence statute did not ban testimony by the defendant's colleagues. However, that same law *did* rule out testimony from the plaintiff's direct relatives, who would, in theory, gain if the court ruled in their favor. The judges said they would disregard the testimony of Udin's family in making their decision.

To answer the question of whether the defendants had committed an illegal act, the judges said they needed to resolve one threshold issue: had the blood been lent to Edy or given voluntarily? The judges concluded that, based on the testimony of a single witness, Udin's uncle, it was "difficult to call the exchange one of lending." The court concluded, "The blood had been given voluntarily based on the belief it would help the police." Having thrown out the family's testimony, the court had made the police's version of the events incontrovertible.

Artidjo and Budi had lost. The court rejected Marsiyem's claim for the cost of Udin's medical care. Since her lawyers, the judges continued, had not demonstrated that any of Edy's superiors, from the police chief to the Indonesian government, was involved in the disposal of the blood, the court would not hold the Bantul police or the government liable for punitive damages. But the court allowed Marsiyem and Legal Aid a tiny victory. The judges concluded that, by throwing the blood into the sea, Edy Wuryanto had "acted against the principles of fairness, propriety, and carefulness toward the public." In other words, Edy had transgressed some generally-accepted sense of moral social standards, and thus deserved some kind of punishment. Judge Mikaela and her colleagues decreed that the detective's restitution would be to tell Marsiyem he was sorry. "The moral damages deemed right and fair as a sentence," they decided, "is that the accused apologize for his act against the law to the plaintiff voluntarily and openly through the print media no later than four days after this decision." The judges instructed Edy to pay the equivalent of four dollars and thirty cents to Udin's widow and twenty-two dollars in court fees: a total of $26.30 in damages.

The Blood Trial thus ended with a verdict overwhelmingly in favor of the police. The entire case had taken three months from the filing of the lawsuit to the verdict. Even though Indonesian civil law recognizes the principle of *respondeat superior* – in which employers are held liable for the negligent or criminal acts of their employees – the police as an institution had not been found responsible although a police officer, on the job, had irresponsibly treated evidence entrusted to him. Instead, Edy was given a light slap on the wrist. His penance would be a printed apology, and the payment of an insignificant fraction of his earnings. "We were annoyed, frustrated." Artidjo recalled feeling, "We couldn't do anything. Because the police, prosecutors, and judges won't move against someone who is part of them."

The outcome of the Blood Trial cast a pall on Iwik's approaching day in court. In the Blood Trial, plainclothed police had intimidated witnesses and police officers had presented questionable testimony in the courtroom, while the judges had looked the other way and delivered to the opposing side the victory. If this was all the courage the lawyers involved in the Udin-related cases could expect to receive from the Bantul court during a *civil* trial, what could they expect from the nearing criminal case? After the Blood Trial, Iwik's future looked a lot darker.

CHAPTER 11

Everything at the Trial

THE BLOOD TRIAL LEFT the journalists and lawyers discouraged and defeated. Marsiyem's lawyers and their allies had wanted to see Indonesia's entire police apparatus punished in the Bantul court. But the case Legal Aid had fashioned was perhaps too ambitious. Judge Mikaela was fair, but she had to be conservative. Based on one detective's disposal of a bag of blood, she and her colleagues were being asked to rule against the entire Indonesian government. Even the most untainted of courts would balk at such a radical decision. Despite the failure, Legal Aid soldiered onward. Shortly after the trial ended, Budi filed an appeal with the Jogjakarta provincial court to review Judge Mikaela's decision.

Worse news arrived the same day of the Blood Trial ruling: the Jogjakarta public prosecutor had yielded to the police. After rejecting the dossier five times in five months, the prosecutor's office had finally accepted the case file. Although the prosecutors still deemed Hadi's work incomplete, they decided that they would conduct their own two-week effort to address the dossier's deficiencies rather than depend on the detective again. The decision meant Iwik would go to trial.

Jogja's journalists jumped to the conclusion that the police had paid the prosecutor or had called in owed favors. How else to explain the sudden reversal in the prosecutor's position? But what the media missed was that many inside the prosecutor's office still remained doubtful that the police had apprehended the right suspect. The decision to accept the case had been taken not because they were convinced of Iwik's guilt, but because many believed in his innocence. The prosecutors could not play ping-pong with the police forever. Nothing in the criminal procedure code limited how many times police investigators could send a case file to a prosecutor, or how many times a prosecutor could reject it. In theory, Iwik's case could stay in this limbo indefinitely, the dossier traveling between investigation and prosecution forever. To end the uncertainty, some inside the prosecutor's office believed Iwik had to go to court, where judges could make a decision on his fate that would be binding on the Jogjakarta police. Only then would Edy and his henchmen leave Iwik alone. "We can't be separated from our humanity. Beyond the law, we are still people," one prosecutor would later admit privately. "From the beginning, my conscience said 'No.' But we received a job: to bring this to trial."

The public prosecutor decided that Iwik did not need to reenter detention. Despite that reprieve and Iwik's own desire for vindication, the prospect of an appearance in court nonetheless disturbed and upset Udin's accused killer. On 17 April, the Dymas driver submitted to a prosecution-ordered medical checkup. To journalists he met on his way out of the examination room, Iwik growled, "I'll reveal everything in my trial." Although the case technically lay within the jurisdiction of the Bantul office, the Jogjakarta provincial prosecutors decided it would supply its own staff to represent the *kabupaten* against Dwi Sumaji. Assistant Public Prosecutor Amrin Naim, who had thirty-two years of experience, would lead a four-man team of prosecutors assembled from all over Jogjakarta.

Amrin promised to prosecute Iwik vigorously. When Adib and Djufri accompanied Iwik to a meeting at Amrin's office, the assistant public prosecutor, according to the lawyers, urged Iwik, "Just confess, Iwik. There are a lot of us against you. Later, we can 'help' during the trial."

"Go ahead and believe that. Just prepare your charges. We'll all meet in court," the hot-headed Djufri challenged the confident assistant prosecutor.

More trouble befell the pro-Iwik-and-Udin alliance that month. Shortly before the Blood Trial's conclusion, *Bernas* publisher Kusfandhi summoned the reporters who had been closely involved in the coverage of the Udin case. He informed each of them that they were to receive new assignments – most located well outside Jogja. Kusfandhi planned to spread the young *Bernas* journalists throughout Central Java: one was to go to Magelang, another to Purworejo, and another to Purwokerto. Moko would be assigned to Wonosobo, a town over a hundred kilometers from the city. The publisher offered a few, such as Achadi, full staff positions, including salary and benefits, in exchange for accepting the new postings. But Achadi would have to move to Semarang, the capital of Central Java province. Tarko, the photographer, was to go to Surakarta, which, although nearer to Jogja than any of his friends' reassignments, required him to shelve his camera and become a reporter.

Although the paper already employed contributors in each of these places, Kusfandhi would later explain that these outlying areas needed coverage if *Bernas* were to be a true regional paper. For the balding, rotund publisher, the decision to transfer the reporters had been a management call: "They must be ready to be assigned anywhere." Kusfandhi told each of the reporters that, if they accepted their reassignments, they could keep their jobs. Only one journalist did not receive that choice: Udin's editor Heru, whom Kusfandhi asked to resign as soon as possible from the newspaper.

An old slur had ended Heru's promising career at *Bernas*. In the 1960s, a family neighbor had accused Heru's father, a member of the schoolteachers' union, of being allied with the Communists. Although Heru's father had worked to clear that slanderous accusation, that whisper apparently remained on record in the local garrison. The morning Kusfandhi asked for Heru's resignation, the publisher had visited the Jogjakarta military command. "There was a rule," the publisher would later explain. "You have to have a 'clean environment.'" That phrase meant a society scrubbed free of Communism's stain, no matter how faint or how faded. Although the *Bernas* owner would not say if the local military had pressured him into dispersing the White Kijang team, Heru was convinced that Kusfandhi would not have cared about his family's past had the local military command not revealed the three-decade-old lie to the publisher.

To Heru's dismay, some of his colleagues supported Kusfandhi's decision. The Jogja media's common interest in bringing Udin's killer to justice had only temporarily masked the deep rivalries, both personal and political, between the PWI and the younger, AJI-aligned journalists. *Bernas*' Putut and the *Free Voice*'s Asril had also learned of Heru's "Communist" credentials from military sources. Privately, Putut and Asril blamed the thirty-three-year-old editor for Udin's death. They were convinced that it had been Heru who had changed the tone of Udin's workaday pieces to antagonize the Bantul government. "He put that edge on those stories," Putut would later claim. In their eyes, Heru had sent Udin to his death as much as if the editor himself had wielded the metal pipe that felled the Bantul correspondent. "To prevent any more victims, you take whatever steps you think necessary," Putut had advised Kusfandhi.

Heru had his explanation for why the stories he edited seemed pointed: "Sharpening a writer's prose is exactly an editor's duty." Heru's bitter dismissal and the reassignments effectively dissolved the White Kijang team. A few of the reassigned reporters, such as Moko, attempted to ignore Kusfandhi's decision and continue reporting from Jogja. That strategy did not work for long. Others, such as Achadi and Tarko, soon quit the paper. Tarko was one of the first. During his meeting with Kusfandhi, the photographer banged his fist on the table and resigned immediately. In the months after Kusfandhi's decision, over a dozen journalists left *Bernas*, including Ndari, who believed she was spared a transfer out of Jogja because she worked on the international desk. Dismayed that her group of friends had been forcibly disbanded, the young journalist decided to find a new job in Jakarta.

Although Ida remained as Jogjakarta correspondent for *Detective & Romance*, and many other non-*Bernas* journalists who orbited the paper's nucleus of reporters stayed at their posts, the White Kijang team's regular gatherings at *Bernas* to discuss the case, the convoys to Bantul and Parangtritis, and the late-night conversations were over. For the journalists, there would be no more tea sessions in the market at Karangtengah or midnight wanderings around Bantul town. Whatever the true reason behind the White Kijang team's dissolution, coverage of Udin's murder in his own paper declined drastically in number and frequency. From April until the beginning of Iwik's trial, only a handful of stories about the case appeared every month, compared to the flurry of pieces readers were used to seeing daily in the pages of the paper.

The team was reunited one last time that year. In late August, close to the one-year anniversary of Udin's death, a fledgling press freedom organization in Jakarta invited Heru, Ida, Achadi, Moko, and more than a dozen other reporters from *Bernas* and other Jogja media to travel to the capital. There, in an emotional ceremony, the reporters received an award for press freedom from Wagiman, the murdered journalist's father and the guest of honor. The award was called the Udin Prize.

On 5 May 1997, Iwik's lawyers sent one final, futile plea to the public prosecutor's office to release their client. Later that month, the Jogjakarta prosecutor's office delivered Iwik's dossier to Bantul prosecutors, with instructions that the case be scheduled for trial in the Bantul court. Yet nearly two more months would pass before Bantul's prosecutor filed the charges against Iwik on 15 July 1997. The long delay, prosecutors would later explain, was an expected scheduling snafu. The Bantul court could not just clear its docket for Iwik's case, no matter how famous it had become.

Those same months also coincided with the once-every-five-years parliamentary elections, which had been scheduled for 29 May 1997, and which occupied the attention of every government official at every level. Activists at Jogjakarta's Legal Aid office had noticed that even the regular anonymous threats they received had changed. Instead of warning them against pursuing controversial cases such as Udin's, this time the disembodied voices told the activists they should not be so vocal in their criticism of government policies. The time was too near to the all-important parliamentary election.

These were the polls for which Sri Roso had started campaigning so vigorously a year earlier. The Bantul *bupati* had not been unique in his devotion to securing a ruling party victory. In the months leading to the elections, local officials all over the archipelago had been promising money to village or *kabupaten* chiefs who could deliver votes for Golkar. In Central Java, Golkar supporters were literally painting towns yellow. Throughout the island, rupiah notes fluttered like confetti at rallies for the ruling party. Suharto's daughter Tutut traveled the countryside to campaign personally for her father. During the voting, government cheating and manipulation ran rampant. In Sumatra, for example, several weeks before voting started, one district had already produced a completed vote count showing a substantial Golkar victory. And after the polls closed, Golkar defeats in *kabupaten* and municipalities magically turned into victories when the ballots were tallied at the provincial level. The military had harassed an independent citizens' group that had tried to organize before the polls to monitor the voting. The organization's secretary-general, a criminology professor, was accused of ties to Communism that the academic never knew existed.

Golkar achieved its goal: a landslide of seventy-four per cent of the vote, which exceeded its 1992 tally by five percentage points. This was a suitably resounding affirmation of the Suharto administration. The ruling party came in first in all but three cities and districts. The showing gave Golkar three hundred seats in parliament. The Unity and Development Party also did well, picking up twenty-three per cent of the vote, but the divided PDI came in at a measly three per cent. Golkar's victory, however, had come at a great cost. The May 1997 elections were the most violent in the country's modern history, reflecting the simmering popular resentment and frustration at how cynical the political process had become. In the weeks before the polls, some two hundred individuals died in election-related violence. On the last day of the campaign, over one hundred lives perished in riots and looting in Kalimantan.

So while the local government and security authorities concentrated on the election ritual, certain lives in Jogjakarta returned to normal. In Samalo, after nearly a year, Marsiyem reopened the shuttered Krisna Photo Studio under the management of Udin's former business partner and neighbor. Iwik and Sunarti moved back to Panasan, where the driver admitted he felt safer than he did in Triyandi's office, despite his lawyer's belief to the contrary. His physical security had come to matter less to Iwik than his psychic comfort. In his home village, he was no longer the center of attention. Among old habits and routines, Iwik could forget what had happened. His old boss had promised that Iwik could return to his job at Dymas. But the driver's former life still remained out of reach; his future was too uncertain for him to make any commitment, even to his previous employer. To earn some extra cash and to occupy his time before the trial, Iwik built a small shack outside his home to sell motorcycle fuel. Sunarti returned to her salon and her sewing.

For the couple, the return to normality passed all too quickly. Three days before his trial for the murder of Udin, Iwik shut down the gasoline kiosk. He had to return to his lawyers' office, because his defense would now dominate his time. He felt it was time to close shop anyway. He could not turn a profit. Too many friends and neighbors bought their fuel on credit. The couple and Bimo moved back to Triyandi's office on Pakuningratan Road, where they would live for the duration of the trial.

Some *dukun* from Surakarta and Central Java had suggested that Iwik begin a regimen to strengthen himself spiritually for the ordeal. A routine would protect Iwik from any magic Edy might attempt to force Iwik to make admissions at trial. On the mystics' instructions, the Dymas driver bathed at midnight, prayed regularly, and avoided eating fish or live creatures. Until the end of his trial, Iwik was to eat only vegetables. As an added precaution, he recited each night the *Ayat Kursi*, the Quran's Verse of the Throne, a passage that the Prophet had said protects its reciter from harm between morning and evening.

The reporters and lawyers would be seeing familiar faces at the hearing. Two of the three judges – Judge Mikaela and Judge Suparno – chosen to hear the case had been on the same panel that decided the outcome of the Blood Trial. This time, Judge Mikaela had a secondary role. The presiding judge would be the assistant chief justice of Bantul, Endang Sri Murwiati. The three had agreed before the trial started that they would refuse any meeting requested by the defense, the prosecution, or even the Bantul government. They could not allow this, Jogjakarta's most important trial in decades, to be compromised by any hint of outside influence.

Iwik's trial opened on 29 July 1997. Just as for the Blood Trial, the police cordoned off the streets surrounding the courthouse. The heavy security did not stop hundreds of people from entering to witness the trial. Dozens jostled for the few seats inside the main courtroom. On the courthouse's front lawn, vendors sold warm cans of soda, flavored ice, and clove cigarettes in a carnival atmosphere. In the throng that day were two former *Bernas* journalists: Achadi, now unemployed, and Heru, who after his resignation for the newspaper began contributing to Ida's magazine, *Detective & Romance*.

Several colorful characters livened up the first hearing. In the opening minutes, a neatly-dressed woman with shoulder-length hair screamed suddenly: "May I interrupt, Your Honor! I know the truth behind the Syafruddin case!" Reporters scrambled over each other to talk to her. But the media soon lost interest after the woman began babbling that she had received a "personal revelation" five years earlier. The journalists' attention turned to a thirty-two-year-old student from a Jogja art college. He had cleverly appeared in the courtroom wearing a red bandanna, a red shirt, and jeans, the same outfit Marsiyem had described Udin's assailant as wearing. The artist had a message to tell the court: that while they tried Iwik, Udin's real killer was still on the loose.

Amrin and his three fellow prosecutors read out their charges. There were four: first-degree murder, second-degree murder, voluntary manslaughter, and manslaughter. The prosecution left it to the court to decide how to classify Iwik's crime. The *kabupaten* had requested harsh penalties: a minimum twenty-year prison sentence or the maximum of death by firing squad.

Amrin's team reviewed the case against Iwik. It restated what Hadi had set forth in the police dossier. The noodle-sellers, Ponikem and Nur Sulaiman, had identified Iwik in a lineup. Iwik's neighbors had only seen the driver at midnight, which meant there were several hours between 6:00 p.m. and midnight when only Iwik's immediate family could testify to his whereabouts. There was the critical forensic evidence: the police crime laboratory had found traces of Udin's blood on Iwik's watch, belt, and denim jacket, as well as on the iron pipe retrieved from Dymas. But the centerpiece of the case remained Iwik's admission of his own guilt. Although Iwik had, since 26 October 1996, denied his involvement in the murder, he did, on at least four occasions before that date, deliver voluntary confessions. Based on witness testimony, physical and forensic evidence, and the accused's own uncompelled admission, the prosecution declared, the court had no choice but to convict him of murder.

Iwik's defense decided to take what Indonesian courts call an "exception." Ordinarily, most trials skip this step, since an exception is only necessary when the defendant seeks to question the court's jurisdiction. If a civilian court had been trying a case involving a soldier, for example, then an exception might have been proper. But in this case, the Bantul court was the natural venue. Nonetheless, Iwik's lawyers saw the opportunity offered by the exception as a chance to get a head start on their defense. On 5 August 1997, Iwik read aloud a ten-page speech he and his lawyers had prepared. "I had been made into a victim for 'political business' and to protect a political mafia," he declared. His lawyers followed with their legal arguments. They questioned the legitimacy of Edy's arrest and accused Hadi of violating procedures. The lawyers requested that the judges dismiss the charges.

The judges did not appreciate the defense's grandstanding. One of the three would later say that the panel believed the defense had filed an exception "just to buy time." At the next hearing, the three judges pointed out that all of the defense's objections to the procedures surrounding the arrest should have been addressed in a pretrial motion, which they had apparently waived. They could no longer raise such complaints when the court could no longer entertain them. The judges underscored a position they would maintain through the entire trial: they could only decide whether the accused before them had committed the crimes with which he was charged, and nothing more. The judges set Iwik's lawyers complaints aside, and declared that the trial should proceed as scheduled.

The judges' curt dismissal crushed the most inexperienced member of the defense team, Djufri. "I saw that the court could no longer objectively comprehend the sense of justice that comes from the people," he would recall feeling. "They could not understand the signs of truth." Triyandi and Eko, however, understood that their speech was just an opening gambit. They knew the court would not throw out the case before a single witness had testified. What they had sought to do instead was set the tone of the trial. To win this case, they would have to give the court reasons to put the police and the government on trial instead of their client.

The prosecution called its first witness, Ponikem. Although Indonesian is the official court language, Judge Endang had to swear in Ponikem in Javanese. The cook could not easily speak formal Indonesian. Judge Endang then began her cross-examination. The first question she asked the old woman: "What happened at Udin's house?"

"Someone died," Ponikem answered.

Judge Endang then urged the sixty-year-old to recount the events of 12 and 13 August 1996. The jurist tried to draw out Ponikem's recollections of her encounter with the suspect the night before the assault, and on the night of Udin's murder.

"Do you still remember what this man was wearing?" the judge asked, referring to Ponikem's encounter with the stranger on the night of 12 August.

"A jacket," said Ponikem.

"What color?"

"It was well-worn."

"But what *color*: red, green or blue?"

"A whitish color."

"If you saw that jacket again, would you still remember it?"

"Maybe," answered Ponikem. A court officer held up Iwik's jacket for the cook to examine. She declared, "The jacket was whiter."

"So this is too blue?"

Some in the audience began to applaud and jeer. The cook and Nur Sulaiman were the only witnesses to pick Iwik out of a lineup. Without their statements, he might not now be on trial. Yet Ponikem could not say for sure if she knew what the suspect had been wearing when she had met him.

"You are deciding someone's fate," one judge reminded the noodle-seller. "Think, please. Was the jacket white? Or blue?"

"Yes, the jacket is like that."

The jeers from the audience grew louder. Confused by the courtroom and ignorant of her role, Ponikem could not summon the conviction the police and the prosecution had put her on the stand to demonstrate. As the judges pressed the elderly cook to describe her recollections of several months earlier, her memory bobbed and weaved. She could not get a precise fix on what she had seen and experienced. As her testimony proceeded, the court could see that the illiterate Ponikem appeared unsure whether to agree with the judges, stick to the account she had delivered to the police, or trust her own now-jumbled recollections. When the prosecution asked her if the man she saw the night before the murder was Iwik, Ponikem answered weakly, "That person wasn't clear to me. I don't remember."

In his cross-examination of Ponikem, Eko, the most fluent Javanese speaker among the three defense lawyers, pointed to his client, Iwik:

"Have you ever seen this person?"

"I've never met him," the cook admitted.

During their own cross-examination of Ponikem, the judges had shown her a photograph from the police lineup in from which she had picked out Iwik. The noodle-seller explained to the judges she had chosen the Dymas driver because of nothing more than "the posture of his body." The witness who followed her, Nur Sulaiman, had even shakier grounds to explain her identification of Iwik. While Ponikem had spoken to the stranger directly on 12 August, Nur Sulaiman had been standing off to the side. So she had even less of a clear look at the stranger than the cook had had in the darkness. She could only note that Iwik's gait was similar to the man who had walked away from them on Parangtritis Road the night before the killing.

"What did this person look like?" Judge Mikaela pressed Nur.

"I don't know. I only saw him leave," she answered.

"Did he look like the accused?"

"It seems so."

"So what were his identifying characteristics?"

"Well, before he was dark-skinned," Nur Sulaiman giggled nervously. "But now he has light skin."

During the defense's cross-examination, Eko pounced on the noodle-seller's careless words: "You say: 'Before he was dark, now he is light?' What does that mean?"

Nur Sulaiman sat mute in her chair before the microphone. She did not answer. Iwik's attorney addressed the judges: "We question Nur's testimony. We ask this witness be reevaluated."

The first day of testimony had turned out well for the defense. With little effort, they had undermined the noodle-sellers, who had signed statements identifying Iwik as the man they had encountered the night before the crime. Their credibility as witnesses had been irredeemably compromised. *Bernas* trumpeted the defense's first-day triumph on their front page the next day. The paper's headline read: "Witnesses Doubtful."

At the next hearing, Amrin summoned Sujarah and Marsiyem. The courtroom audience had not thinned, nor did its members' attention diminish, despite the fact that both witnesses that day would recap much of the same details as the noodle-sellers had at the previous hearing. Sujarah, however, told his story in a way that was particularly entertaining. His delivery was frank, earthy, and humorous. When Judge Endang asked the reporter's neighbor why, after he saw Udin's body, he had gone inside his house to get a weapon, Sujarah quipped: "Rather than let my enemies stick it to me, it's better to stick it to them first!" Later in his testimony, after Judge Mikaela asked him to recall what he was doing before he heard Marsiyem's cries for help, he answered, without embarrassment: "At that time, I was looking to cuddle with my wife."

Even Judge Endang could not hide a smile as she admonished Sujarah that although he was under oath, there were some affairs he could keep private. The judges, however, sought a straight answer to their main question: was Iwik the man Sujarah had met the night before the murder?

"When you faced the stranger, it was not Iwik, was it?" Judge Suparno asked him.

"No."

"He did not have his features?"

"No."

"Not his skin?"

"No."

"So your conclusion is that Udin's killer was not Iwik?"

"Yes."

Sujarah's cross-examination took several hours to complete, as both prosecution and defense asked him to relate the events of both nights in Samalo. When the prosecutors and lawyers ran out of questions, Sujarah left his seat behind the microphone.

It was now Marsiyem's turn. Before her appearance at the court, some journalists had doubted Udin's wife would appear to testify. Since the beginning of the investigation, she had considered the arrest of Iwik and his subsequent prosecution a farce in which she refused to participate.

Given her depression, she also had a medical excuse to skip the trial.

But Udin's widow had arrived at the court promptly. She had waited patiently in a back room until being summoned for her testimony. Marsiyem wore a headscarf that surrounded her face from forehead to shoulder. It fell around her thin, pinched features like a shroud. As she began answering the judges' questions, the courtroom grew quiet. This day was the first time that many in the audience heard her tell, in her own voice, the story of how she had asked her husband to greet his killer.

"At 10:00 p.m., my husband came home from work," she began. "At that time I had just started my ironing. He came home and wanted to play on the computer. He didn't tell me anything special. Nothing was happening that was out of the ordinary. Then at around 10:40 p.m., someone knocked on the door."

"When you opened the door, did you ask the person his business?" Judge Endang asked.

"It seemed it was something very important. I asked: 'Who is it?' From the outside, I could hear: 'It's me, ma'am.' Then I opened the door and asked: 'What do you need?' 'Is Udin in?' 'He's here. Why do you want him?' 'I want to store my motorcycle with him. My motorcycle is broken.'"

"Did you see his motorcycle?"

"I didn't. Sujarah's fuel stall was blocking my view, and my house is set back a little from the road."

"Did he show you anything?"

"He showed me a shiny metal pipe."

"And then?"

"I told the man to wait, then I called Udin. 'What does the man want?' he asked. 'I don't know.' At that time he was ready to go to bed. He changed his pants – so he looked presentable – before going outside. I went back to my ironing, because my iron was still hot. Then after a few minutes I thought: 'Why isn't there any sound?' It's as if the visitor wasn't there. Just as I was about to leave my ironing to go outside, I heard a thud. I ran straight to the front."

"What did you see?"

"I saw Udin…He was sprawled out on the ground."

"Did you see his wounds? How were his wounds?" the judge pressed.

Marsiyem began to speak, but stopped. She stayed quiet for more than a full minute. Then she put her face in her hands and started to sob. Not a word issued from the judges, lawyers, journalists, or audience. The entire courtroom was silent, listening as one young woman wept for her dead husband.

Judge Endang gently asked Udin's wife, "Are you strong enough to continue?" She asked a court officer to fetch some water. More minutes passed as Marsiyem wiped away her tears. Then the judge continued: "Before the incident, did you see this man from the front?"

"I was right there!" Udin's wife answered firmly. Her tone had changed. No longer was she the grieving widow. She was now the defiant wife, seeking justice for her wronged husband.

"If you met this person again, would you still recognize him?"

"Yes."

"Please take a good look at the defendant."

"He's not the same at all, Your Honor! I know in the deepest part of me he was not Iwik!" Marsiyem cried.

In her testimony, Marsiyem insisted that the red shirt that the killer had been wearing looked nothing like Iwik's, which had been brought by the prosecution as evidence. When prosecutors showed her the rusty metal bar they claimed was the murder weapon, she insisted the piece of metal she had seen had been narrower and shinier. But once the judges began probing into her family life, Marsiyem's disposition turned from defiance to annoyance. During her testimony, she had tried raising the issue of the *kabupaten*'s persecution of her husband for his reporting on the IDT funds. But the judges showed more interest in the details of the couple's married life. They asked the year she and the reporter had wed and how many children they had raised together. Marsiyem lost her patience: "What connection do these questions have to this case?" she snapped.

"When the panel asks, just answer what you know," Judge Endang answered. "The judges would like to understand the condition of your household. Did you know if he had a girlfriend? Did he ever tell you he was having an affair? Did you ever suspect him of having an affair?"

"Never!"

"After you married, was there even a shadow of an old girlfriend?"

"No."

"You don't know – or you didn't want to know?"

"It's not that I didn't want to know. There were never any secrets between us."

During the defense's cross-examination, Triyandi asked for permission from the bench to show Marsiyem a picture of the businessman Nizar, clipped from the same magazine he had shown many months ago to Iwik. Triyandi wanted Udin's widow to confirm if the man who had visited her at the end of October was the same "boss" Iwik had met at Parangtritis. Triyandi, like Marsiyem, also hoped to use this opportunity to draw the court's attention away from Iwik to other theories about the murder. But the court would not follow.

"This is irrelevant!" Amrin objected.

"Counsel, ask only what the witness experienced, what she knows," Judge Endang told Triyandi.

"We object if the prosecution only seeks to steer the accused to a preordained sentence." Triyandi argued. "We also want to expose the facts: how far did those people involved go in setting up Iwik?"

"This court is not here to find out who is the real killer," Judge Endang reminded Iwik's lawyer. "The responsibility of this court is to ascertain Iwik's guilt. As for the identity of the killer, that is the responsibility of the police."

Their attempt stymied, Iwik's defense wondered if their first day in court, so filled with potential, might instead have raised their hopes too high. A fast start often means that the path ahead slopes downhill.

As the trial progressed, Triyandi tried repeatedly to draw the court to speculate about the Bantul *bupati*'s involvement. On 8 September 1997, Sri Roso's nephew Kuncung appeared in court for his testimony. Controversy had shadowed the young village official since the murder. But unlike his uncle, Kuncung seemed eager to speak to journalists. The previous December, he had received ten reporters the night before a police interrogation. "So many people say so many things without first meeting with us," he had complained at the time. "If you have some kind of interest, just contact me, so everything is clear." To reporters, he continued to deny accusations that he had attempted to bribe Yani to admit to an affair with the deceased reporter. "Just getting new tires for my car is difficult," he said. "How can I offer someone a house and everything?"

Perhaps because he had repeated his explanations so often, Kuncung arrived at his court appointment the most prepared of the witnesses. He was full of self-confidence. He recounted the same details he had told the press many months before: the volleyball game that he and his friends had watched, Akung's invitation to go out for noodles, the trip down Parangtritis Road, the sudden halt in front of the panicked ladies of Ponikem's noodle stall, and then the delivery of Udin's bloody, broken body to the Bantul hospital.

"How could you still go ahead and still eat those noodles?" Judge Endang wondered.

"At the time I didn't know how bad he was. My friends didn't know either. By bringing him to the hospital we felt we had done our civic duty." Kuncung said smoothly.

"Why didn't you check on his condition?"

"I never thought that he would die. I never thought it would go that far."

During the defense's turn, Triyandi cross-examined Kuncung about his visit to Yani. "What was the intent in asking her to admit to an affair with Udin?" the lawyer demanded.

"Let me explain," Kuncung replied. "One day, a lot of police were waiting for me at my home. Someone from the precinct arrived: Edy Wuryanto. I was told to ask Tri Sumaryani whether she had been near the Bantul courthouse that Monday before the crime. I never expected her to accuse me. I only helped the police."

The defense did not manage to get Kuncung to reveal anything he had not said before in other contexts. His friends, also called to testify he following week, added nothing of value. "I didn't feel satisfied," Triyandi would later reflect on their handling of the early days of the trial. "We couldn't expose anything in its totality." When the last youth left the witness seat, no one still knew whether the presence of Sri Roso's nephew at the scene so soon after the assault was due to coincidence or to conspiracy.

As the defense in a criminal case, Triyandi's expected strategy was to introduce doubt in the judges' minds about his client's guilt by alluding to other possible suspects. The judges' reaction was equally predictable: they had seen lawyers perform this trick before, and they were tired of it. They would only examine and rule on the evidence presented; deciding on anything else would be a guess or a grab. It was not their fault that the wrong case – even the wrong suspect – was before them. They had a job to do, and it certainly was not to catch Udin's "real" killer. That was law enforcement's responsibility.

Beginning with Kuncung's questioning, the trial adopted a regular schedule. Every Monday and Thursday, the judges heard testimony. In the trial's early weeks, each hearing lasted up to five hours, from midmorning until well after lunchtime. Every day that a hearing was scheduled, the courtroom would prove too small to contain the spectators. The audience would spill out into the hallway and into the court's front yard, where people listened to the judges and the witnesses over a set of loudspeakers. The reactions of the audience largely favored Iwik. Each time a witness mentioned something that supported the defense, people clapped or shouted.

Although Triyandi was the lead defense counsel, he allowed Eko, Adib, and Djufri to participate actively in the cross-examinations. For Djufri, this opportunity to participate in a nationally famous case came once in a career. Before each scheduled hearing, he studied the police reports of each witness' interrogation, probing for possible uncertainties or exploitable contradictions in their stories. He prepared dozens of questions for each witness. He never missed a hearing.

By mid-September, nearly all the main witnesses had been questioned. Not one had testified for certain they had seen Iwik at the scene. Two witnesses, Sujarah and Marsiyem, had stated adamantly that the man they had met could not be Iwik. Still, the prosecution possessed two powerful items of evidence: the supposed murder weapon, with its traces of blood that led back to the victim. They also had Iwik's unretracted confession. Witness memory could be unreliable. But the rusty metal bar with the trace evidence was hard, physical, and incontrovertible. And the suspect's own words could still send him back to prison, if not to his execution.

When Dymas' secretary Ratna Ismariana took her seat before the microphone, the metal pipe became a critical issue. Under questioning from Judge Mikaela, Ratna revealed that police officers had once showed her a length of pipe they had retrieved from the scrap piles around the office. Triyandi, Eko, and Djufri recalled that when they had accompanied the detectives on their initial search of Iwik's workplace on 22 October 1996, none of them remembered any of the detectives presenting an employee of Dymas with the metal pipe Iwik had picked out. But if the billboard company's secretary had not seen the pipe that day, then why was she insisting to the court that she had?

The defense realized that if Ratna's recollection was correct, then police detectives had possibly made *another* trip to Iwik's workplace and taken *another* pipe to be used as evidence. Triyandi asked Ratna if what she remembered was accurate. "The police did come several times to Dymas," the secretary insisted. "I don't remember when they showed the pipe to me. What I'm sure is that I was in the office."

"Take ten seconds to look closely: was this piece of iron really the one showed to you on that day – the shape, the length? Look closely," Djufri joined in.

"I'm not sure about its length and width. I only saw it for a moment…"

"Can I conclude that you doubt this piece of evidence?"

"It's true I don't know for sure. I only saw it for a moment."

Triyandi looked closely at the length of pipe on exhibit in the courthouse. It was a narrow, straight, rusty tube of metal. Although he had seen the pipe unsealed, unwrapped, and presented to the court, the lawyer had never felt comfortable about this piece of metal. All the time he had thought the pipe confiscated on 22 October was shorter, thinner, and rustier. He remembered that one end had been bent at a right angle and had a serrated edge, as if the pipe had been cut from a longer length of metal. None of these characteristics, especially the distinctive bend, he noticed in the piece presented at the court. The secretary's testimony confirmed his doubts. The police's efforts to pin the crime on Iwik now seemed even more ridiculous, for the pipe presented to the court was neither the one Iwik had picked up nor the real murder weapon. Perhaps the police had worried that Marsiyem would find unfamiliar the piece of metal Iwik had picked at random on 22 October 1996, and thus decided to supply a more "credible" murder weapon.

"According to my experience, this is called manipulation of evidence," Triyandi told journalists the day of Ratna's revelation. "During the seizure of evidence at Dymas, I was the one who held that pipe after Iwik. And it was different in size, shape, and condition." With the metal pipe under suspicion, he told the media, the prosecution's case had become tissue-thin. It rested solely on Iwik's confession. "The prosecution's charges," Triyandi pointed out, "cannot be supported by the prosecution's own witnesses."

The last witnesses scheduled to face the court were the neighbors and friends of Iwik and Sunarti. But instead of helping the prosecution establish motive – Sunarti's affair with Udin – the witnesses assisted the defense by confirming the couple's alibis. Three of the couple's neighbors said they were certain Iwik had been at home on 13 August. They said the driver could not have traveled the eighty kilometers to Bantul and back on his run-down Vespa between the times the police had established. "I can often hear when Iwik throttles that Vespa," the couple's neighbor Heri told Judge Endang. "It can be more than ten, fifteen times before it starts."

On 22 September, Sunarti recounted the couple's activities the night of the assault, and the day before. She explained Iwik's asthma, which would have made it difficult for him to brave the midnight chill down to Samalo. Sunarti admitted that she sometimes argued with Iwik, but it was usually over Bimo, who "was still rather spoiled." But, she insisted, no other person, especially not another lover, had ever come between them.

Sunarti's longtime friend from Bantul, Isnani, confirmed that there had never been anything going on between Udin and Sunarti, even in high school.

"Did you ever see Udin visiting Sunarti?" Judge Endang asked Isnani.

"In God's name, no!" she answered.

"Did Sunarti ever tell you she had another boyfriend besides Iwik?"

"In God's name, she never did!"

"You don't need to use the words, 'in God's name.'" Judge Endang reminded her. "You're already under oath."

Each time *Bernas* summarized a witness' testimony for its readers, the paper reminded them that not one had verified either Iwik's guilt or Sunarti's adultery. The trial had become a subject for national discussion; an opportunity for all individuals, from peasant farmers to citified intellectuals, to comment on the state of their nation. Despite the tight security, student protesters gathered regularly outside each hearing. Prominent Muslim leaders and human-rights commission members often attended each demonstration and sometimes sat through the hearings. In opinion pieces and news reports in the local and national press, journalists used the Iwik trial to review the sorry state of press freedom. Lawyers referred to the ongoing case to score points in arguments over necessary reforms to the legal system. Activists reflected on how the developing drama in the Bantul courthouse reflected the suffocating selfishness of their government.

"If the public prosecutor represents the public interest in bringing Iwik before the court," one legal scholar asked in a *Bernas* essay, "then exactly what public interest does he represent?" Several forensic specialists debated the evidence: whether the blood that had been found on the pipe could have been taken from the bag Edy had borrowed from the reporter's family. Others attempted to comment on larger issues in a more unique fashion. A group of Jogja artists installed at Legal Aid's office a single bust of Udin and an array of ninety other identical sculptures, each of a head without eyes, ears and a brain, and whose mouth had been plastered over. Inside the courtroom, the judges could maintain a strict boundary between the facts of the case and its charged political context. But outside the Bantul courthouse, the situation was very different.

Despite the vast attention the case was receiving, something disturbed Udin's fellow journalists and the lawyers. They had tried their best to make the trial a chance to reopen the long-stalled inquiry into the Bantul government's alleged involvement and the police department's supposed cover-up. Yet the judges' strict focus on deciding only Iwik's guilt or innocence meant that very little could be exposed about Udin's death in this trial. The court case generated much heat but shone no light at all on the murder that spawned it. Marsiyem, too, had realized that whatever was going on at the Bantul courthouse brought no one nearer to solving her husband's death. So she had relived the night of her deepest pain for little purpose. "How can justice be achieved in this country?" she asked an audience of students at a local campus. "What's important these days are what the investigators want, and what those in power desire."

The entire apparatus of law and order in Jogjakarta – the police, prosecutors, and judges – seemed so wrapped up in Iwik's case that no one was looking anymore for the true assassin. If those behind Udin's murder had desired protection from exposure, they had succeeded magnificently. As each day of Iwik's trial passed, the trail of clues leading to the true killer grew colder.

One day during the hearing, Ida picked up her eight-year-old son from school. She drove around idly to see if she could find a local thug Titet had mentioned lived in the neighborhood and who might possibly be Udin's real killer. She spotted her quarry's car come out of a side road. She quickly pulled her vehicle around to follow him. "At the Tungkak intersection he turned east towards the bus terminal," she would later recall. "Then he disappeared in that direction. I couldn't follow him anymore." Worried about her son, Ida turned around and went home.

Ida's brief encounter with an alternative suspect was a microcosm of Iwik's trial. The spectacle had practically buried Udin's murder. Just as the real killer had somehow magically escaped the night of the assault, now, all the attention surrounding the scapegoat had ensured that the real murderer of Udin would have long vanished.

CHAPTER 12

A Country of Law

HALFWAY THROUGH the trial, Triyandi was ready to declare victory. The prosecution's own witnesses had helped Iwik far more than they had the police or the public prosecutor. The noodle sellers had bungled their identification of Iwik, while the two crucial figures, Sujarah and Marsiyem, had rejected the driver as a suspect. Other witnesses cast doubt on several aspects of the prosecution's case, from the likelihood that Iwik's Vespa could be the getaway vehicle to whether the murder weapon presented in the courtroom had really been the one Iwik had picked up from Dymas. "The picture was complete of where Iwik was at the time of the crime," Triyandi could tell himself. "He wasn't the killer." Djufri felt equally satisfied. "We finished them off," he would later recall feeling. "We really killed them."

When the prosecution's final two scheduled witnesses, the police serology laboratory chief Tunggono and DNA expert Djaya Surya-atmadja, appeared in court at the end of September, their testimony seemed almost superfluous. Although blood that matched the victim's blood type and DNA profile had been found on Iwik's possessions and the murder weapon, both experts admitted they could not conclude that the blood had come from Udin himself. Both could not deny the possibility that the blood traces had been placed on the evidence on purpose. "As an expert," Judge Mikaela had asked Djaya, "can you tell the difference between blood that sticks to something as a result of a crime and blood that has been intentionally applied?"

"When examined at the DNA level, there is no difference," Djaya answered.

Djaya had been the last on the list of witnesses in the dossier Hadi had provided. Throughout the trial, most of Amrin's team had seemed unconvinced by its own case. Early in the hearings, Judge Endang admonished the four for allowing the judges and the defense to dominate the cross-examinations. Indeed, to most who had observed the trial, the prosecutors seemed as if they had shown up in court just so Iwik's trial could proceed. With the possible exception of Amrin, their hearts were not into ensuring a guilty verdict.

At the end of the expert witnesses' testimony, the lead prosecutor asked the judges to allow him to summon additional witnesses. On his list, along with other names the defense did not recognize, were several police officers, including Edy and Hadi. Iwik's defense counsel immediately protested the presentation of new testimony, on the same grounds Marsiyem's lawyers had cited during the Blood Trial. The policemen, they declared, were biased, whose accounts could only serve to prejudice the court against their client. Nonetheless, the judges accepted the prosecution's request. The trial was not yet over.

Once the new witnesses were permitted to testify, the atmosphere in the court changed. Instead of the ordinary citizens who had attended the first half of the trial, the audience now consisted mainly of men with crewcuts and muscular builds – plainclothed police, there to support their colleagues in a case the result of which implicated their entire organization. Sprinkled among the males were a few women who wore khaki skirts, part of the standard female police officer uniform. By 6:30 a.m. on each trial date, police officers had seized all the seats in the courtroom. Some lay across several chairs so no one but their colleagues could take them. Edged out by the new, police-packed audience, the usual trial watchers found themselves shunted off to the courthouse lawn or the back parking lot.

Iwik's lawyers sensed the change in the courtroom atmosphere as they entered the room on 2 October 1997 to hear the first of the new witnesses. When the attorneys took their seats, the audience hissed insults:

"Dog!"

"Pig!"

"Two-bit attorneys!"

Iwik thought he heard the same voices that bawled threats at him from outside his detention cell in the first weeks of his imprisonment. Triyandi later protested the courtroom harassments to the Bantul police chief. But Yotje replied he could neither discipline nor restrain his men and women, since the officers were there in a personal capacity to support their colleagues.

None of the defense lawyers knew anything about the first witness but his name, Diharjo Purboko. A short, chubby man with pencil mustache, Diharjo's most distinguishing feature was his dark, glossy skin, which made him appear more Indian than Javanese. The regular courtroom ritual of judge's cross-examination, followed by the prosecution and the defense, had shifted. In this phase, Amrin would have first crack at each new witness for the prosecution.

"Witness, have you ever met the accused?" the lead prosecutor asked Diharjo.

"Yes. At the Hotel Queen."

"In what capacity were you at the Hotel Queen?"

"I was asked by Franky to play a 'boss.'"

On 21 October 1996, Diharjo told the court, Edy's deputies met Diharjo near Parangtritis to ask for his help. They wanted him to participate in a sting operation to capture a suspect responsible for the famous Udin murder. When Diharjo agreed, Edy took him to the Queen of the South Hotel and introduced him to Iwik.

At first, Diharjo recalled, the Dymas driver was silent. But when the three of them entered a hotel room to talk, the dark-skinned man continued, Iwik asked Diharjo if they might speak privately. "Iwik cried in my lap. I told him to sit beside me," Diharjo recounted to the court.

"He said: 'I have a big problem, sir.' I asked: 'What problem?' 'I beat up Udin.'"

The courtroom cheered, hooted, and clapped. In previous hearings, when Marsiyem and Sujarah rejected the Dymas driver, the courtroom audience had applauded. Gales of laughter had also greeted the noodle-sellers' confusion. Now the observers who surrounded Iwik and his lawyers had taken a position opposite to that of the first audience. They praised every testimony that brought the hapless driver a step closer to a possible death sentence.

Diharjo said that Iwik told him he did not want to go to jail, or that his wife and child would find out what had happened.

"He spoke from his conscience?" Amrin asked the witness.

"Yes."

Later, one of Iwik's defense lawyers would ask Iwik if Diharjo was indeed the boss he had met at Parangtritis. The Dymas driver shook his head. "His face seemed similar," Iwik would recall. "But his body was not big enough, and the man I met before had a light complexion. This one was too dark." To Triyandi, Diharjo's presence confirmed the information that he had received more than eight months earlier – that a different "boss" other than Nizar would be found for the trial. Indeed, Triyandi had persuaded himself that Marsiyem's visitor and "Jendra" was the same person. Despite the fact that the witness before them had the kind of coal-black skin someone like Iwik might have plausibly perceived as "Indian," and could have been the "Jendra" in Edy's plan, the attorneys were skeptical that this witness had actually been present during Iwik's capture. So when the judges turned Diharjo over to the defense for cross-examination, the lawyers decided that before confirming the details of Diharjo's stint as Edy's "boss," they would first attempt to unmask this apparent pretender.

"Your education?" Triyandi asked Diharjo.

"Bachelor of Laws," the witness replied proudly, and named Gadjah Mada University as his alma mater.

"Occupation?"

"Raising livestock."

In their cross-examination, Triyandi and his co-counsel prodded Diharjo to describe his encounter down to the details: What was Iwik wearing? What was Edy wearing? Who arrived at the hotel first, the Dymas driver or the detective? To the court, the defense must have seemed obsessed about minor matters of fact – of distance, clothing, and weather. But the lawyers were convinced Diharjo was a liar. They wanted to get this man to slip, so they could catch the actor in the act of acting.

"What special skill did you have in solving this case?" Djufri asked Diharjo.

"I was not there to 'solve' the case," the witness responded. "I helped. As a citizen when the police ask me for help, I am always ready!"

Although none of the three extracted an admission from Diharjo that he had not in fact been at the Queen of the South, the defense lawyers managed to infect the judges with doubt. During their cross-examination, the jurists became curious how a livestock salesman could persuade a driver, even one as dim as Iwik, that he ran an offshore drilling company.

"Do you know anything about drilling?" Judge Endang asked.

"I don't."

"Then how can you talk about offshore drilling?"

When the defense bluntly confronted him as well with their skepticism, Diharjo insisted that the role had been played by him and not by Nizar, "I'm sorry, but there is a lot in the papers that doesn't make sense," he said. "I read: 'Offshore Drilling Boss Discovered.' I was surprised! I thought everyone knew it was me. The reporting is wrong."

The second witness that day, Edy's deputy Slamet Wijayanto, asserted that the Bantul team had indeed chosen Diharjo for the operation. "Yes, Diharjo was asked to help in the investigation in the murder of Udin," he said, answering one of Amrin's questions. "He was given the responsibility of being our 'boss.'"

Slamet, Edy's aide, explained how the Bantul police had made Iwik a suspect. While investigating the reporter's background, he said, they received some information that the day before the assault, Udin had been seen carrying a woman on his motorcycle outside the Bantul courthouse. The source of that news was a woman he knew named Windarmiyati. To confirm her information, Slamet took Windarmiyati to Sunarti's salon. Apparently, Slamet's informant had been the woman in a civil servant's uniform who had her hair cut that day in Panasan. In Sunarti's salon, Slamet said Iwik's wife had replied, to a question about the dead journalist: "He was my friend! He was just about to get rich. He had a new Tiger motorcycle, he had a computer, and he asked me to 'get back together' with him."

One of Iwik's lawyers queried: "When you asked Windarmiyati whether the woman in the salon was the same one on Udin's motorcycle, what did she say?"

"She said it wasn't," replied Slamet. "The woman on the motorcycle had long hair."

Judge Mikaela noted Slamet's response. She interrupted to ask: "So why was Iwik taken when Windarmiyati was not sure that the person on the motorcycle was Sunarti?"

"At the time we took him, we were still in the process of investigation."

"So why was he arrested?"

"Because he confessed to Diharjo."

"But wasn't there a – what do you call it – a 'performance' before that?"

"It wasn't a performance!" responded Slamet.

"Well, what would you call all that play-acting if it wasn't a performance?"

As the judges pressed him, Slamet could not explain why, if Windarmiyati could not say for sure whether she had really seen Sunarti on the reporter's motorcycle, the Bantul police had not immediately discarded Iwik as their primary target.

"So was the basis for suspecting Iwik just your instinct?" Judge Endang asked in wonder.

"Yes...just our instinct."

Eko demanded to know why the police continued to target a man against whom it had no evidence. "Edy can explain it all later," Slamet said lamely.

At the end of Slamet's testimony, the judges turned back to Diharjo. They asked the livestock salesman to show them his identity card and his student credentials to confirm his biographical information for court documents. His identification, however, indicated that he was still a student, undermining his claim that he was a law graduate. When the judges began questioning Diharjo whether what he had said under oath was correct, the color drained out of the dark man's face. "Under the rules of this court, I request Your Honor to detain this witness," Triyandi shouted triumphantly.

The court exploded in uproar of whispers. The audience murmured to each other, as did the judges, lawyers and prosecutors. Judge Endang finally concluded that Diharjo's perjury was harmless: "His statement appears to concern only himself and his own background. There does not seem to be anything in our criminal laws to detain him on that basis." Triyandi was satisfied. Although they had not contradicted the witness' testimony, they had cast enough doubt on Diharjo's credibility to undermine his account of Iwik's capture.

The next witness was Slamet's informant, Windarmiyati. She told the court that she had been at the Bantul courthouse on 12 August to attend a hearing involving one of her relatives. When she left the court, she noticed a woman riding on the back of a motorcycle of a man she had often seen covering trials in the building. During the extensive coverage after the reporter's murder, she told the court, she realized that the man she had seen was Udin, but that the woman with him was not his wife.

"When I read the newspapers and watched TV, I thought: 'Why is the person crying different? So who was that riding?'" she told the judges.

She had mentioned her story to her younger sister, who reported it to the police. Afterward, Slamet brought Windarmiyati a picture of Sunarti to match against her recollection of the rider. When she could not determine from Sunarti's photo whether it depicted the woman she saw on the back of Udin's motorcycle, the detectives took her to Sunarti's salon to see Iwik's wife in person. There, just as Slamet had testified earlier, she was surprised to find that Sunarti had short-cropped locks, although her height seemed about the same as Udin's passenger.

The discrediting of Diharjo had now colored the judges' approach to the remaining witnesses. To the pleasant surprise of Iwik's attorneys, the jurists joined the lawyers in scrutinizing both the information delivered as well as the credibility of the messengers. Windarmiyati had attended the hearing in a headscarf, the garb of pious Muslim woman. That image was not in line with her account, since a devout Muslim woman would not have gone in the company of another man to Sunarti's salon without her husband. At one point, Judge Mikaela made her suspicions about Windarmiyati rudely clear.

"Are you a 'friend' of Slamet's?" she asked the witness. No, insisted Windarmiyati vehemently.

The last witness of the day was Retno, the teenage prostitute who had met Iwik at the Agung Inn. She described how Iwik had entered the rest house with several men. She remembered they had ordered three bottles of beer, which she poured into four glasses. She said Iwik only had finished half a glass before the two of them went into a room together.

"Did Iwik invite you in?" asked Amrin.

"Yes," Retno answered.

"What did you do?"

"We just talked."

"Did you have sex?"

"No. Just some kissing."

In Indonesian criminal trials, after each witness speaks, the court gives the accused a chance to object to any part of the testimony. Iwik had used this traditional privilege sparingly. He had sat through each testimony impassively, without indicating a response. But when Retno finished, Iwik spoke in anger. They did not kiss, he insisted to the court. Nothing had happened between them. Indeed, months earlier, Retno had told the *Bernas* reporters that all Iwik had done was fall asleep after some conversation. Either she had changed her story since then, or she had not been truthful when she had first spoken to the reporters.

Although it enraged the defendant, Retno's testimony on whether or not she and Iwik had engaged in any physical contact was a tangential issue. The next witness scheduled to appear was far more important to his case: Edy Wuryanto.

On 6 October 1997, Edy swaggered into the courtroom. The Bantul detective oozed confidence. Perhaps it was because, as rumored, the detective's personal *dukun* had joined the audience to support Edy, or because Edy just felt that he controlled the courtroom, with or without his *dukun*'s magic. Plainclothed operatives and policemen, just as they had for the previous sessions, occupied all the available seating so Iwik's lawyers could not find a single sympathetic face in the audience. Some members still hissed threats at them. One man shouted at them in the slick, extended vowels of sarcasm: "Hey, why are you defending a murderer?" Before the hearing began, the judges had two men in crew cuts removed for brawling. That move did not seem to disturb the mood of the rest of the audience. They had come to support Edy – and Edy knew the audience was firmly behind him.

Amrin began asking questions of the detective. Edy told Amrin his superiors had told him to investigate all possible motives behind Udin's murder. "We started with his news, then we looked at his personal life." Edy said. The latter line of inquiry turned out to be the most promising. First, he said, their suspicion fell on Yani. "We got information that Udin gave a ride to a woman one evening on Parangtritis Road towards Jogja. This person said: 'Hey, someone's asking if Udin still has that 'backpack'.' We went and looked into who this 'backpack' was. We found out that this 'backpack' was Tri Sumaryani."

"So I went to Tri Sumaryani. She was evasive. I cross-examined her, and in the end she admitted she had hitched a ride that evening. I wondered: 'Why so late?' So we checked: does Tri Sumaryani have a boyfriend? It turned out she did, and they were about to get married."

"Then I got information from some of Udin's old friends that Udin was often paired with Sunarti at school. We found out Sunarti was a Bantul girl, who married someone from Sleman. So I went to the religious affairs office in her area to confirm, and borrowed from the director her photo and address in Sleman."

"I wanted to know who these people Dwi Sumaji and Sunarti were...When I first saw Dwi Sumaji, in my heart I thought, hey, this man looks suspicious. He fits the description. But to get close to him, I had to know his job and where he worked. So I often ate noodles at Heri Karyono's stall. I got information from Heri and the neighbors about Dwi Sumaji. Because I knew where he worked and where he lived, I came to Sunarti's place to get a haircut. When Sunarti talked to me, I pretended I was from Jakarta."

The assistant public prosecutor interrupted Edy's fluent and confident palaver. "What name did you give?"

"She hadn't asked me."

"What name did you give the accused?"

"I was 'Franky,'" Edy nattered on. "So I asked Sunarti, 'Why is Jogja so full of talk about this journalist?' 'That man was from my village.' 'Oh, so you are from Bantul?' 'Yeah, and he was a good man. Udin was really a good man and a good friend of mine.' Then she continued talking about how often Udin came to her house – I heard this all myself – and he was about to be rich. He had a Honda Tiger motorcycle. He had a computer, he showed her his press card, and he told her he wanted to 'get back together' with her. I told her: 'Don't be so loud. What if your husband hears?' She said that he had left for work and she wanted to let him know anyway."

"So how did you get close to the defendant so he got to be so comfortable with you?" asked Amrin.

"I was in control of his whole identity," Edy said proudly. "I knew even about his twin older brothers in Jakarta. I showed I really knew him. I talked about his work and how when he goes out of town for work, he doesn't come home, that he gets sixty-four dollars a month working morning until night. I thought: how do I get closer? So I ordered a billboard. At the time, I hadn't planned it. It was spontaneous. He accepted but said not to let his company find out. He said he knew how much a billboard cost. He would take care of having it made and getting the paint and everything. I went to look for an example of a billboard, and then I went to find Dwi Sumaji but didn't find him. I gave his friend this message: 'Here's a letter for him. If there's anything, have him call me. The main thing is that Dwi Sumaji handle this himself. I'll arrange a meeting for him with my boss later.'"

"So I came to his house on Monday, 21 October 1996. When we got there, he had already left. We were told he had taken public transportation. So we chased him, but he had already caught a bus and was hanging off the back of it. At the turnoff there was a red light, and I stopped on the side of the road. 'Dwi!' He said: 'Hey, Frank.' He got down on his own and told me I hadn't called. 'Huh? I was waiting for your call too! How about it if we meet my boss right now?'"

"We went straight to Parangtritis Road. Dwi Sumaji asked where my boss was, and I said he was staying at a hotel in Parangtritis. When we got to Parangtritis, I went into the Agung Inn. There was that girl Retno and another whose name I didn't know."

"On entering this place, did you order drinks or not?" asked Amrin.

"I asked Dwi if he wanted tea or coffee and he boasted: 'I can drink a lot and not throw up.'" The audience guffawed. Edy grinned, pleased with himself, and continued. "At the time, we had three bottles of beer among five people, and we mixed the beer with Red Bull and divided the drinks equally. Then, he embraced one of the women while doing this." Edy rubbed his fingers together in one hand as the crowd chortled.

"What does that mean?"

"Maybe it means 'money' or whatever, but I told him everything would be taken care of. Then I left him while going around thinking what to do next. I got together with my friends and thought who would be the best to be a 'boss' among us. Fat Jono's haircut looked fit for a boss but he looked like a mess, so it wouldn't work. Among us detectives, I'd have to say I was the best-looking and most suitable." Once again, the courtroom laughed. His audience was enjoying this retelling.

"So why was someone else chosen?"

"There was a suggestion from Tarjo that his friend Diharjo would fit because he wore a lot of gold jewelry. Diharjo came at about 2:00 p.m. I saw that he was the right guy. I asked him for his help because I suspected someone of killing Udin. 'Help me and be my boss' – the boss of offshore drilling. Diharjo went to the Hotel Queen because it wouldn't work for the boss to be in the Agung Inn. I went there and Iwik hadn't come out yet. In the end, he came out. I gave him about eight dollars to give to Retno then I said: 'Come on, my boss is here.' I saw that Dwi Sumaji looked nervous but I didn't know why."

"Maybe he was drunk," said Amrin.

"No, sir, if he was drunk it'd be obvious...so I talked with Dwi Sumaji. Maybe he was thinking that he did have a problem. Dwi Sumaji talked to the boss, who said Dwi Sumaji wanted to speak face-to-face with him. I went outside."

"You didn't hear what was discussed?"

"No. After some minutes I was called in by Diharjo, who said, 'Your friend does have a problem. He beat up Udin.' When he said this, I had to confirm this information with details I had picked up in the field. I had to know why Dwi Sumaji confessed to the 'boss.' If his story didn't fit, then he was lying."

"What had been said?"

"He asked the 'boss' for help, that he not be tried and his case not end up in the papers," said the detective.

"Was this confession forced or voluntary?" asked Amrin.

"It came from his conscience."

Edy had been polite, even collegial toward the lead prosecutor. But when the defense lawyer Triyandi began his cross-examination, Edy became visibly vicious.

"Witness," Triyandi asked, "on what evidence did you bring this investigation to this conclusion?"

"As a lawyer you should know," the detective shot back.

Annoyed, Triyandi turned to Judge Endang: "Please tell the witness I'm the one asking questions!" She nodded, and reminded Edy to be polite in his answers.

"On 21 October," Triyandi continued, "Why did you invite Iwik?"

"I didn't invite him. He came down off the bus himself."

"Did you invite him, kidnap him, or did he go voluntarily?"

"Honorable counsel, I think you know better what constitutes a 'kidnapping.'" The audience clapped and hooted.

Triyandi tried another line of questioning. "When you took Iwik to Parangtritis, did you identify yourself as a policeman?"

"I did not."

"Under our criminal law, you were supposed to show your papers to the defendant. Why didn't you do that?"

"In detective work, there is something you call techniques of observation, of tailing. There is also undercover work. It's there, in criminal law!"

"You took Iwik to Parangtritis, then you brought Retno to him, then you gave him alcohol. Was this allowed under the rules of investigation?"

"I've already testified that Dwi himself asked for the beer. And we drank it. If there really was a setup, then just point it out!"

"I'm not accusing you of a setup. What I mean is: are procedures like this considered correct?"

"Figure it out yourself from what I just said."

The crowd cheered, as if he had scored a goal during a game of soccer. Even after Judge Endang stepped in to remind Edy that he was in a court of law, and was obligated to answer each question respectfully, the detective continued testing the lawyer's patience.

"At first you wanted to talk about business," asked Triyandi. "How was it that you came to be talking about the Udin case? Did you invite him to do so?"

"No. I came with Dwi to the Agung Inn not to discuss Udin."

"How is it possible that you can make such a denial?"

"I'm telling what happened, by God."

"You can say that, but we have our own beliefs about you," Triyandi spluttered.

"Well, that's your prerogative, isn't it?"

"What I asked is why Dwi Sumaji submitted to what you wanted?"

"Because I had become close to him."

"Did you promise him anything?"

"I never promised him!"

"Witness, you are under oath!"

"It's true! I swear. What do you want to make of it?"

"And what were the Bantul police chief's promises?

"He said he was ready to help, and that the most important thing was that Iwik would not go to court."

"And is that what happened?"

"That was *detective work*!"

"We note down – may the judges note down – that those promises were never kept and now the defendant is being tried!"

"Counsel, just questions please," Judge Endang cautioned.

During the judges' cross-examination, Edy toned down his hostility.

"Who directed the whole scenario in which Diharjo was made the 'boss?'" Judge Endang asked.

"I did."

"A 'boss' of oil drilling?"

"No, just drilling in the ocean."

"The place of Nyai Roro Kidul?"

"Oh, *no*," Edy answered, laughing.

Outside, the journalist Achadi was listening. "These are the most outrageous lies," he thought to himself. An Indonesian police detective handbook does say that undercover work is "a very useful technique in exposing organized crime, such as subversion, smuggling, organized theft, extortion, kidnapping, etc." Edy could not explain to the court, however, why undercover work was necessary to nab Iwik, who was not a subversive, a smuggler, a thief, an extortionist, or a kidnapper. Edy still had not justified why his team had focused so much attention on the driver on the basis of so little evidence. He answered the judges' and Triyandi's questions by repeatedly stating that it had not been his role to check the evidence or make the right fit. His job, it seemed, was only to find a suspect for the police – not the most likely one.

If that was so, then Edy must have been blessed with a string of exceptionally fortunate circumstances. A chance bit of information about a woman who had ridden home with Udin led him to conclude that Udin was having an affair. In exploring that affair – which he could never confirm – he had stumbled on a man who looked suspicious enough to be a suspect. Then, in the most fortunate happenstance of all, that suspect spontaneously confessed, rescuing Edy from the responsibility of gathering any more evidence.

Perhaps that bag of Udin's blood, which the reporter had thrown that *Kliwon* Tuesday eve into Nyai Roro Kidul's realm, had indeed worked. From deep inside her invisible palace, the demon queen had taken his blood offering and had led this suspect to him. And thus one poor, ill-educated man confessed to a murder in a hotel perched on the edge of her realm, while the surf of the Southern Ocean crashed in the distance.

When Sunarti heard the police witnesses' testimony, she was horrified. Although she had told both Edy and his deputy that she had known Udin and had joked with him, they had perverted her sentences to hint at an altogether different meaning. How could they conclude that she was having an affair from the few words she had so carelessly tossed away? Her confusion, however, could not rival her husband's anger. He felt a sense of deep betrayal; he had been made a fool by this detective.

When Judge Endang asked him for his objections, Iwik stood up and spoke. "Before my meeting with the boss, Franky made up a scenario that I was to confess to murdering Udin," he said. "He said it was political business. He said it was to protect one official in Bantul!" Iwik stabbed his finger at Edy. His voice, at first calm and measured, grew steadily louder. At the end, he did not realize he was shouting.

❦

In the courtroom, Edy had exhibited an arrogant bravado that perhaps he hoped masked the many incongruities in his testimony. His explanation for why he had arrested Iwik only underlined the importance of Iwik's confession, which had become the fundamental reason why he had arrested Iwik. So instead of expanding the prosecution's case, the new witnesses' testimony had narrowed it down to this one issue: the voluntariness of Iwik's confession. If the confession were shown to be compelled, then the police and the prosecution had no good reason why Iwik had been made a suspect in the first place. So Hadi, who had handled most of Iwik's interrogations, had the unenviable task of persuading the court that Iwik's confession was valid. Hadi would be the last witness for the prosecution.

Infuriated by Edy's testimony, Iwik's attorneys went for Hadi's jugular. During their cross-examination, they dug into the detective mercilessly. They demanded to know why the police had violated so many procedures in the investigation, from the search for and seizure of the "murder weapon" at Dymas to the failure to inform Iwik's counsel of critical events that involved their client.

"In the first lineup, we were there. Why weren't we informed about this second lineup? What was the reason?" Triyandi told the judges. "Note it down that we were not there. This was really peculiar."

Hadi answered each question fearlessly. But in the end, his simmering resentment of Udin's widow for complicating what should have been a cakewalk of a case finally brimmed over.

"The defendant was questioned eight times. In all of those eight times, did he give the same information?" Judge Mikaela asked Hadi.

"Four times the accused admitted openly," Hadi answered, "But after 'big shot' Marsiyem said that the suspect was not Dwi Sumaji, he changed his mind, Your Honor."

"Marsiyem is a 'big shot?'" Judge Mikaela asked sharply.

"Yes, she always has people around her. She's gotten a lot of money. She's become a big shot." When the judges' expressions showed him that they did not appreciate his answer, Hadi hastily revised it. "Let me emphasize," he continued, "the defendant began to change his mind after meeting often with his counsel, and his counsel gave him a lot of suggestions."

In blaming Marsiyem and Triyandi, Hadi had exposed the police force's resentment for all to see. Hadi, Edy, and Mulyono had all believed they had a solution to the Udin murder mystery. They had a criminal in custody. They had his confession. They had secured forensic evidence, confirmed by a Western expert. Then their plans fell apart because a few people, people who were supposed to have no role in an investigation – Udin's stubborn-as-hell widow, Udin's journalist friends and these damned lawyers – had chosen to doubt their capabilities and their authority.

When the chastened Hadi finished his testimony, the lawyers presented a letter they had obtained from Gadjah Mada University. The university confirmed that Diharjo had yet to receive his law degree. The defense knew the revelation had no relation to the case. But the more they could discredit the prosecution's witnesses, the stronger their final argument would be. Since the beginning of the Iwik affair, the credibility of the police had eroded. The detectives and police chief might blame Udin's relatives, the media, or grandstanding lawyers for the collapse of the case they had carefully assembled against the Dymas driver. But most people in Jogjakarta and perhaps even the rest of Indonesia seemed to believe the blame for botching the Udin investigation lay with police officials themselves. During the trial, a police representative from Jakarta headquarters pleaded to a skeptical Jogja campus audience: "When this incident appeared, it was already planted in the mind of the public that it a 'high official' was behind it.

But we studied the victim's news clippings. And the result did not lead in that 'high official's' direction."

Yet whatever reasonable explanation the police could present for why it had chosen to pursue Iwik instead of Sri Roso, they had undermined themselves – when plainclothed officers made threats to witnesses during the trial, when Edy showed his disrespect for the legal process, and when the police played fast and loose with the evidence. *Bernas* printed several stories quoting lawyers and law professors who complained about how rudely they felt the enforcers of order had treated the institutions of law. After Edy's testimony, a retired police lieutenant general came to the *Bernas* office to complain in person: "I am angry, offended, and resentful. Just vomiting and defecating. How can there be police who act like this in a courtroom?"

After the prosecution had exhausted its list of witnesses, the defense called its own. Sunarti's mother appeared to say that Iwik had not left the house the night of Udin's murder. The couple's neighbor, Betha Meirawan, also testified that Iwik never acted like someone guilty of a crime: "If someone had just done something wrong, especially killing someone, it's obvious. But what I saw, Iwik never showed any strangeness in the office or at home. When all those police brought Iwik to the office, my work colleagues and I just laughed. These police got the wrong person."

Two of Iwik's coworkers confirmed that the pipe they had seen Hadi and the police take on 22 October 1996 was not the same one presented as evidence a year later at trial. Their testimony supported the conclusion that the defense wanted the judges to draw from Ratna's testimony, which is that the police had arrived on another occasion to take another pipe to be a more appropriate "murder weapon." Iwik's defense team also summoned *Jogja Post* reporter Sumadiyono to repeat that story he had told *Bernas* a year earlier that it had been him – not Sunarti or another woman – riding with Udin the day before the murder. Iwik's lawyers would have summoned many more people to verify the couple's alibi but many refused to help out of fear. "Just to get them to testify is a job that's really trying," Eko would later recall. "There were many, many people that saw what happened or knew what happened. A lot didn't want to become witnesses."

In any case, the most important witness they had was Iwik himself. The night before his testimony, scheduled for 20 October 1997, almost exactly a year after his arrest, Iwik sat down with his wife to review the memories of the evening of 13 August 1996, to fix all the details in his memory. He continued to practice the routine he had followed since the trial began, which was to bathe at midnight and pray the Verse of the Throne before sleeping. Months before the beginning of the trial, he had told reporters he would "reveal everything" at his trial. Now, he would make good on that promise.

In two hours of testimony, Iwik told the court that he had only admitted to killing Udin because "Franky" had coerced him: "He said this would be to protect a Bantul official. He said later I would get a reward from this official."

"What official?" asked Judge Endang.

"The *bupati*."

This was the first time Sri Roso's name had been directly linked to Iwik's arrest. Under oath, Iwik had put Bantul's chief executive under the spotlight. If the *bupati* had not been involved in the murder, then why had his name been mentioned as someone who would supply a "reward" in the cover-up? To those in the courtroom, there were two probable explanations. First, Edy and Sri Roso had worked together to frame Iwik. Second, and perhaps the one more likely, Edy had invoked the *bupati*'s name without the Bantul executive's knowledge or permission. The detective had merely woven another thread into the net of lies he needed to snare his quarry. But the court was not the place to resolve the issue. Judge Endang made no sign she had noted Iwik's revelation.

"You were promised a job, work, and a reward. Weren't you at least tempted by these things?" she asked.

"I wasn't tempted – I was frightened."

"Didn't you think at the time that if you confessed that in the end you would be in a trial?"

"No, Your Honor."

"Was there in your mind the hope that if you followed Edy's instructions then your life would be happy?"

"I was just afraid of being shot. I was confused. Franky also said that the police had found my wife's photo in Udin's wallet."

"On 26 October, why did you suddenly say that you didn't do it?"

"Because my previous confessions went against my conscience."

"How did you have the courage?"

"My heart rebelled," Iwik said. "The promise to me was that I would not go to prison, but instead, there I was. I was no longer strong, especially in the place that I was. That's how I got the courage."

"You weren't afraid of getting shot?"

"No. Let me be shot, I didn't care."

The lead prosecutor, Amrin, would not allow Iwik to escape responsibility for his earlier confession as easily. He recalled for the court Iwik's initial confession, after his arrest. He pointed out that Edy had only been present at that first interrogation.

"So Edy was there on the twenty-first, until the evening?" he asked Iwik.

"Yes."

"On the twenty-second?"

"No."

"On the twenty-third?"

"No."

"The twenty-fourth?"

"No."

"So why did you continue to confess?"

"Because the investigators said if I said one thing before, but later it's different, my punishment would be heavier."

"So how could you say one thing in front of the investigators and now say another?"

"I retract my confession from the twenty-first to the twenty-fourth, because it does not correspond to truth or my conscience."

"So what is the truth then?"

"I did not attack Udin."

At the end of Iwik's testimony, Amrin's team of prosecutors requested three weeks to prepare their closing argument. The judges allowed two weeks, although Amrin's team had needed the time to assemble a united front. The defense lawyers' source inside the public prosecutor's office told them that the prosecutors had split. Most on the prosecution team felt that they had long ago lost this case, and might as well acknowledge its weaknesses. At most, the closing argument to them would be a formality. But Amrin, the supposed lone holdout, wanted to push forward and demand at least a fifteen-year jail sentence for Iwik. The reputation of the prosecutor's office was valuable; it would not look good to give up so easily.

Ignorant of the tug-of-war within the prosecution team over whether to demand conviction or acknowledge defeat, the public had already reached a verdict. On 26 October 1997, *Bernas* printed the results of a poll of people randomly chosen from the Jogjakarta telephone directory. Eighty-four per cent of the respondents said they followed the Iwik trial. Of that group, 88.5 per cent believed Udin had been killed because of his reporting. Nearly all said that they did not believe there had ever been an affair – and 92.55 per cent did not think that Iwik was the killer. The poll was hardly scientific, but it captured perfectly the mood of the moment.

The story enraged Bantul Police Chief Yotje, who told the paper: "This published news seeks to influence opinions and will have a negative impact. As the party responsible in Bantul for guarding law and order during the trial, we ask *Bernas* not to print news connected to opinion, which is not supported by facts." He told the paper to wait for the verdict. He cited a refrain many New Order officials had repeated throughout the three decades of Suharto's government: "Our country is a country of law." But after what Jogjakarta's citizens had witnessed in the Bantul courtroom, that phrase rang hollow.

The city waited anxiously for the result of the trial. One law professor fretted to *Bernas* that the chance of conviction or acquittal still seemed fifty-fifty. Iwik worried that his fate was soon to be decided. Whether he would join the ranks of other victims of the New Order's inherent injustices – among them Sum Kuning, the *Petrus* victims, and Marsinah – was now up to three judges. "I often contemplate myself what I have done," he told a reporter. "I weep when I think about my child, wife, and family. Everything is messed up. My son's schooling is messed up, my wife's work is messed up, and my family is all messed up."

The date set for the prosecution's closing argument was 3 November 1997. On that day, Amrin arrived late for the hearing. As both prosecution and defense sat down in their usual seats, Eko noticed one of the prosecutors grin and give him a surreptitious thumbs-up signal. The lawyer understood the import of that gesture halfway through the prosecution's reading of their summation. After spending most of seven hours reviewing the evidence and testimony presented at the trial, the prosecutors presented the court with a surprising request. They asked the judges to declare Iwik innocent of the crime.

The prosecution admitted that all it had been able to prove was that a murder had been committed, but it had been unsuccessful in establishing that Iwik had been the one who committed the crime. This was a particularly skillful argument. It allowed the prosecution to save face by claiming that the trial had been a worthwhile endeavor, while at the same time, granting that the case against the Dymas driver had been faulty from the start. The canniness of the argument led many to believe what had been rumored. In one version Iwik's lawyers and reporters had heard, Amrin had arrived late for the hearing because he had received a copy of his closing argument prepared directly by a team sent to Jogja by the prosecutor-general's office in Jakarta. Amrin had supposedly written his own closing argument, which included his demand for a guilty verdict and a fifteen-year prison sentence for Iwik, but his superiors had supposedly instructed him to replace whatever he had written with one that requested a not-guilty verdict.

The prosecution asked the court to release Iwik, return all evidence seized, and rule that the state should shoulder all of his court expenses. The judges seemed taken aback by the prosecution's admission that the case had fallen through. Rare in Indonesia are cases in which the public prosecutor's office drops all charges, especially at the end of a lengthy trial. As the prosecutors completed their reading, *Bernas* reported, Iwik "hid his face with both his hands and wiped away his tears." Long after the trial ended, many in the Jogjakarta police would blame the prosecution for this final capitulation. "In the end, we asked: 'What was going on?'" Hadi would complain. "The prosecutors should have an active role. They have to support this duty of investigation, they must be responsible towards this case. But in reality, the prosecutors didn't go forth. They didn't attack."

Yet after the prosecution's surrender, National Police Chief Dibyo hinted that Iwik's ordeal was hardly finished. "It's just the prosecutor," he told reporters in Jakarta. "Wait for the final decision from the judges." In fact, such is the Indonesian legal system that even if prosecutors decide they had no case, judges could still find that there was enough credible evidence to declare a suspect guilty.

The judges were scheduled to reveal their decision on 27 November 1997. In the meantime, Iwik's defense delivered its own closing argument. Just as they did during the exception, both Iwik and his lawyers read their own prepared speeches. In his, Iwik explained that his hostility was not towards the law enforcement community as a whole, but directed to a few of its members and associates. "The testimony of witnesses Edy Wuryanto, Slamet Wijayanto and Diharjo Purboko, who said that they would swear on the safety of seven generations of their grandchildren," Iwik read aloud to the court, "May that be heard and acknowledged by God the All-Knowing." His entire arrest, detention, and trial, he said, "was just the setup of one irresponsible officer: Edy Wuryanto."

The four attorneys reminded the judges that, of the twenty-five witnesses the prosecution had presented, not one could identify Iwik as the killer. Not only was the evidence, such as the blood-spattered metal pipe, that the prosecution had presented questionable, the witnesses for the prosecution were not believable. "It is rather clear there is a forcing of proof," the lawyers argued. "What is demanded of us is not to be carried away by the thinking that someone who has been investigated and accused *has* to be convicted."

When the day of the verdict arrived, an air of electric anticipation blanketed the town of Bantul. Police set up roadblocks around the courthouse in a radius of two hundred meters. As a precaution, Triyandi asked Sunarti not to stay until the end of the hearing. She was to leave the courthouse early, and wait at his house with her parents and son Bimo, in case a guilty verdict led to trouble. The reporters were also worried. Rumors flew fast and loose that the judges had been paid off and that they would find Iwik guilty despite the prosecution's decision.

At 9:45 a.m., the three judges began reading their opinion. The first issue they decided was whether to accept Iwik's retraction. Since Edy had admitted he had involved Diharjo, Slamet, and others in a scheme to ensnare Iwik, the judges told the packed courtroom, "the accused's confession in front of investigators on 21, 22, 23 and 24 October 1996 was only the product of this scenario." Thus, they had decided that, "the said retraction is accepted."

The judges observed that no witness had seen Iwik on Parangtritis Road, but that several could confirm that he must have been asleep in his house in Sleman. Since witnesses disagreed whether the metal pipe presented in court was the murder weapon, the judges continued, the evidence presented was likely "not the weapon used by the assailant." The judges set aside all the material evidence – Iwik's belt, watch, jean jacket, shoes, white T-shirt, slacks, and Vespa – the prosecution had presented. The prosecutors had not demonstrated persuasively that these items had been present at the crime scene. After a marathon three and one-half-hour reading, the judges reached the essence of their ruling:

"Given all the considerations above…it is the opinion of this bench that it has been proven that Dwi Sumaji, alias Iwik, is not the actor behind the crime in this case." The judges instructed the prosecutor's office to revoke all charges and grant Iwik his freedom.

A chorus of cheers from both inside and outside the courtroom drowned out the judges' last words. Someone began singing a patriotic song, which everyone joined in and chanted. Another person launched into the opening bars of the Indonesian national anthem. Several audience members shouted:

"Long live the judges!"

"Long live Iwik!"

"Long live the lawyers!"

As the judges completed reading their opinion, Iwik rose from his seat, turned towards the audience and raised his arms in a gesture of victory. Thirteen months and six days had elapsed since his arrest and this moment, and he wanted to savor the feeling of freedom. Before he left the courtroom, carried on the shoulders of several in the audience, the judges and even a few prosecutors approached the Dymas driver to congratulate him.

At Triyandi's house, a thanksgiving feast of fried chicken, rice, satay, and stir-fried vegetables had been prepared. The journalists who had covered Udin's murder and Iwik's trial had also been invited. But many could not come. With the announcement of the verdict, they had deadlines to meet and stories to file on the public reaction, which had been substantial and often emotional. One housewife called the *Bernas* office to say she had wept upon seeing Iwik on television because she had imagined herself in his place, accused of a crime by an unjust system. Another woman from Bantul muttered: "Whoever's behind this dirty setup, just burn them alive!" One *Bernas* reporter went straight to the heart of the entire saga: Udin's family home in Trirenggo. The imam, Wagiman, had not attended Iwik's trial. He watched the end of the trial on television.

Wagiman appeared to sense the real consequences of the court victory. Iwik may have been set free. But Udin's murderer still remained at large, somewhere. In a week or so, the jubilation over the verdict would be forgotten. And nothing would have really changed: not the police or its habits, not the judges or their usual cowardice, not the government and its disregard for its people. Indonesia would still be in the grip of its age of madness – and his son would still be dead because he had tried to do the job for which he had been hired. "These days are the days of people playing with power, when power is meant to serve the people, not for self gratification," Wagiman told the reporter sadly. "If this goes on…perhaps one day, God will give a warning."

EPILOGUE

Like Dust Blown Away by the Wind

ONE JUNE NIGHT a year and a half after the verdict, five figures emerged from a car parked on the Central Java plain. The hour was long past midnight, well into the shivering hours of the early morning. Above the group of four men and one short, stocky woman, the inky sky glistened with stars. To the group's left, Mount Merapi's smoldering cone blew puffs of smoke somewhere on the shadowy horizon. Prambanan's ancient array of temples, invisible, lurked a short distance away from where the group was standing in the predawn darkness.

The five walked towards a lighted house. Their shoes crunched sand and gravel. From the driveway, they could see bulbs still burning at this early hour. The house, which was meticulously clean, appeared sparse and unfurnished. Although a television crackling in the kitchen and the low hum of a refrigerator revealed that the inhabitants had a steady income, nothing cluttered the white-tiled space inside the front door, save a coffee table and a large, curved sofa. Instead of chairs, the home's occupants had spread straw mats on the floor. Several young Javanese males, swaddled in sarongs and T-shirts, sat sipping tea and watching the glowing screen.

The house's middle-aged master, a man nicknamed "Cengkek," gave his visitors a welcoming look from the sofa and murmured a greeting in a relaxed drawl. Throughout Central Java, the lanky Cengkek was a renowned *dukun*. People recognized his name as far away as Semarang.

He could summon essences of human beings, jinni, ghosts, and demons – any life force from a creature, natural or supernatural. Cengkek could even borrow the souls of living people as they slept. The young men who drank his tea and watched his television were his apprentices. He had trained them to enter into trances that made their bodies and tongues temporary vessels for the summoned spirits. The shades supposedly entered through the back of the neck. "Like a big wind weighing down my shoulders, followed by the feeling of pins and needles," would be how one of his students described his possession. Complete unconsciousness followed that first rush, and then darkness. After the session, the apprentice would awake with no recollection of what had happened.

Cengkek's clients visited him so they could contact dead, missing, or estranged relatives. He often received visits from detectives or policemen, who wanted to be put in contact with fugitive burglars or suspected murderers. The chronically ill asked for one-on-one sessions with famous but busy specialists from local hospitals. The *dukun*, a former truck driver, claimed he could grant all these requests, with a few limitations. A client must know the name and location of the person whose spirit was to be summoned, and, since Cengkek's powers decreased over distance, the target must live or have died on Java.

Although he could borrow a living soul at any moment, the *dukun* preferred to do so late at night or unreasonably early in the morning, when most people were asleep, to avoid accidents caused by drivers whose souls were borrowed from their bodies. Cengkek could not guarantee success, especially if the target had his or her own protective enchantments. The simplest and most powerful spell, he would chuckle, was to say God's name before going to bed. "How many of us forget to do that?"

Cengkek knew one of his five visitors: Bambang Tiong, a reporter for the Sunday edition of the *People's Sovereignty*. Bambang lived nearby, a few rice paddies away. Bambang introduced his four companions: Heru, Ida, Achadi, and Heru Nugroho, the Jogja correspondent for the

Surabaya paper *Surya*. At this time, in mid-1998, both Heru Prasetya and Ida were working for *Detective & Romance*, while Achadi had returned to his studies at his Islamic teacher's training college.

Everyone in the room, including Cengkek and his students, had just been through the most uncertain days in Indonesia's modern history. A few weeks before, on Thursday, 21 May 1998, Suharto had finally resigned, some two months after he had been elected to a seventh five-year term. He was just eight days shy of his seventy-seventh birthday. Just as both prophets and political scientists had foretold, Suharto's end had come cataclysmically. Nine days before, his soldiers had shot dead four student protesters at a Jakarta university. Mere hours later, arson, riots, and looting spread across the capital and cities in Sumatra and Java, such as Surakarta. Jogja escaped the chaos when the sultan himself appeared in public to plead for order. In Jakarta alone, over twelve-hundred people were reported killed in the riots. Damage to property was estimated at half a billion dollars. During those crucial days, as columns of black smoke rose over the country's largest cities, the army and the police did largely nothing. No one knew if that inaction could be attributed to a behind-the-scenes power struggle, or whether the armed forces were simply too afraid to impose order on the chaos.

Following the riots, student demonstrators occupied the parliament building. They demanded that the speaker of the upper house request Suharto's resignation. That speaker happened to be the craven Information Minister Harmoko. He meekly did so on 18 May and betrayed his oldest patron. Bereft of any remaining claim to popular legitimacy, President Suharto resigned three days later.

More than just dead student protesters had brought Suharto down. His resignation had capped a year seething with political unrest, economic troubles, and social crises. Since mid-1997, as Iwik and his lawyers struggled to win his trial, bureaucrats in Jakarta had been fighting futilely to save the country's sputtering economy. Foreign capitalists, who had finally realized that Indonesia's rampant corruption and political uncertainty made the country too risky a bet, fled the currency and stock markets. The government emptied the treasury to buoy the rupiah and bail out local banks and companies, although among the first to be saved were those connected to the First Family. In late December 1997, reports of Suharto's ill health led to an even steeper plunge in the rupiah's value. As the dive turned into a free fall, food and fuel prices skyrocketed. Throughout the country, desperate farmers and workers raided shop houses and stalls. Mobs targeted ethnic Chinese merchants, the unfortunate scapegoats for the excesses of both their wealthier kin and of Suharto's native Indonesian cronies. By March 1998, the country's currency was worth just one-fourth of its value against the U.S. dollar a year earlier. The Suharto government turned to the International Monetary Fund. The Fund prescribed a stringent reduction in state expenditures, a program criticized for paying too much attention to balancing the government's books than to the sensitive political situation. The Fund-directed elimination of fuel subsidies immediately preceded the May riots.

For years after 1998, debate would rage over exactly how and in what proportion these varied elements had contributed to the dictator's downfall. How badly had foreign meddling wrecked the economy? Had Suharto's children and cronies conspired and schemed against their father and patron to save their political careers and vast business empires? Had the master puppeteer, in the end, been betrayed by his puppets? For Indonesia's *dukun*, Suharto's political demise could be explained easily. They accused the aged president, who in his last years began to turn more toward Islam, of having abandoned the traditional Javanese magic that had sustained him. His last mistake, according to one, was that Suharto had sworn in his final, crisis cabinet on a "kick-the-corpse" day, a *sampar wangké*.

In the shadow of the national turmoil, the four journalists visiting Cengkek wanted to see what would happen in their own small corner of Indonesia, to the unsolved murder that had occupied them for more than two years. They submitted five names connected to the Udin case and asked the *dukun* to summon the individuals. To prepare for the ritual, several of Cengkek's pupils took seats on the straw mats. As their heads nodded, Ida pulled out her notebook and pressed a button on her tape recorder. His apprentices then began their meditation. Ida imagined Sri Roso sleeping soundly in his bed in the *bupati*'s official residence, undisturbed by Udin's death, the accusations of his involvement, or the spectacular failure of the case against Iwik.

Sri Roso would not be sleeping at that official residence for much longer, however. He was to suffer a fate remarkably similar to that of Suharto. On 2 June, twelve days after the president's resignation, about fifty students from twelve Jogjakarta universities staged a sit-in at the *bupati*'s compound. Inspired by the success of their counterparts in Jakarta, the students moved their protest to the Bantul assembly building, where they insisted they would not leave until the council cut short Sri Roso's second term as *bupati*. On 6 June 1998, just as Harmoko had asked Suharto to resign weeks earlier, forty-four of the assembly's members voted to request the Interior Ministry to remove Sri Roso from his office. They gave as their reason the *bupati*'s violation of his oath of office by attempting to bribe the Dharmais Foundation. The only council member to vote against the measure was Sri Roso's older brother, Gunawan.

His promise to pay one billion rupiah to Suharto's charity put Sri Roso in front of a military tribunal for bribery and corruption. On 2 July 1999, after the testimony of fifteen witnesses, the tribunal sentenced the ex-*bupati* to nine months in prison. Sri Roso, who had attended all the hearings in full military uniform, paled as the guilty verdict was read. The colonel, however, never served his sentence. Unnoticed by a media preoccupied by the troubled post-Suharto transition, a higher court reversed his conviction. As of mid-2002, Sri Roso was living quietly with his family in a suburb of Jogja. According to one of his lawyers, the now-retired colonel still refuses requests for interviews relating to the Udin case. He intends his silence to be a statement: that he had, from the very beginning, never been involved in the murder.

Suharto achieved a similarly serene retirement as well. Despite demands by Indonesian citizens' groups and intellectuals for the ex-dictator and his family members to be tried for corruption, successive presidents, including Megawati Sukarnoputri, refrained from prosecuting Suharto. On 10 October 1999, during the brief rule of Suharto's vice president B.J. Habibie, the prosecutor-general formally halted the investigation into Suharto's corruption. In August 2000, under Habibie's successor, Suharto was finally charged with embezzling $550 million donated to his charitable foundations, including Dharmais. But the case collapsed when a Jakarta court judged the former president too infirm to stand trial.

Despite these figures' escape from justice, no Indonesian envied either Suharto or Sri Roso. In Jogja and Jakarta, even the most devout Muslims use a word associated with Hinduism when talking about these individuals' lives since leaving office. That word is karma. The ex-general would spend his last years surrounded by his treacherous, spoiled children and a retinue of bandits, gangsters and goons, the ragtag remnants of his once-invincible secret security apparatus. He had seen his grand illusion of development for Indonesia dispelled; the scrim pulled back to reveal his regime as supported only by the strength of its arms and the weakness of its morals.

Sri Roso's youngest son fell victim to a roadside accident not long after the Iwik case ended. The boy spent an agonizing two months in the hospital before dying. Despite never having been tried for involvement in Udin's death, Sri Roso's name in Indonesia has become synonymous with bribery in local elections and the murder of the journalist. Although both Sri Roso and Suharto had been born on different days and *wuku*, each of their horoscopes shared one aspect. Both contained the same Javanese phrase to describe their fates: "*Lebu katiyup angin.*"

It means: "Like dust blown away by the wind."

༄༅

Jogja's chapter of the PWI did not formally disband its Fact-Finding Team. Many Jogja journalists active in covering the case, such as Heru and Ida, also remained ardent followers of further developments. The rival journalists' groups kept in close contact with Triyandi's Legal Defenders and Budi's Legal Aid office. A few days after Iwik's verdict, Legal Aid and Legal Defenders signed a joint letter calling on the police to investigate at least twenty-one individuals for both the murder of Udin and the subsequent cover-up. Among the names on the list were ex-Bantul Police Chief Adé and police detectives Edy, Hadi, and Slamet. After Iwik's acquittal, journalists and activists expected Legal Defenders and Iwik to sue Edy and the police. Another court case – this time argued on stronger legal grounds than the Blood Trial – seemed to be the next and necessary step to forcing the Indonesian police apparatus to reveal the extent of its officers' responsibility in a sloppy investigation, if not an outright miscarriage of justice.

But the crusading journalists and legal activists were disappointed. Although his lawyers had prepared a complaint demanding the equivalent of $61,500 from the Jogjakarta Police District for wrongful arrest and loss of income, Iwik no longer wished to be a hero. For some time after his trial, he and his wife continued to live at Triyandi's office, where they still received hissed threats over the phone. "Don't be too encouraged," one unidentified caller told him. "This is not the end." The end, however, was exactly what the couple wanted. Three weeks after her husband's acquittal, Sunarti gave birth to a son. The couple gave the child the name Triyandi, followed by the words "Andi Kurnia Purna Yudha," which mean, "The Reward at the End of Struggle." Their struggle had exhausted thirteen months of their lives. "If we sued, it wouldn't be over in a month or two months. It would take years," Iwik would later explain. "When was I ever going to live free? Who would guarantee my safety if I faced the police?"

In late December, Triyandi arranged a meeting at a Jogja hotel between Iwik and Yotje. The Bantul police chief promised the impoverished couple the equivalent of over ten thousand dollars to drop a planned lawsuit. Without formalizing the settlement, Triyandi prematurely asked Eko to fax to his police contacts a statement Iwik had prepared in case he decided to abandon the case. On 29 December 1997, Indonesian National Police Chief Dibyo read the driver's letter to a group of astonished journalists. In the statement, Iwik declared that he wished now to concentrate on his family life, which for over a year had been in chaos. He would not commence legal action.

Triyandi's enthusiasm was understandable. Yotje's proposed settlement provided the lawyer with the solution to the dilemma that had worried his office since their first meeting a year before with Iwik. By backing down from a lawsuit, Triyandi could start rebuilding his damaged relationship with the police. His client, who had already indicated he never wanted to see the inside of a courtroom again, would receive an immediate financial benefit. Yet after Dibyo received and read aloud Iwik's statement, Iwik and Sunarti did not receive the full settlement they had been promised. They returned to their lives in Panasan almost as poor as when they started. It would take some time as well before Iwik's life could return to normal. For three years after the case, Iwik felt he could not go back to work. Fame still imprisoned him; he disliked the celebrity the case had brought him. Strangers would still call his name out in the street in Jogja or even when he visited Surabaya. In 2000, he felt he felt he had reacquired enough anonymity to once again make a living. He went back to driving, maneuvering a minibus back and forth on a route linking four villages on the slopes of Mount Merapi.

Triyandi returned to fulltime practice. Both Eko and Djufri left Triyandi & Associates to start their own successful law practices. The Iwik trial turned out to be Legal Defenders' first and last famous case. Never again would the firm on Pakuningratan Road receive the same kind of attention, although the fame of its lawyers continued to draw in clients.

After Iwik's settlement allowed Legal Defenders to drop out of the picture, Legal Aid and the journalists decided to focus on prosecuting Edy. Legal Aid pursued its appeal of the Blood Trial decision all the way to the Indonesian Supreme Court. An appellate tribunal confirmed

Judge Mikaela's decision, as did the Indonesian Supreme Court. But to Marsiyem's lawyers' astonishment, the supreme court only affirmed the original decision in part. The court relieved Edy of his obligation to apologize publicly to Udin's widow. So the detective was never required to make a public apology in Jogja's newspapers, as Judge Mikaela had instructed. On 20 May 1997, the detective still sent a smarmy personal letter of apology to Marsiyem, which read:

> My intention in writing this letter is none other than my desire to offer my deep apologies if, during the time I knew your family, there have been any words or attitudes that have offended your feelings or that of your family. All of this is not because I intended or wanted it.

After Iwik's trial, the Jogjakarta Police District announced an internal investigation into whether the detective had violated procedures when he had arrested Iwik. But a year later, in December 1998, the Jogjakarta police chief told reporters that "Edy Wuryanto did not 'set up' anything." So Legal Aid decided to begin its own action against the detective. While the Blood Trial was being appealed, the bureau also filed a complaint against Edy with the military police. Edy had taken Udin's notebooks and never returned them, and could be found guilty for hiding evidence in a criminal investigation. A Jogjakarta military court put the Bantul detective and his deputy, Slamet, on trial. Edy brazenly ignored all but one summons to interviews by military prosecutors as well as three calls by the military court to appear before it. The journalists who covered the case against Edy often commented that the Bantul detective must still have some strong magic behind him. In one oft-told tale, after the detective had once again refused to show up for his testimony, a military judge at one hearing supposedly complained loudly that the police officer had no respect for the law. At that moment, a flag in the courtroom suddenly fell from the wall. Not long afterward, the story went, the judge died of a heart attack.

During the entire military court case against him, the Jogjakarta police refused to allow Edy to be questioned. "Edy Protected by 'Mantras'" read one *Bernas* headline. As the case continued, the detective received a transfer to Jakarta to work at the national police headquarters. In August 2001, the Jogjakarta military court sentenced Edy to ten months in prison and Slamet to one month. But just as in Sri Roso's case, Edy dodged the bullet on appeal. In 2002, an military appellate court ruled that the military prosecutor had committed prejudicial, procedural errors at trial. The Jogjakarta court was ordered to retry his case. The Jogjakarta Police District argued that this placed the detective in risk of being tried twice for the same crime. His case lapsed into a judicial limbo.

Despite the controversy the Udin case generated, many of the officers involved received promotions. Mulyono won the prized post of Jakarta police chief in 1998, while Hadi received his own precinct in Jogja before being appointed Bantul's chief detective. Many in the Jogjakarta police continue to blame Udin's widow, the press, or local legal aid groups for helping Iwik get away. As late as the end of 2000, four years after Udin's murder and three after Iwik's acquittal, a Jogjakarta police chief would comment: "Marsiyem must be questioned again. How is it that this Iwik could have been set free?"

As for Marsiyem, she has moved past the tragedy. She remarried in 2000 and had a child with her new husband, Udin's ex-partner in the Krisna Photo Studio. With the donations that came in after Udin's death, Marsiyem was able to open a second photo-developing shop in a house a short walk from the Trirenggo village graveyard. One rule of life she has learned, she says, is "never again trust strangers."

After every new Jogjakarta or Bantul police chief is inaugurated, journalists in Jogja ask if the investigation into Udin's murder will continue. Yet despite successive promises to find and prosecute the killer, no other suspects have been produced. The case has been practically abandoned. "We have carried out the lawyers' suggestions, we have carried out suggestions from the PWI team," Hadi said in a 2001 interview. "Everything is still zero. There is no result. Everything is at a dead end." The annual commemorations of Udin's passing by Legal Aid and *Bernas* have thus turned into rituals less of remembrance than of self-protection, much like a performance of the *wayang*. The reporter's name is mentioned to ward off evil, to remind the authorities to treat the media with more respect, and to care for their protection.

Still, reporting in Indonesia has not become any safer. On 11 June 1997, a journalist for the *Makassar Post* in Sulawesi died from injuries supposedly sustained during a motorcycle accident. His family claimed that he had been beaten. The victim, too, had been reporting on the embezzlement of IDT funds, as well as on timber theft and illegal logging. On 25 July 1997, just before Iwik's trial opened, a journalist for a Jakarta newsweekly was found stabbed dead in his car in Kalimantan. He had published reports on timber smuggling that involved local officials. In 1999, two journalists, one Dutch and the other Indonesian, were killed within four days of each other while covering the conflict in East Timor after its vote for independence from Indonesia. Both were believed shot by members of the Indonesian military or by military-backed militias. In 2001, three journalists died under mysterious circumstances. One of them had died while in police custody.

Back at Cengkek's home, four of the spirits requested by his visitors had been successfully retrieved. But the interviews were not going well. Ida had asked apprentices hosting the souls of Mulyono and Adé what had really happened to the murder investigation. Both, she would recall, responded that they had been "following orders." Meanwhile, the student hosting Sri Roso's soul had been so tight-lipped and unresponsive that afterward, Ida could not even remember what he had answered. Of the four, Edy's soul had been the toughest for Cengkek to summon. The five journalists watched the young man hosting Edy's essence perspire and squirm, as if the act of bearing the detective's soul physically burdened his body. But like the others, the spirit that appeared in front of the reporters insisted that the detective had done everything according to procedure.

That night, the only soul Cengkek could not conjure for the reporters was the one that belonged to Noto Suwito. The enchantments protecting him – that strong Suharto family magic – were simply too powerful for the *dukun* to penetrate. Of all the officials accused of involvement in Udin's death, Noto Suwito has emerged the most unscathed by the scandal. No evidence connects Suharto's brother to the death of the reporter. But the Indonesian habit to see "puppeteers" remains so potent that few in Jogjakarta can discuss the Udin murder without mentioning the deceptively frail village chief of Argomulyo. Many still believe the one reason why the murder remains unsolved is because Noto Suwito does not wish for the truth to surface.

The four journalists left Cengkek's home an hour before dawn. The sky had lightened from a deep black to a luminous blue. The vast void surrounding the *dukun*'s home had evaporated in the morning light, leaving an endless carpet of brilliant green rice fields that appeared tacked to the glimmering horizon. As they returned to their car, the reporters mused on their varied impressions of their encounter. "I was between believing and not believing," Ida would recall. The *Surya* correspondent Heru Nugroho marveled at how well Cengkek's pupils had mimicked the voices of Bantul and police officials. But for both Heru Prasetya and Achadi, what they saw was nothing more than several impressionable young village men who had been taught to act as if they had assumed alternate personalities. Whether the enchantment was real or not, the reporters had no idea.

"The problem with *dukun* is that you don't know what you get," Achadi would say, sitting in a Jogja café six years after the murder. What they had witnessed that morning, he thought, was not magic but a performance. The journalists might have spoken to the spirits of Mulyono, Adé, Edy, and Sri Roso – or no "spirits" at all.

"What they told us," Achadi shrugged, "was nothing more than what they could have read in the papers."

SOURCES

MUCH OF THIS BOOK emerged out of two 1997 cases: *Marsiyem v. Government of Indonesia* (Case no. 01/Pdt.G/1997/PN Btl) and *Government v. Dwi Sumaji al. Iwik* (Case no. 16/Pid/B/1997/PN Btl). The linked investigations and trials produced hundreds of pages of court opinions, legal memoranda, witness testimony, and police reports, from which I obtained many of the facts of this story. To assure myself that the printed page accurately reflected the words spoken at the time, I compared the official transcripts of Iwik's trial with original audio recordings of the hearings. To confirm or expand on the events these documents described, I also combed through hundreds of archived Indonesian newspaper articles published between 1995 and 2002. The vast majority appeared in *Bernas*, but I also referred frequently to *Jawa Pos*, *Kompas*, *Forum Wartawan Independen*, *Republika*, *Solo Pos*, *Media Indonesia*, and *Kedaulatan Rakyat*. Many of the pieces I read bore Udin's sole or joint byline. The statistics that appear here come from official publications by Indonesia's National Development Planning Agency, Interior Ministry, or Central Statistics Office.

I personally interviewed most of the people involved in the cases or who had covered it, with the notable exception of Sri Roso Sudarmo and Edy Wuryanto. Sri Roso turned down several interview requests over a period of two years, while Edy rebuffed or did not respond to similar appeals over the same period. Frequent transfers of personnel also made tracking or arranging time difficult with several key police individuals, such as former Bantul Police Chief Adé Sudarban, who had been transferred from Irian Jaya by the time I began work on this book, and former Jogjakarta Police Chief Mulyono Sulaiman.

Books written about the Udin case in English and Indonesian helped fill in much of the resulting lacunae. I consulted, in particular: Heru Prasetya, ed., *Kasus Udin: Liputan Bawah Tanah* (Jakarta, 1999); Alliance of Independent Journalists, *Journalist Slain: The Case of Fuad Muhammad Syafruddin* (Jakarta, 1997); and Noorca M. Massardi, ed., *Udin, Darah Wartawan: Liputan Menjelang Kematian* (Jakarta, 1997), which is a posthumous collection of Udin's *Bernas* articles. The Asia Foundation's 2001 "Survey Report on Citizens' Participation of the Indonesian Justice Sector: Preliminary Findings and Recommendations" provided the data I quote in this volumes on popular perceptions of the legal system.

I found several books, academic journal articles, and essay collections particularly useful. Since this is not an academic volume, I could not footnote in the text the titles to which I owe a clear debt. I list them here both to acknowledge my gratitude for their authors' meticulous research and excellent analysis and to point interested readers to further sources.

Javanese history and culture. Aside from the standard works on the subject – Koentjaraningrat, *Javanese Culture* (Singapore, 1985); and Clifford Geertz, *The Religion of Java* (Chicago, 1976) – works by Franz Magnis-Suseno, *Javanese Ethics and World-View: The Javanese Idea of the Good Life* (Jakarta, 1997), and John Pemberton, *On the Subject of "Java"* (Ithaca, 1994), provided some valuable, contrasting insights on the culture: one a canonical view, the other a smart and critical deconstruction of the prevailing images of Java. Y. Argo Twikromo, *Ratu Kidul* (Jogjakarta, 2000), helped me learn more about the legend of the demon queen. The portion of the Jayabaya prophecy I quote in the Introduction comes from a version found at http://www.mastoni.com.

Local and national politics. Hans Antlöv and Sven Cederroth, eds., *Leadership on Java: Gentle Hints, Authoritarian Rule* (Richmond, Surrey,

1994); and Hans Antlöv, *Exemplary Centre, Administrative Periphery: Rural Leadership and the New Order in Java* (Richmond, Surrey, 1994); sketched the workings of the Indonesian bureaucracy at the local level in helpful detail. For national politics, I consulted the standard works on Suharto's Indonesia, among them Adam Schwarz, *A Nation in Waiting* (St. Leonards, New South Wales, 1999) and John Bresnan, *Managing Indonesia: The Modern Political Economy* (New York, 1993). Two biographies – J.D. Legge, *Sukarno: A Political Biography* (Sydney, 1984); and R.E. Elson, *Suharto: A Political Biography* (Cambridge, UK, 2001) – are invaluable to anyone researching the lives and influence of Indonesia's two major post-independence leaders. Given the importance of the 1965 coup in Indonesian history, much has been written on the subject, but several essays provided me with key descriptive facts and theories: Jacques Leclerc, 'Girls, Girls, Girls and Crocodiles', in *Outward Appearances: Dressing State and Society in Indonesia*, ed. Henke Schulte Nordholt (Leiden, 1997); Benedict R. O'G. Anderson, 'How Did the Generals Die?', *Indonesia* 43 (1987); and Pipit Rochijat, 'Am I PKI or Non-PKI?', *Indonesia* 40 (1985), a famous eyewitness account of the massacres. The New Order's crackdown on the Indonesian Democratic Party is described in Alliance of Independent Journalists, *Jakarta Crackdown* (Jakarta, 1997). Veven Wardhana and Herry Barus, *Para Superkaya Indonesia: Sebuah Dokumentasi Gaya Hidup* (Jakarta, 1998), paints a revealing portrait of the lifestyles of the New Order elite.

Crime and law. George Quinn, 'The Javanese Science of Burglary', *Review of Indonesian & Malaysian Affairs* 9 (1975); remains an entertaining and informative source in English about "traditional" criminal in Java. The essays, especially those by Daniel Lev, John Pemberton, Henke Schulte Nordholt, Margreet van Till, and James T. Siegel, in Vicente L. Rafael, ed., *Figures of Criminality in Indonesia, the Philippines and Colonial Vietnam* (Ithaca, 1999); were incredibly rich, creative and insightful pieces about Indonesian crime and its constructions. Hans Thoolen, ed., *Indonesia and the Rule of Law: 20*

Years of 'New Order' Government (London, 1987); and Timothy Lindsey, *Indonesia: Law and Society* (Sydney, 1999) are good introductions to the intricacies and challenges of Indonesian law, with Lindsey's the most comprehensive and the most level-headed. I found most useful "Aspects of Criminal Justice," J. t'Hart's contribution to Thoolen's volume, and Saraswati Sunindyo's "Murder, Gender and the Media: Sexualizing Politics and Violence" in Lindsey's collection. To describe the Sum Kuning and Marsinah cases, I drew from two books in Indonesian: Indonesian Legal Aid Foundation, *Kekerasan Penyidikan Dalam Kasus Marsinah: Catatan Bagi Revisi KUHAP* (Jakarta, 1995); and Kamajaya, *Sum Kuning, Korban Pentjulikan, Pemerkosaan: Proses Perkaranya Dengan Tuduhan Telah Menyiarkan Kabar Bohong* (Jogjakarta, 1971). Finally, Simon Cole's well-researched *Suspect Identities: A History of Fingerprinting and Criminal Identification* (Cambridge, MA, 2001) laid out for me the basic principles behind DNA fingerprinting.

The press. Aside from the journalists themselves and my own experiences in Indonesia, two Australian academics contributed a great deal to my understanding of the challenges Indonesian journalists face. The first is David T. Hill, who wrote *The Press in New Order Indonesia* (Nedlands, Western Australia, 1994). The second is Angela Romano, who graciously sent me her unpublished PhD thesis: "Journalistic Identity and Practices in Late New Order Indonesia."

The police state. The best description I found of the various institutions and techniques of Suharto's surveillance state is in Richard Tanter, 'The Totalitarian Ambition: Intelligence Organizations in the Indonesian State', in *State and Civil Society in Indonesia*, ed. Arief Budiman (Clayton, Victoria, 1990). In addition, Benedict R. O'G.Anderson, ed., *Violence and the State in Suharto's Indonesia* (Ithaca, 2001); included many helpful articles, such as Joshua Barker's "State of Fear: Controlling the Criminal Contagion in Suharto's New Order" and Loren Ryter's "Pemuda Pancasila: The Last Loyalist Free Men of Suharto's Order?"

Printed in the United States
89651LV00004B/219/A